TUBERCULOSIS AND THE VICTORIAN LITERARY IMAGINATION

Tuberculosis was a widespread and deadly disease which devastated the British population in the nineteenth century: consequently it also had a huge impact upon public consciousness. This text explores the representations of tuberculosis in nineteenth-century literature and culture. Fears about gender roles, degeneration, national efficiency and sexual transgression all play their part in the portrayal of 'consumption', a disease which encompassed a variety of cultural associations. Through an examination of a range of Victorian texts, from well-known and popular novels by Charles Dickens and Elizabeth Gaskell to critically neglected works by Mrs Humphry Ward and Charles Reade, this work reveals the metaphors of illness which surrounded tuberculosis and the ways those metaphors were used in the fiction of the day. The book also contains detailed analysis of the substantial body of writing by nineteenth-century physicians which exists about this disease, and examines the complex relationship between medical 'fact' and literary fiction.

KATHERINE BYRNE is Lecturer in English at the University of Ulster, Coleraine.

T0371049

CAMBRIDGE STUDIES IN NINETEENTH-CENTURY
LITERATURE AND CULTURE

General editor
Gillian Beer, *University of Cambridge*

Nineteenth-century British literature and culture have been rich fields for inter-disciplinary studies. Since the turn of the twentieth century, scholars and critics have tracked the intersections and tensions between Victorian literature and the visual arts, politics, social organization, economic life, technical innovations, scientific thought – in short, culture in its broadest sense. In recent years, theoretical challenges and historiographical shifts have unsettled the assumptions of previous scholarly synthesis and called into question the terms of older debates. Whereas the tendency in much past literary critical interpretation was to use the metaphor of culture as 'background', feminist, Foucauldian, and other analyses have employed more dynamic models that raise questions of power and of circulation. Such developments have reanimated the field. This series aims to accommodate and promote the most interesting work being undertaken on the frontiers of the field of nineteenth-century literary studies: work which intersects fruitfully with other fields of study such as history, or literary theory, or the history of science. Comparative as well as interdisciplinary approaches are welcomed.

A complete list of titles published will be found at the end of the book.

TUBERCULOSIS AND THE VICTORIAN LITERARY IMAGINATION

KATHERINE BYRNE

CAMBRIDGE
UNIVERSITY PRESS

CAMBRIDGE UNIVERSITY PRESS
Cambridge, New York, Melbourne, Madrid, Cape Town,
Singapore, São Paulo, Delhi, Mexico City

Cambridge University Press
The Edinburgh Building, Cambridge CB2 8RU, UK

Published in the United States of America by Cambridge University Press, New York

www.cambridge.org
Information on this title: www.cambridge.org/9781107672802

First published 2011
First paperback edition 2013

A catalogue record for this publication is available from the British Library

Library of Congress Cataloguing in Publication Data
Byrne, Katherine, 1978–
Tuberculosis and the Victorian literary imagination / Katherine Byrne.
p. ; cm. – (Cambridge studies in nineteenth-century literature and culture ; 74)
Includes bibliographical references and index.
ISBN 978-0-521-76667-8 (hardback)
1. English literature–History and criticism.   2. Tuberculosis in literature.
3. Literature and medicine–Great Britain–History.
4. Communicable diseases in literature.
I. Title.   II. Series: Cambridge studies in nineteenth-century
literature and culture ; 74.
PR149.T83B97 2011
820.9'3561–dc22   2010035791

ISBN 978-0-521-76667-8 Hardback
ISBN 978-1-107-67280-2 Paperback

For my parents, with love and thanks

Contents

Illustrations

Beata Beatrix (oil on canvas) by Dante Charles Gabriel
Rossetti (1828–82) © Birmingham Museums and
Art Gallery / The Bridgeman Art Library   *page* 102

Acknowledgements

My first thanks go to Dr Tim Marshall and Dr Cath Sharrock at the University of East Anglia, where this book began its life. I greatly appreciate all their advice and support, and their considerable wisdom compensated somewhat for my lack of experience. Thanks also to Professor Roger Sales and Dr Tom Smith for their ideas and suggestions regarding Chapter 5. Professor William Hughes has been, and continues to be, a valuable source of inspiration.

In the later stages of this project I am grateful to, and for, my wonderful colleagues at the University of Ulster, in particular Kevin De Ornellas and James Ward. Thanks to the British Library – archives there have been essential to this work – and to the Bridgeman Art Library, for the use of the cover image. An earlier and abbreviated version of Chapter 2 appeared in *Nineteenth-Century Contexts* in 2007: thanks to Routledge (Taylor & Francis) for allowing me to reproduce this. Linda Bree and Elizabeth Hanlon at Cambridge University Press have made this book possible.

Finally, but most importantly, my thanks go to all my family, in particular my endlessly patient father, for support both financial and practical, and everything else besides, and to Jonathan, my tech support and long-suffering ear, who now knows an awful lot more about consumption than he ever wanted to.

Introduction

Pulmonary tuberculosis has played an influential but analytically understated part in social and cultural formation throughout human history. It has of course formed a perpetual accompaniment to that history, for the disease known to the ancient Greeks as phthisis[1] can be traced back to at least 3000 BC,[2] and – despite the hope for eradication which accompanied vaccination and the antibiotic revolution in the middle of the twentieth century – remains one of the biggest global killers even today. In this book, however, my interest is confined to the western world and the latter stages of this disease's existence. The full significance of this tiny bacteria can best be displayed through its impact upon the nineteenth century, as this was the last age in which tuberculosis was at its height in Europe, and this is the rationale behind the historical framework of this work, which covers the seventy years of Queen Victoria's reign.[3] I am concerned here with revealing the ways in which tuberculosis influenced the construction of the nineteenth-century social body through its pathologising of the gender, class, and economic and aesthetic status of the individual body. The health of a nation is necessarily dependent upon the health of its citizens; disease disrupts social functioning by negatively intervening in the lives of the people. It also fractures society's view of itself as a robust, operational, organic whole, causing a separation between healthy sections as 'Self' and diseased bodies as 'Other', and the tensions this pathological split creates are at the heart of this study.

In the Victorian era consumption killed more people than cholera and smallpox combined, and was equalled only by syphilis in the extent of its effect upon the contemporary political and literary imagination. Tuberculosis and syphilis functioned as sites of social anxiety in Victorian times as cancer and HIV/AIDS do in ours, and as such provided entry into a whole world of sexual and social as well as medical discourse. Fears about femininity, (hereditary) inheritance, degeneration, national efficiency and sexual transgression are all epitomised by consumption, mainly because it

I

is, as Susan Sontag suggests in *Illness as Metaphor,* a 'disease of individuals', an infection which singles out its victims rather than affecting the whole community like the fever epidemics.[4] Thus the consumptive seems to be set apart from his neighbours: his disease is different, therefore by implication he is in some way different too.

Disease becomes invested with a particular significance when it is not the common affliction of the whole community. This significance was very clear in the case of syphilis, a disease well known to be a consequence of sexual contact, as it indicated that the sufferer had overindulged in (probably illicit) sexual behaviour, or was the offspring or spouse of someone who had. Syphilis's physical symptoms contributed to this sense of moral certainty about its cause, for the primary chancre usually appeared at the site of initial infection and this frequently confirmed the sexual nature of its means of transmission. This enabled syphilis to be used as a political and moral tool against potentially deviant, subversive sexualities, making it, as Claude Quetel has pointed out, the 'most social of social diseases' in terms of the extent of the cultural and political response it has generated.[5] However, Sontag has described syphilis as 'limited as a metaphor because the disease itself was not mysterious, only awful', and it is true that the disease's meanings and its means of transmission were and are irrevocably linked.[6]

Tuberculosis's metaphors, in contrast, were anything but 'limited'. This disease encompassed a remarkable fluidity of meaning and associations, largely because its origins were shrouded in mystery. Tuberculosis took many forms and affected many different parts of the body – brain, spine, stomach and skin as well as lungs – with the result that it resembled a number of different diseases rather than a single killer, though it is only the most common, pulmonary form of the disease which concerns me in this study. Its one known 'calling card', internal lesions, frequently varied from soft cheesy pustules to hard chalked cavities, depending on the progression of the disease, and this complicated even its post-mortem diagnosis. It had thus evaded the medical profession for centuries, and it was not until Robert Koch's identification of the tuberculosis bacillus in 1882 that its cause and means of transmission finally became known. Even when its infectiousness was established this did not account for the seemingly random distribution of victims, however, as frequently those exposed to and infected by the disease did not go on to become actively tubercular. While 'it is possible that a near totality of the population of many large European cities in the nineteenth century . . . would have tested positive for exposure to the tubercle bacillus', only a small proportion of those would have actually become consumptive, and this inscrutable selection of victims added to the elusiveness of the disease.[7] As it was apparent to doctors and laymen alike that consumption's infectiousness worked differently from that of other diseases, individual susceptibility seemed dictated by an unknown X-factor which could be perceived as the workings of fate or Providence, or which could be the result of the victim's own actions, a comment on the inherent pathogenicity of their behaviour or their lives. There seemed to be a metaphysical element involved in the propagation of tuberculosis, and this enhanced its symbolic potential by allowing it to encompass a number of different meanings.

Consumption's capacity to act as a manifold metaphor made it a malleable vehicle for social expression and discussion in the art and literature of the nineteenth century. Tuberculous subjects are plentiful in the Victorian era and some of the traits associated with them have persevered to the extent of becoming part of our cultural and literary history. As this study will reveal, the disease has been associated, often simultaneously though not always congruously, with youth and purity, with genius, with heightened sensibility and with increased sexual appetites. The resulting images have become famous textual tropes: the languishing consumptive poet whose thwarted desires and personal frustrations seem to have brought about his illness; the Christlike innocence of the child who dies because they are too pure for the world; the beautiful but wan and pining girl whose decline owes as much to her broken heart as to the bacilli invading her body. Hence the inclusion of consumption in any text engages that text with the wider cultural associations that surround the disease.

This book focuses upon the Victorian novel, as this was the artistic medium through which consumption was most commonly explored and its myths and meanings disseminated throughout nineteenth-century society. No other cultural form touched and informed people across the classes to the extent that the novel did, and hence it is the best means of examining how the disease was represented and understood in popular culture in this era. It is true that much could also be said about consumption's influence on other branches of the creative arts – in particular French theatre and opera[8] – but an examination of such diverse forms is necessarily beyond the scope of the present work. However, in order to explore all the possible manifestations of consumptive imagery, I do invoke and discuss some of the representations of phthisis in British poetry and painting of the period where it is relevant to and bears upon my argument, in particular Dante

Gabriel Rossetti's paintings of his wife, which owing to their important influence on the consumptive aesthetic I explore in some detail in Chapter 4.

I have also chosen to confine this work to an examination of British texts. There is a substantial body of tubercular literature in the United States in the nineteenth century, with the novels of Louisa May Alcott, L. M. Montgomery and Harriet Beecher Stowe all containing important consumptive characters,[9] but while these have many points in common with those I explore here, it is clearly not possible to assume a continuity of the meanings and metaphors which surround the disease. This is especially true regarding the perspective of the American medical profession, whose opinions on the cause and treatment of the disease differed from those of their British counterparts. Hence my concern remains with the English experience of the illness, the only exception among the novels being Henry James's *Portrait of a Lady*, which, as it was written and set in England, asserts itself as a product of British discourse about consumption despite the nationality of its author. As regards the body of medical writing about the disease, it is impossible to discount the work of several influential European physicians, particularly those colleagues of Koch who were involved in the identification of the tubercle bacillus, but I have only used as sources those works which were published in Britain, in English, and which therefore were accessible contributions to the Victorian medical profession's views about phthisis.

Chapter 1 is introductory in nature and sets out to establish a medical framework for the study, by interrogating the substantial body of literature written about consumption by physicians in the nineteenth century. I establish here a paradigm which is central to this whole argument: that a complex and symbiotic relationship seems to exist between medical writing and the popular fiction of the time. I explore the origins and nature of this relationship and the ways that the two genres interact with one another to construct the dominant stereotype of the consumptive and to produce widely held assumptions about the disease. As we shall see, a detailed examination of medical publications reveals how, through debates on the cause, diagnosis, and treatment of consumption, doctors consolidated and validated some existing cultural myths about this illness, and developed or even created others. This chapter identifies a number of the most enduring medical theories about the illness, particularly the belief that it was not infectious, that a certain type of person was likely to become consumptive, and that a lifestyle that was socially deviant in any way encouraged tuberculosis to flourish. I discuss how these representations are the attempts of struggling physicians to cope with a mysterious and incurable disease, and are made to serve certain political and personal agendas, namely to facilitate the social management of the illness and to validate and reinforce the authority and importance of the medical profession.

The second chapter begins my exploration of the Victorian novel. I have taken as my starting point the Condition of England novels of the 1840s and 1850s, as they are the first body of Victorian literature in which tuberculosis appears as a recurrent and central theme. Through their preoccupation with the class system, the effects of industrialisation and the state of the social body these novels reveal one of the most intriguing aspects of consumption: its association with capitalism. My argument here is that consumption works as both a disruptor of the capitalist, commercial world, and a metaphor for it, and that this produces interesting tensions within the industrial novel. This synthesis of disease and economics in the context of class issues is clearly not a new one in academic terms, and there is a huge body of work concerned with the pathologising of the industrial working class in this era. However, the majority of this criticism, from Kate Flint's *The Victorian Novelist: Social Problems and Social Change* to Anthony Wohl's *Endangered Lives,* focuses on the diseases most obviously linked to industrialisation and urbanisation – cholera, typhoid and typhus.[10] Yet consumption possessed symbolic potential as a metaphor for the consequences of capitalism in a way that these miasmic infections could not. Fevers were limited as metaphors because they represented such specific problems and issues, such as the sanitation debates, the need for improvement of the physical – and moral – cleanliness of the masses, and middle-class guilt at working-class suffering. Hence their inclusion in a novel must invoke these kinds of questions. Tuberculosis in contrast could not be used as a simple signifier for social conflict and social responsibility, for it did not have an identifiable environmental cause and it was not, despite a definite link with impoverishment, a disease of poverty and squalor which was confined to the lower classes. Consumption's ability to infect all social spheres rendered it a perfect symbol for the capitalist system as a whole, rather than just a means of expressing its effect upon one section of the population. In Dickens's *Dombey and Son* the presence of tuberculosis among the bourgeoisie indicates that the effects of industrialism extend beyond contaminated water or cramped living conditions, and suggest that it may have a harmful impact upon the soul of the capitalist as it does upon the body of the worker. Similarly, while Elizabeth Gaskell's *North and South* associates phthisis with the factory system, it also suggests that this disease is not only about the deprivation born of exhaustion and overwork. Bessy Higgins's illness may be contracted in her workplace, but is also linked to the use and ingestion of luxury goods. The process of consumption – which was of course shared by all classes – is as dangerous as the process of production: capitalism, it seems, is pathological at any stage in the system.

The focus of tuberculous literature appears to undergo a shift from the pathologising of economic status to the pathologising of femininity as the century progresses. Class remains a concern, but questions of gender predominate. In the most general sense, the rest of my study is therefore centred around the consequences of the social perception of tuberculosis as a female disease, in the context of the sexual anxieties that surrounded the approach of the *fin de siècle*. It is difficult to establish conclusively from the statistical evidence whether or not consumption actually was 'female', or, in other words, whether it did affect substantially more women than men. It certainly seems to have done in some regions of Britain, as Scotland and Ireland both have higher mean death rates from pulmonary tuberculosis for women until the turn of the century, but this does not seem to be true of England itself. Any gender difference in incidence of the disease was probably due to environmental factors, but it was still utilised as a signifier of increased female susceptibility to the disease. With some significant and usually emasculated exceptions (like the subject of my final chapter, Ralph Touchett in Henry James's *The Portrait of a Lady*) the classic literary consumptive is inevitably a woman in the Victorian era.

Huge critical attention has been given to the figure of the sickly woman in literature, but this has also been focused upon diseases other than consumption, namely syphilis, hysteria and anorexia.[11] Tuberculosis has significant links with these illnesses, and here I am concerned with revealing how it interacts with them to construct and reveal new pathologies of femininity. Consumption was traditionally associated with mental disorders and was regarded by the medical profession as more likely to afflict those with a certain personality type, or those suffering emotional distress. Hence it became viewed as the concrete physical manifestation of psychological problems: a kind of hysteria made flesh. As consumption signified heightened sensibility, its sufferers were portrayed as refined, intelligent and sensitive members of the upper classes – a desirable identification – yet through its association with subversive, self-inflicted diseases like anorexia, they could also be regarded as a social threat. Chapter 3 explores these and other complex and paradoxical attitudes towards the Victorian invalid through a reading of a best-selling but critically neglected late-century novel, Mrs Humphry Ward's *Eleanor*.[12] An examination of this text's consumptive central character reveals phthisis's unique ability to act as a signifier of purity and spirituality on the one hand, and sexual deviance on the other. Eleanor herself is consumed by unreciprocated love and desire as much as by tuberculosis, and this compromises her virtuous femininity, as she becomes less passive and less self-restrained. Her desires are even more unacceptable because to satisfy them, to marry and reproduce, would perpetuate her disease and contaminate the bloodline of an old family (there are clear parallels with syphilis here). She is socially pathological in other ways too, for she is able to undermine patriarchal authority because of the powers of persuasion and manipulation which her invalid status grant her. However, this novel reveals how the consumptive patient can also function as the self-sacrificing female ideal. *Eleanor* utilises the cultural myths of spirituality which surround the disease in order to engage in debates about sin, punishment and the possibility of redemption. Ward represents her dying heroine as a Magdalen figure who, through the cleansing effect of her illness-induced suffering – and through the partly self-induced wasting of her body – transforms herself from fallen woman into a kind of female messiah.

These questions about the power and appeal of the consumptive woman are developed further in Chapter 4, on the rise of the tubercular aesthetic, which explores how such a painful, debilitating and fatal disease became a fashionable, even sought-after illness in the Victorian era. In this chapter I build upon the work of Bram Dijkstra in the influential *Idols of Perversity* by examining how the nineteenth century's 'cult of invalidism' developed into the consumptive aesthetic. This phenomenon was strongly influenced by the art and literature of the period, which glamorised consumptive women and portrayed them as ethereal rather than emaciated, graceful rather than ghostly. Perhaps the most persuasive tubercular images were the pallid and fragile models and muses of the Pre-Raphaelite movement, and in this chapter I, like Elizabeth Bronfen in *Over Her Dead Body*, include a case study of one of the most famous: the sickly wife of Dante Gabriel Rossetti, Elizabeth Siddal. I discuss here the ways in which Siddal's disease was much more than an unfortunate affliction, suggesting that it was in fact a useful and powerful force which assisted her dramatic social rise, created her distinctive appearance, and lent her a romantically mysterious and tragic public persona. Post-Siddal, the tubercular look soon became the prevalent form of fashionable beauty, a process facilitated by the rise in popularity of the corset, a deeply political garment which fashioned its wearer into a stylishly fragile near-invalid who resembled the classic consumptive. This deliberate, constructed pathologising of the female body is highly revealing, raising questions about the nature of art, fashion and the physically damaging pursuit of an aesthetic ideal in relation to femininity and disease. I therefore regard the corset as an important contributor to tubercular culture, especially as there is also a link between corsetry and capitalism, as corset-making was big business in the Victorian era. This forms another instance of industry's capacity to produce disease, or, indeed, of disease's ability to generate industry in order to meet its demands. The corset thus produced consumption (or more specifically the appearance of consumption, though the actual pathological effect of tight lacing was also the subject of much medical debate) as well as trade and capital.[13] The power of the consumptive aesthetic and the dangerous consequences of such a fashion are central topics in the two novels I discuss in this chapter. George Du Maurier's hugely popular *Trilby* and Charles Reade's lesser-known *A Simpleton* represent two very different views of female beauty and reveal the complex and ambivalent attitudes which surrounded the tubercular 'look' and the tight lacing which helped emulate it.

This book suggests that consumption was set apart from other diseases by its unique ability to act as a hyperbolic signifier, something which made it a valuable symbolic medium in fictional texts. Chapter 5 is concerned with examining one of the most sinister 'metaphors of illness' which surround this disease: the creation of a link between phthisis and vampirism. I suggest that this association was a traditional one forged in centuries of folklore, but is picked up by and developed further in the late Victorian novel in order to articulate anxieties about the newly discovered communicability of the illness and the impact this might have on the nation and indeed the empire. Through a reading of Bram Stoker's *Dracula*, and with reference to several other popular vampire stories of the time, I reveal how not only the vampire's wasted victim, but the vampire him/herself, resembles the archetypal consumptive. This identification is a useful means of blurring the line between realism and science fiction for the authors who utilise it in their texts, but it clearly has negative repercussions for real-life patients. Through association with the vampire, the consumptive ceases to be a passive recipient of disease – though indeed, as previous chapters show, this was never really an accepted picture of the tubercular patient – and becomes a willing embracer of it, and one who will infect others in turn in order to survive. That this view of the consumptive was not limited to the fictional sphere is revealed by an examination of a number of late-century medical texts, whose rhetoric and images suggest that physicians too have been influenced by the vampiric association. This of course had tangible consequences for their patients, whose treatments – like the recommended consumption of fresh blood – frequently had their basis in superstition rather than scientific fact.

The final chapter concludes my examination of the gendering of tuberculosis by looking in detail at one of the few male consumptives in nineteenth-century fiction, Ralph Touchett in Henry James's *The Portrait of a Lady*. James's choice of a disease traditionally perceived as female to afflict his central male character is a deliberate one, for consumption is the perfect vehicle through which to explore the crisis of masculinity which he suggests exists in contemporary society. Consumption, a disease associated with capitalism and luxury, becomes in this novel symbolic of the moral and emotional sickness which manifests itself in the men in *Portrait* and which is presented as the inevitable consequence of the idleness and indulgence inherent in affluent middle- and upper-class existence. Just as phthisis compromises the reproductive capacity of its sufferers – Ralph indicates that it is inadvisable for him to have children for eugenic reasons – the men in the novel are rendered physically and creatively sterile by their circumstances: they consume *objects d'art* and women, but produce nothing.

James uses topical medical and social debates about the best choice of lifestyle for the consumptive patient in order to interrogate possible solutions to the problem raised by masculinity in the text. The book juxtaposes the bourgeois recipe for health – work, marriage and domesticity – against the conventional invalid lifestyle of nomadism and bachelorhood which Ralph leads, a life which also happens to be shared by all the affluent young men in *Portrait*. It is useful for James's purposes that of all diseases tuberculosis responded especially well to the cosseted invalid lifestyle of rest and indulgence: it was not a disease of gradual inevitable decline like cancer but one whose uncertain progress could be repeatedly halted through careful living. This regime of invalidism offered the only available hope of complete recovery, but paradoxically it also needed to be faithfully maintained throughout life to avoid the danger of a relapse. Hypochondria was in a sense an essential component of the consumptive's quest for health, and the pursuit of longevity thus became recognised as a long-term, full-time occupation. This of course has problematic consequences for the consumptive male, whose gender success was conventionally defined by activity and productivity, and we can see the implications of this in Ralph, whose disease becomes a poor substitute for a career. However, as I will show, James proposes that even this subversive existence is in a sense more spiritually 'healthy' than that experienced by the physically well men in the novel. In particular, he makes us aware that, for certain men and particularly for the artist, invalidism has its own benefits and advantages, and they are worth some sacrifice of conventional masculine roles. This is most plainly revealed through an examination of the relationship between Ralph and

Isabel Archer and its real-life inspiration, that between James and his dying cousin, Minny Temple. With reference to James's personal letters, I suggest how consumptive illness may be useful to Ralph and also to his creator, as a means of escaping the unappealing responsibilities and everyday domesticities which accompany health. This very autobiographical novel provides an insight not only into James's view of a pathological society, but also into his personal attitudes about marriage, creativity and the dangerously consuming nature of sexual desire.

A number of authors have worked with the study of tuberculosis's social and cultural impact over the many years of its long history. Perhaps most important of these is Susan Sontag, whose classic *Illness as Metaphor* delineates the symbolic associations and images that surround tuberculosis, syphilis and cancer. Sontag's work, which identifies the ways in which illness is regarded, represented and even transformed by its social context, must be a vital starting point for any exploration of tuberculosis. However, while she does quote from fictional texts to illustrate her observations about consumption's persona, there is much more to be said about the literary production of the disease than her short book can cover. Other explorations of tuberculosis manifest the same lack of detailed engagement with tubercular fiction. Thomas Dormandy's fascinating medical and social history of tuberculosis, *The White Death*, for example, includes much on the lives and deaths of its famous victims, many of whom are writers and artists, but, presumably because its author is a doctor rather than a literary critic, does not explore the potentially revealing work these consumptives left behind. Similarly F. B. Smith's *The Retreat of Tuberculosis*, Frank Ryan's *Tuberculosis: The Greatest Story Never Told*, David Barnes's *The Making of a Social Disease* and Katherine Ott's *Fevered Lives* all concentrate on the factual aspects of phthisis, namely its political impact and the medical response it has provoked. These are of course the essential foundations for any dialogue about this disease, but by by-passing its representation in fiction these works are missing an important source of information about the illness's cultural as well as medical existence. Only Clark Lawlor's recent *Consumption and Literature: The Making of the Romantic Disease* has so far set out to fill this gap. Lawlor's text explores the literary history of the disease from the Renaissance, through the Enlightenment and into the nineteenth century, with particular focus on the Romantic poets and their legacy. Like Sontag, he examines the cultural associations that surround tuberculosis and investigates their literary origins, and his detailed reading of Samuel Richardson's *Clarissa* forms an essential backdrop for my exploration of the consumptive aesthetic in Chapter 4. *Consumption and Literature* does not however, deal, with the later nineteenth century or the Victorian novel, and thus to some degree this book begins where Lawlor's leaves off.

One of the most notable aspects of the studies of tuberculosis listed above is their time frame, for they are all published within the last twenty years. This suggests how an examination of the tubercular literature of the past may be even more relevant today, for the appearance of a recent crop of new tubercular investigations indicates the renewed sense of urgency and importance which is becoming attached to this malady. Tuberculosis today threatens one third of the world's population, and was declared a global health emergency in 1993.[14] Its resurgence was facilitated by the arrival of the AIDS pandemic, for ever-opportunistic tuberculosis has seized the opportunity offered by immune-deficient sections of the population today in the same way that it leapt upon the consequences of the Industrial Revolution in the nineteenth century. It is interesting that this, the most 'spiritual' of illnesses, has maintained its seemingly incongruous link with diseases that symbolise sexual 'deviancy': syphilis may have given way to HIV and AIDS in the twentieth century, but their silent partner, tuberculosis, endures throughout. The appearance of certain lethal, drug-resistant strains of the disease further indicates that even the limited (in that it is confined to affluent societies who can afford the drugs) medical victory represented by the antibiotic revolution has only been a temporary one, spanning in actuality rather less than forty years, and that tuberculosis is likely to form a part of our future as it has of our past. The revival of the study of TB's cultural meanings has been influenced by HIV/AIDS, which has generated new interest in the epistemology of illness by emphasising the significance of infectious diseases in our society, and it reflects a need to understand the social impact of a disease which is clearly not going to go away. As I will show in the following chapters, TB's myths and metaphors change to reflect and indeed produce the anxieties and preoccupations of its community: it is 'the perfect expression of an imperfect civilisation'.[15] Behind this sense of it as a 'social disease', however, should be an awareness of its ability to endure, to triumph over medical progress and to transcend the actual passage of time.[16] Wealth and technological advances may temporarily contain tuberculosis, but cannot eradicate it, and so it remains a powerful symbol of the frailty and mortality of humanity in general.

CHAPTER I

Nineteenth-century medical discourse on tuberculosis

A study of the medical writing published on consumption in the nineteenth century reveals a surprising and intriguing paradox, which takes the form of an unexpected divergence between the history of the disease and the history of its textual representation by physicians. We might expect the interest the medical profession showed in the disease to reflect the extent of the national problem it created, but in fact there is no correlation between the percentage of the population affected by consumption in Britain in the nineteenth century and the numbers of physicians writing about it in a given year. Phthisis had been at the height of its destructive power in the early decades of the century, when a fifth of all deaths in England were attributed to it.[1] The numbers of consumptive deaths began to fall around 1830, and continued to decrease slowly but steadily throughout the rest of the century[2] (though it remained throughout the Victorian era the biggest single killer of men and women in their physical and productive prime, or, more specifically, of those aged between fifteen and thirty-five). Yet there is relatively little published on the disease before 1840, compared to the proliferation of work that emerged after this date (see Appendix B).

The number of medical publications about consumption seems to triple between the 1830s and the 1840s, the very decade when the disease was in decline for the first time since the Industrial Revolution began. This change in medical interest cannot be considered so much a reflection of the *actual* pathological importance of the disease, then, as a reflection of its newly awakening, *perceived* social significance. These books, pamphlets and articles published on phthisis are not only concerned with the numbers of people it consumes and destroys, but also with what it creates and produces: symbols and metaphors, political and eugenic fears, and the transfer of power and wealth. Physicians who had previously been silent on the topic of consumption suddenly began to consider it an important subject for discussion around 1840. That a resurgence of interest had taken place in recent years was acknowledged in the 1870s by Horace Dobell,

Chief Physician to the Royal Infirmary for Diseases of the Chest, who suggested that it was the result of the writings of just a few men:

For many years . . . the subject of tubercle and consumption had been almost dead in the professional mind . . . even to write upon the subject of consumption was looked upon with suspicion; it being assumed that the science of the subject was so completely settled, and that a writer upon it could now have no other object than to produce 'a bait for practice'.

Now all this is changed. In 1859 the late Dr Hughes-Bennett published his book on consumption. In the *Lancet* of September 1864 I published my first Report . . . In 1865 and 1866 my friend and coadjutor M. Villemin gave . . . the startling results of his experiments. In consequence of these and other productions – or at the least coincidently with their appearance – the whole profession began to stir on the subject of tuberculosis and from that time to this the interest and agitation have acquired yearly increasing impetus.[3]

Dobell's opinion is revealing because it implies that the discussion of this disease was in a sense reclaimed and reintroduced from within the medical profession, by several exceptional doctors, himself among them, whose writing paved the way for others to follow. There seems to be a touch of professional anxiety here, for in locating the cause of this new discussion solely within medical discourse he ignores and rejects the other possible factors which might have influenced it. It does seem likely that the publications of these influential physicians on phthisis consolidated and validated the new importance of the disease in medical thought, but they clearly could not have pre-empted a revival of interest which my research suggests began in the 1840s, not more than ten years later as Dobell states.

It is important to note that these works which mushroomed in the 1840s were not motivated by a need to share, discuss or advertise therapeutic advances, for there was little real headway in the medical treatment of the disease until artificial pneumothorax began to be introduced in the 1890s. Hence there was nothing promising or ground-breaking to report in these earlier texts. The aforementioned Bennett's only suggestion for a cure, for example, was that much-discussed old faithful, cod-liver oil. This lack of progress goes some way towards explaining the reluctance of early nineteenth-century physicians to write about consumption, for a number of book reviews in *The Lancet* reveal that those who did take up the subject in this period were frequently greeted with contempt and cynicism. This was because the disease was believed to be untreatable and hence any discussion of it was regarded as pointless. For example, a *Lancet* book review of 18 November 1826 criticises the work of a Dr Whitlock Nicholl for 'drivelling out 11 pages of balderdash on the prevention of phthisis . . . although there is not an idea in it which has not been known to the public for ages'.[4] The implication in this article is that Nicholl has set out to exploit an incurable disease for financial gain, as his writing seems to be merely, in Dobell's words, a 'bait for practice' with no constructive medical reason behind it. In this context Dobell's statement that early nineteenth-century physicians who wrote on consumption were viewed with 'suspicion' by the rest of the profession seems to be an accurate one, as their motives for publishing without having any new knowledge to share could be called into question. Dobell does not attempt to explain, however, why after 1840 it became more acceptable to publish on this disease even in the absence of scientific advancement, and why the medical profession felt the need to establish a discourse around consumption even though it remained mysterious and impenetrable until the 1880s, and incurable for another whole century. This was not an accidental revival of interest, either, but a determined effort on the part of the medical profession, as indicated by the words of controversial physician Charles Scudamore in 1841. He expresses the desire for a change in the way consumption is thought of and investigated by doctors 'in the hope [that it] will be better understood and not so much despaired of than formerly'.[5] More radically, Dr P. C. A. Louis, writing in *The Lancet* in 1844, calls for the 'associated efforts of a great number of medical men' to struggle with the disease: 'In a word, nothing less than an actual *crusade* would suffice.'[6]

So what did inspire this dawn of a new or at least newly prolific body of medical writing about consumption, if not progress in the medical understanding or treatment of the disease? Some answers are suggested by David Barnes's exploration of tuberculosis in nineteenth-century France, *The Making of a Social Disease*, which uncovers a similar situation across the Channel half a century later (pp. 13–20). Barnes charts an increase in medical publications and corresponding government interest in tuberculosis in France at the end of the nineteenth century, also a time when death rates from the disease had recently begun to fall. He locates the French 'War on Tuberculosis' (which lasted from the late 1890s to 1906) within the context of national social unrest, showing that at this period the Republic was coming under attack from political factions from both Left and Right, there was widespread class-related violence and strikes among workers, and, in addition, the falling birthrate seemed to present a threat to the future survival and prosperity of the nation. Barnes argues that tuberculosis 'was the most familiar face of death in nineteenth-century France' and so 'became a vessel into which could flow a variety of fears, grievances, and emotions'

(p. 251). Hence a newly vehement attack on the disease becomes an attack on the social problems it symbolises – problems more diverse and therefore less manageable that the disease itself.

> Birthrates, mortality, moral decay, political subversion, the filth and danger represented by the working class in bourgeois eyes – tuberculosis allowed all these diverse and threatening themes to be assembled into a single coherent package. (p. 19)

An interesting parallel between the two countries emerges here, for as regards class conflict, strikes, civil unrest, and threats to the status of the bourgeoisie, *fin de siècle* France has much in common with England in the 'hungry forties'. Both countries display a connection between a period of social turbulence and a revival of interest in consumption. The disease becomes a valuable symbol for the body politic, for it represents the consuming and wasting and weakening of a nation from subversive elements within it.

It is of course undeniable that not only phthisis but disease in *general* occupied a dominant place in English public consciousness in the 1840s, a decade ravaged by repeated and major epidemics of typhus, typhoid, cholera and smallpox.[7] With the death rate on the increase for the first time since the seventeenth century, the need to learn more about all killer diseases became of pressing importance. In addition, the medical profession's reputation became at once more legitimate and more scientific in this period, and the popularity and impact of medical publications such as *The Lancet* increased in consequence. Hence the growth of medical writing on consumption could be due to these factors alone. However, we would expect phthisis, as an old and familiar illness, to be overlooked by doctors in the flurry of public concern over the new (in the case of cholera) and more pressing health issues the fevers represented.[8] Why then was consumption, among the most ancient of human ailments, singled out for increased investigation at a time when medicine had its hands full with more virulent diseases?

The writings of Victorian physicians do not provide a definite answer to this question. It is certain, however, that within the space of a few years the disease goes from being avoided and silenced by a frustrated medical profession[9] – with writing on the subject being 'looked upon with suspicion', as Dobell suggests – to being a popular topic for debate and discussion. Physicians who formerly 'shrink from contending with the disease'[10] begin to consider it an acceptable subject for investigation. I suggest that this

new sense of consumption as a more respectable, even bourgeois disease
was created at least in part by the literary fiction of the period, which transformed the public's perception of the illness. The social problem novel was
an important medium for drawing public attention to the social and pathological consequences of class division and poverty in the 1840s and 1850s. As
they are realist texts dealing with the industrial poor it is not surprising that
these novels often represent a number of the diseases of deprivation which
plagued this section of society, but it is important to note that consumption
has a special role to play within them. As a disease of individuals rather than
the masses, consumption is the perfect vehicle for the social problem novel,
a form which was preoccupied with the interaction between society and the
individual, and by their repeated use of consumptive characters it can be
argued that these popular novels are responsible for bringing consumption
into the general public's consciousness. Gaskell's *Mary Barton* and *North
and South*, Charlotte Tonna's *Helen Fleetwood*, Brontë's *Jane Eyre* and Dickens's *Oliver Twist* and *Dombey and Son* all describe a number of diseases but
their consumptive characters are singled out by the plot and rendered more
important within the text than the plentiful victims of fever also represented
there. As I discussed in my introduction, consumption is used in literature
as a means of identifying the innocent, spiritual and worthy characters and
separating them from the squalid diseased masses. Dickens's consumptives,
Paul Dombey and little Dick in *Oliver Twist*, are angelic, too-good-to-live
child heroes: of all the diseases of deprivation which stalk the workhouse
in which he lives, consumption is the one which carries the pious Dick off.
Jane Eyre's Helen Burns is a Christlike portrait of resigned, uncomplaining
suffering, and it is notable that her death, from consumption, has more
meaning – to Jane, to the reader, and even to Miss Temple, who shares
her room so she may nurse her personally – than those of dozens of others
who die around her in the typhoid epidemic. Gaskell's Bessy Higgins in
North and South, although working class, functions as an instrument of
cross-class communication and reconciliation because of her refined, bourgeois sensitivity, thoughtfulness and religiosity, and the gradual, reconciled
nature of her 'good' death reflects this. It also, of course, contrasts markedly
with the sudden, brutal and squalid death from fever of, for example, Ben
Davenport in *Mary Barton*.

What emerges from these novels is a compelling fictional picture of
the consumptive as a socially desirable patient, a worthy recipient of the
bourgeois physician's care and attention. These popular works consolidated
and publicised the stereotype of the idealised consumptive whose moral
worth merited an increase in medical concern for their condition. Their

plots also suggested that this disease was in a sense more significant and important than other illnesses which were denied the same textual status. The new importance that the medical profession gave to the disease in this decade was mirrored by its representation by the novels of the time, and, I suggest, may have been influenced by them. After all, as Richard D. Altick has pointed out, 'because of the special requirements of their daily work, as well as the general cultural tradition of the professional class', physicians, along with teachers and civil servants, 'constituted an important audience for reading matter' in the Victorian period as never before.[11] An increase in leisure time, coupled with (owing to the rise of Evangelism) increased limitations on the ways in which that time could be respectably spent, contributed to the rise of novel-reading among the professional classes.[12] So did increasing urbanisation and the growth of the railways, which facilitated commuting and hence provided daily opportunities for perusing fiction.

That fiction was not only read by physicians but also had an important influence over Victorian medical thought is indicated by an examination of the writings of several physicians who reveal an interest in literature and even an awareness of its use to the profession. One such example was late Victorian doctor Norman Moore,[13] a physician and lecturer at St Bartholomew's Hospital, who published at the turn of the century an exploration of the relationship between medicine and English literature which is worth discussing in some detail here. Moore examines the ways in which doctors may learn from literary texts: 'my object in this address has been to show how we who are acquainted with medicine may use literature as one of the many means of improving ourselves in our own subject'.[14] He argues that to be a good physician a man must have a knowledge of much more than medicine, and that 'for those who are to engage in the practice of our far-reaching and all-absorbing art' it is desirable to possess the 'widest possible basis of education'.[15] 'Far-reaching and all-absorbing' suggests that medicine cannot be considered merely a study of the body, but must assimilate a wide variety of different branches of knowledge to be able to treat the extensive problems of the human condition. His use of the word 'art', in turn, implies a rejection of the recent (mid-nineteenth-century) separation between definitions of scientific and artistic skills, which associated medicine with 'utility' rather than 'imagination', with the pursuit of facts rather than of creativity. Moore invokes the intellectual versatility of Renaissance Man when he goes on to state that an understanding of grammar, rhetoric, logic and philosophy are all vital constituents in a doctor's ability to 'treat the whole' person – an opinion shared by other physicians.[16] As these accomplishments are of a specifically literary nature, they suggest a link between the physician and the author of fiction. Successful practitioners of these seemingly different 'arts' must share similar attributes. Literature is not only a means of creating more versatile, socially minded and sympathetic doctors, however, but according to Moore has a more concrete didactic value for physicians as well. Books are a medium through which medical issues can be recorded and explored – Moore cites Boswell's *Life of Johnson* as a literary chronicle of historical disease which is still of value to the modern-day physician – and, most importantly, disseminated to the reading public. Moore acknowledges the extent of the influence of the literary author over the population, aware that they have an ability to reach people about medical issues in a way that medical science cannot. He uses Daniel Defoe as an example:

Defoe's *History of the Plague* is a Work of imagination ... [yet] it is to this unhistorical 'History' of the Plague, which so well illustrates the remark of Fielding that works of imagination may have more absolute truth in them than histories, that we owe the fact that almost every child in England has heard of the great plague of London ... such is the power of good literature ...[17]

It is not the physician but the author of fiction who can inform and educate 'almost every child in England' about disease, for medical texts are much less accessible to the general public.

Novelistic treatment of the character of the doctor himself is also of interest and use to the medical reader, as those texts which 'relate to the histories or characters of physicians ... afford abundant material for consideration and some of them ... almost belong to the actual illustration of medical study and observation in our literature'.[18] The fictional physician, then, is an object of fascination for his real-life counterpart, as both a means of reflecting on the important persona of the doctor and a method of observing how members of the profession are viewed by the public. The significance of literature's part in constructing disease and doctors alike is reinforced by Sir Humphry Rolleston's observation some thirty years later that 'there is a great literary tradition in British medicine'.[19] Rolleston also suggests that 'the representations of medical men in literature and fiction are historically useful as evidence of contemporary opinion' in medical matters, and cites Dickens as an especially useful source owing to his interest in medicine and his associations with Victorian physicians.[20]

Other physicians have admitted the influence of literary fiction on Victorian medical thought with specific reference to consumption. Alfred Hillier, a personal friend and colleague of Robert Koch, begins both of his influential medical books about phthisis with an exploration of the literary representation of the disease by authors such as George Sand and Chateaubriand. By this inclusion Hillier acknowledges the importance of the artistic influence on social and medical thinking about the illness, but he is aware that this influence may be a dangerous one. He is particularly concerned about the the role certain pervasive and persuasive literary myths have played in the medical identification of a tubercular diathesis:

Tennyson's 'May Queen', than whom there was none so fair 'in all the land, they say', with her bright eye, brilliant gaiety, and pathetic death, is sometimes taken to be a typical description of the tuberculous constitution. But on the other hand, how frequently do we see patients suffering from pulmonary tuberculosis obviously not fashioned with that ethereal delicacy which tradition – begot, perchance, of the bereavement of parents – has associated with the so-called 'consumptive tendency'.[21]

Hillier sets out here to destabilise the assumptions which literature and 'tradition' have together forged about the consumptive, revealing that the reality of the disease may be much more prosaic. 'Tuberculosis reflects the large in build, the coarse in feature, the dull and sluggish, as freely as the fairest and brightest in the land' he concludes.[22] Hillier is aware that reliance on the stereotypical view of the consumptive type was a common means of diagnosis throughout the period, and one which might lead the physician astray.

It is notable here that even those physicians like Hillier, who presented a deliberate, conscious attempt to claim authority over the disease through a more scientific approach based on – in the absence of concrete fact – careful observation and long personal experience, and who set out to challenge the traditional fictions of consumption, must still battle with the metaphors and images which literature had made an unavoidable accompaniment to the disease. 'Superstition and prejudice have agreed in their creation . . . in the supposed causes of consumption, and it is a task of great difficulty in the present day to separate the real from the unreal' observed Dr Edwin Alabone in 1880.[23] This is reinforced by medical texts right throughout the century, in which consumption frequently functions as a powerful signifier on many levels, a likely legacy from its representation by the fiction of the period. I have mentioned phthisis's association with the pious, the angelic and the refined in literature, and how novels single out consumptives as special, yet these views are frequently replicated in medical texts and used there as *facts* about patients, facts which form diagnostic tools with which to identify consumption. Physicians like John Balbirne declare that 'amiability is a usual characteristic of the consumptive'[24] and T. R. Allinson states that phthisis affects 'the talented, gifted and beautiful more often than coarser humanity'.[25] In addition, an assertion by Balbirne that 'the intellectual facilities indeed seem prematurely developed – they are remarked as apt, wise and knowing beyond their years . . .'[26] is reminiscent of consumptive literary heroes and heroines, like little Paul Dombey, who thinks like an 'old, old' man, and the religious mystic Helen Burns.[27]

There is an interesting medical dependence here on cultural myths – either created or perpetuated by literature – rather than on science. But, of course, fiction must be especially hard to dismiss when facts themselves are in short supply. Because of the absence of accurate information about the disease, for most of the century medical thinking about consumption was a rather unscientific mix of speculation and hypothesis. There was little new knowledge with which to update or alter the enduring, culturally persuasive literary portrait of phthisis. Unfortunately, the necessity of searching for a cure, without really understanding the nature of the disease, meant that many of these medical writings were a kind of fiction in themselves. A large number of these texts were written to make claims about their authors' knowledge and skill as physicians, and frequently put forward new ideas about or possible treatments for consumption, which demanded the faith of readers and patients alike, yet were usually unsupported by any kind of real evidence, and had little hope of success. The whole canon of Victorian medical writing on consumption reveals the struggles of a frustrated profession with a deadly and mysterious disease, a search towards truth hampered by lack of certainties and facts, and confused by a proliferation of myths and assumptions. The absence of this truth meant that out of necessity was born a reluctant open-mindedness towards other possible sources of information about the disease, as a Dr Elliotson revealed in *The Lancet*: 'I cannot cure phthisis; I shall therefore put to the test any-thing that I hear of from a respectable source, or which appears in itself plausible . . .'[28]

I have been attempting to show in these pages that there was an important dialogue or relationship between Victorian medical writing about consumption and literary fiction. At the very least, both genres were writing about the same disease at the same time, and we would expect interesting similarities and differences to exist. At the most, they directly influence one another in significant ways. I am dealing mainly in this chapter with the ways in which medical literature may have been shaped by fiction, as the rest of the study will concentrate upon novels and their relation and use of contemporary medicine. This work as a whole takes as its central concern the fictional literature about consumption, and in the following chapters sets out to interpret and investigate that literature by reading it in the context of the medical writing that helped produce its portrayal of the disease. However, as I have shown, this was not a one-way process: medical discourses are not constructed in a vacuum and are in fact shaped by the same social and political forces as the novel. I now intend to provide a brief overview of the most important issues and themes in Victorian medical writing on consumption, but I also wish to uncover the political objectives and assumptions and the gender and class concerns which lie behind these issues. This is undertaken with a view to revealing how the medical treatise, like the novel, can function as a revealing and informative portrait of its age.

INFECTIOUS OR INHERITED?

The single most important concern in the whole canon of medical writing on consumption was the debate over whether it was hereditary or infectious, a question which preoccupied doctors throughout the Victorian era and beyond. For centuries opinion had been more or less settled on the matter, with physicians from Aristotle onward convinced that it was a transmissible disease. However, this changed with the advent of the nineteenth century: 'From 1800 on, with some very few exceptions, Medical opinion and Public opinion have been gradually becoming settled in opposition to the theory of contagion.'[29] Much of Europe did still consider phthisis to be infectious and accordingly took administrative measures to prevent the spread of the disease, but this view was shared by a only few physicians in Britain and America. Among them was the professor of clinical medicine at Harvard, Henry Bowditch, who argued in 1864 in support of the contagion theory in *Is Consumption ever Contagious?*, reporting that his own experience had showed him that consumption could be passed between married couples. The British medical profession as a whole, however, clung to their belief in hereditary transmission for most of the century.

We might expect that after Koch's identification of the tubercle bacillus in 1882 this controversy would come to an end, but an examination of medical writing from the 1880s and 1890s reveals that scepticism about the infectiousness of phthisis remained. 'Thanks to certain wary qualities and certain social considerations, Britain has not been driven into accepting all the logical consequences [of Koch's discovery],' said Dr Candler in 1887.[30] This was at least partly so because it seemed apparent that while consumption had been shown to be *transmissible* it was not *contagious* in the way other diseases, like typhoid or cholera, were: it did not strike down whole communities at once, rather singling out certain people and frequently leaving those in close contact with them unscathed. The continuation of the infection debate is indicated by texts like *Reasons for Believing in the Contagiousness of Phthisis* by W. A. Webb, published in 1884. As the title of this work suggests, contagion theory was still not accepted without reservation, even post-Koch. That phthisis was not included in the Infectious Diseases Notification Act of 1889 – which made it compulsory to notify the authorities when a contagious disease was diagnosed – reflected further the ambiguous nature of public feeling about this question.

The motivation behind this rejection of the contagion theory is complex and multifaceted. The primary 'social consideration' which encouraged British physicians to be cynical about the consequences of Koch's discovery was an awareness of the public panic and fear that would result if phthisis was known to be infectious, and hence there is a clear political motive for silencing this aspect of the disease. It is difficult to control the spread of a gradual, chronic illness: contagion could only be managed by the enforced isolation and confinement of the patient for many years. This was clearly not an attractive solution from a social point of view, as it would necessitate heavy government interference in private life, and result in the splitting up of families. Such quarantine had problematic economic consequences as well, for it must involve removing the patient from his job even while he remained well enough to work, adding to the already heavy financial burden which phthisis had laid upon the working classes. An acceptance of contagiousness was also threatening to the more affluent sections of society, for the increased chances of recovery they benefited from depended on the availability of certain resources, namely attentive nursing care, a certain luxurious standard of living, and emotional support by family and friends. All this would be threatened by fear of contagion which would demand removal and isolation of the consumptive from the society which had previously served him and assisted in his recovery. Frédéric Chopin, whose final days were rendered much more traumatic by his treatment in Majorca, was a fearful testament to what middle- and upper-class consumptives might expect if their disease was accepted as infectious. Even money and friends could not ensure good treatment for him on an island which, like much of Europe outside Britain, believed that phthisis was infectious, and which consequently treated its sufferers like lepers.[31] Then there was the difficulty, equally pertinent for all classes, that the psychological disturbance caused by such isolation was considered a major threat to the recovery of consumptive patients, 'whose cure was dependent on freedom from mental anxiety'.[32] If phthisis really was infectious, then any attempt to protect the healthy from catching the disease meant further endangering the wellbeing of those who were already consumptive, and further reducing their quality of life.

The medical profession had other, more complex reasons for continuing to construct phthisis as a hereditary disease, however, and this is revealed by the shifting nature of medical thinking about infectiousness by the end of the century. After 1882 physicians slowly came to accept that consumption was caused by a transmissible bacillus, but this merely redefined the hereditary debate in terms of germ theory, as debate arose about whether the bacteria could be passed from parent to child. Comparisons were made with syphilis, which was also an infectious disease and yet could be transmitted congenitally, passed down through families for generations. As part of this hereditary/congenital debate, studies were done on children who were removed from their consumptive (and working-class) parents at birth, placed in healthier surroundings, and observed for a number of years to see if they developed symptoms of the illness. They frequently did not, and though this was not for many considered conclusive evidence against parental transmission medicine began to look for other explanations for the seemingly arbitrary selection of victims. Physicians were preoccupied with the unanswerable question which seemed to be key to an understanding of consumption: why did a disease which seemed almost permanently present in the air and was transmitted every time its hosts breathed or talked not infect the entire population, considering that a huge number of people must inhale it every day? Why did it afflict only certain, unfortunate individuals who seemed singled out to become victims? Did they have an innate physical weakness which rendered them liable to infection? And if so, was this susceptibility inherited, even if the tubercle bacillus itself was not?

These questions represented a return to the most persistent, politicised theory about phthisis, which had, significantly, its roots in the consumptive characters of the Victorian novel. This was the long-enduring belief that there was a consumptive 'type', a group of classic, stereotypical victims whose bodies were innately susceptible to the disease. The appeal of this theory is clear: even if the disease was infectious, it was not random, but personal. Consumptives were not simply unlucky people who had inhaled the germ, but had been selected for a mysterious reason, as popular opinion had always believed, and fiction reinforced. Of course this 'reason' for illness was open to interpretation, and thus the romance that literature and culture had always associated with consumption was back. The existence of a diathesis meant that it was again medically legitimate to seek to identify or diagnose consumptives by their outward appearance or their personality. Physicality and behaviour were thought to be bound up with the disease. And, of course, if a consumptive type existed, then the stereotypical victims of fiction – the innocent child, the beautiful, spiritual young woman, the lovesick poet, the impoverished but talented artist – could no longer be considered merely literary tropes but could actually be accepted as potentially accurate representations of diathesis. The myths, both literary and cultural, which had always accompanied the disease could become validated. Literary fiction had traditionally represented consumption as not contagious, because its value to the novel was based on its existence as a disease of individuals, associated not with contagion but with personal characteristics, behaviour and lifestyle, so that it might function as a cultural signifier. This becomes apparent when one considers that even those late-century, post-Koch novels which accept that consumption is passed from one person to another hold factors other than mere infection responsible. In Mrs Henry Wood's best-selling 1900 novel *East Lynne*, for example, the consumption which kills the heroine, Isabel, is clearly contracted while nursing her son, but within the world of the novel her death is represented as the consequence of her guilt and suffering: when asked what is killing her, she says 'a broken heart'.[33] Her miserable and lonely existence as a fallen woman renders her physically and mentally weak and hence vulnerable to a disease which does not spread to anyone else in the household.

Of course this tubercular diathesis, as perpetuated by both medicine and literature, has disturbing implications for the consumptive patient. Germ theory in general represented a movement away from this internalist way of approaching illness, as it became accepted that the disease could be caused by agents outside the body, which penetrated it and then caused havoc in a previously healthy organism. It was, therefore, not the individual body's 'fault'. But it was known that the tuberculous bacillus could enter the body and have no effect, for post-mortems had often revealed old, healed tubercle deposits in individuals who had lived healthy lives and died of unrelated illnesses. This shifted the emphasis back to the individual, for if the bacillus did not automatically cause disease, then those who succumbed to it were, it seemed, in some way responsible for their own illness. The consumptive *was* consumptive not just because he or she had become infected, but because they had either inherited the taint of susceptibility to the disease, were marked for it from birth, or else had acquired the diathesis through their lifestyle or behaviour, like the doomed Isabel.

It is apparent then that the inheritance question is not simply a medical issue about how one becomes ill, but in fact has serious consequences for the patient. The whole issue about susceptibility and responsibility transforms the consumptive from passive victim to self-pathologising social deviant whose behaviour and lifestyle invite his or her disease. This is of course frequently a means of viewing the patient afflicted with a sexually transmitted disease: it was a common way of thinking about syphilis in the Victorian era as it still is about HIV/AIDS today. It is significant, however, that consumption, despite its reputation as the most 'spiritual' of all illnesses, was also portrayed by medical literature as an illness bound up with the behaviour of its sufferer long before it was known to be infectious to all and yet only fatal to some. As early as 1859 John Hughes Bennett revealed in *The Pathology and Treatment of Pulmonary Consumption* why it was thought of in this way. A professor of medicine at Edinburgh University who, as already mentioned, was heralded by Horace Dobell as the man who began the Victorian revival of medical interest in consumption, Bennett is a substantial early authority on the disease. He believed that consumption was caused by a lack of fats in the body, and was thus 'almost invariably [the consequence of] such circumstances as induce impoverished nutrition'.[34] As he points out, among the poor malnutrition was an unavoidable condition, but members of the more affluent classes had only themselves to blame for their unhealthy diet. Consumption was

ushered in with a bad and capricious appetite . . . unusual acidity of the stomach, [and] anorexia . . . (p. 17)

Such individuals [consumptives] have a most capricious appetite, frequently loathe all kinds of animal food, and it will be found that even when they say that their appetite is good, and that they live well, the diet is actually either deficient in quantity, or in quality. (p. 114)

It is significant here that the consumptive is defined not only as a faddy eater, but also as secretive and deceptive about their eating habits: the picture drawn here is reminiscent of the behaviour exhibited by patients with anorexia nervosa.[35] Bennett does not limit personal responsibility for illness to diet, however. He also discusses the disastrous effects of what he terms other 'intemperate habits', which include alcoholic drink and 'the attractions of fashion' (p. 133), in other words late-night parties and other social gatherings which 'the young can seldom resist . . . they return to their homes late at night, exposed to the chill air, the injurious effect of which is augmented by the previous heat and foul air of crowded assemblies' (p. 133). In this way it is clear to see the origins of consumption's existence as a 'fashionable disease', for it is associated with indulgence in the pleasures of the social round. In this way its treatment is not so much about fighting the illness as changing the lifestyle, for, as Bennett indicates, the latter is held responsible for the former:

In the treatment of this disease the physician has to struggle not only with the deadly nature of the disorder, but with numerous difficulties over which he has no control such as, among the poorer classes, the impossibility of procuring good diet, and the thousands of imprudences which not only they, but the majority of invalids, are ever committing. (p. 137)

There is a touch of medical manipulation here, for this implies that it is only the patient's circumstances and behaviour which get in the way of a cure, that it is only poverty and irrepressible human nature which is beyond the physician's 'control', when in fact he had little influence over their actual disease either. In fact this whole 'responsibility of lifestyle' theory which was advocated by Bennett and many other physicians[36] was extremely useful to the medical profession, which utilised it to disguise the absence of any scientific evidence about the true cause of the disease. By shifting the emphasis from the disease to the patient it was possible to play down medicine's inability to successfully treat consumption, for if it is lifestyle that is to blame then it becomes the patient's fault for being ill rather than the physician's fault for failing to cure. It was also, even more importantly, a means of extending medical power within Victorian society. Treatment for phthisis was no longer only a matter of letting blood or giving out drugs, but necessitated control over almost every aspect of their patients' lives and, in consequence, frequently the lives of their families as well. Diet, rest, habitation, clothing, social life, personal relationships: all needed to be under a doctor's influence for a cure to have every chance of success. The case studies Bennett lists reveal that his patients are in remission while following his advice and relapse when they return to their dissipated lives. The message here is that respectability – frequently in the form of abstinence from drink, alcohol being it seems the greatest threat to a consumptive's health – and obedience to the physician bring their own rewards.

The kinds of medical judgements found in these texts begin to uncover the wide spectrum of attitudes that are directed towards the consumptive persona. It might be observed that the physician's view seems to be setting out to resist the prevalent cultural and literary version of the disease: far from being pure, ethereal and spiritual, Bennett's consumptives are self-indulgent, deceitful, pleasure-seeking and stubborn. This portrayal of the

patient as subversive and troublesome, needing to be cured morally as well
as physically, runs through a large number of medical texts. Dr Ludwig
Rohden, for instance, wrote in 1875 about the 'well known and dangerous indiscretion of pulmonary patients' which 'leads almost all on every
opportunity into transgressions, which in no affliction are less tardy in their
revenge than in phthisis' (p. 531). What these 'transgressions' might be is
not specified, but a hint is given by the mention of unsuitable appetites:
Rohden condemns the 'usual gluttony of convalescents at seaside health
resorts' (p. 526), an unusual criticism when one considers that consumption was normally associated with the failure to eat. Bennett is clearly not
the only doctor to believe that consumptive patients are likely to misbehave,
and also likely to be punished for their misbehaviour by the worsening of
their illness. In Braun's text too, the disease functions as both a morally
corrupting force which leads its sufferers into dissipation and an instrument of social control which rapidly seeks 'revenge' for any behaviour that
undermines the obedience and docility necessary for physical and moral
health.

This creates a rather ambiguous view of consumption as at once socially
subversive and a means of ensuring good behaviour, a view which is reflected
in the figure of the consumptive himself, as an examination of the work of
several other physicians reveals. The paradox at the heart of the metaphorical representation of the disease is revealed here, for there is a struggle in
this medical writing, as in literary fiction, between the idea that any diseased body is socially subversive and deviant because unhealthy, and the
traditional conception of the consumptive as a spiritually pure, even holy,
victim of the White Plague. It is interesting that several writers display
the usual physician's distaste for, and exasperation with, the troublesome
phthisis patient, and yet simultaneously accept and reinforce the idealised
literary and cultural stereotype associated with the illness. Alabone's text
is a good example of this condemnation of the pathological behaviour of
the consumptive. Alabone cites female vanity as a major cause of phthisis
in women, and explains that their desire to display themselves through
'extravagancies in dress' (p. 27) leads them to ignore his advice, with fatal
results (he is particularly disapproving of the bare flesh exposed by fashionable gowns). He also emphasises the importance of physical cleanliness,
as if consumption was associated with bodily dirt: 'in no class of disease is
the thorough cleansing of the skin so necessary as in this', he states (p. 60).
The implications of a link between sexual immorality and consumption
here are strong. Yet later in the same text, he describes what he believes

to be the tubercular diathesis in terms that would not be out of place in a novel by Dickens:

The taint of consumption can in many cases be easily recognised by physical signs . . . The eyes . . . possess a most remarkable brilliancy . . . the nervous system is especially developed, hence it is a frequent thing for consumptive patients to be of a most refined nature . . . being remarkable for the gentleness of their disposition, the amiability of their character, and the great purity of their moral feeling . . . (p. 24)

This idealisation of the consumptive figure seems to neatly match the classic, 'too good to live' cultural stereotype: the disease may be a physical 'taint', but is a spiritual blessing, for the afflicted possesses moral strengths to compensate for the weakness of body. This represents an almost total reversal of opinion within the same text, as Alabone sees the consumptive as socially deviant, and yet also 'remarkable for . . . great purity'. These kinds of dichotomies resound throughout a number of the medical texts, and seem to present something of a problem for the Victorian physician, who was preoccupied with establishing the personality of the consumptive, and depended on such identifications for diagnosis. The Victorian novel, on the other hand, could readily embrace such contradictions, and utilise them. Novels like Mrs Ward's *Eleanor* and du Maurier's *Trilby* represented consumptives as naturally and innately superior beings, who temporarily fell into depravity, but became suitably punished and then finally elevated into saintly spirituality by their disease. The redemption plot at the heart of these books, and the narrative of illness that illustrates it, are essentially one and the same.

Also significant about the personality described by Alabone above is the mention of a highly developed nervous system, which is of course meant to be read as a representation of increased sensibility. Alabone goes on to link consumption with emotional state, stating that 'depressing passions and violent emotions of the mind pre-dispose greatly to this disease' (p. 24). This association between phthisis and mental health is forged, as Clark Lawlor points out, in both literature and medicine as far back as the Renaissance period, and continues into the long eighteenth century: Lawlor traces 'consumptive love melancholy' from Benedick in Shakespeare's *Much Ado About Nothing* to Richardson's *Clarissa*.[37] It is unsurprising, then, to see this link perpetuated by Victorian physicians who are drawing on long-held, traditional beliefs about the disease. Of course, Victorian fiction picks up on the psychological dimension of consumption as well, for it enables the literary trope of 'dying of a broken heart' to take on a tangible physical meaning, through a disease which preyed on the suffering and grief-stricken. This useful plot device is put to work in novels like *East Lynne, Eleanor* and *Wuthering Heights*, where, as in *Clarissa,* the disease of (inevitably female) consumptives functions as an outward expression of their inward suffering. Whereas Richardson's heroine may be absolved from blame, however,[38] in the Victorian period tubercular melancholy is really another form of the responsibility theory: the consumptive becomes ill because their psychological instability and over-indulgence in grief makes them vulnerable to the disease, as we shall see.

It is notable that the fictional consumptives in the novels mentioned above are all middle or upper class. Alabone's analysis works to construct phthisis as largely a disorder of the higher classes, since the working population were not thought to be sensitive enough to experience problems with their 'nerves'.[39] To be upper class, then, was to have 'a refined nature', to be emotional and vulnerable to mental upset, but this in turn rendered one susceptible to phthisis. It is in fact clear from the whole direction of Alabone's writing that he is only concerned with affluent consumptives, for all the treatments he proposes – special diets, warm surroundings, travel abroad – assume that wealth and leisure are abundant resources for his patients. Hence the text has the overall effect of constructing phthisis as an aristocratic disease, so totally are the poor excluded from his exploration. It is possible, however, that this is not so much an oversight as an acknowledgement of the widely held belief that phthisis was a different illness for different classes. Physician to the Norfolk and Norwich Hospital F. W. Burton-Fanning discusses this separation in his book on the disease: 'There are two kinds of consumption – that of the rich and that of the poor. The former is sometimes cured, the latter never.'[40] This is on one level a pragmatic acceptance that the best treatment for phthisis was denied to the poor, because they lacked the money to facilitate their treatment – and, of course, to pay the illustrious physician whose advice provided the best means of a cure. Later in his argument, however, Burton-Fanning hints that there may actually be a difference not just in the social experience of the disease, but in the disease itself: 'amongst the poor, [tuberculosis] is a strictly infectious disorder, but it attacks the well-to-do classes more or less sporadically'.[41] This seems to suggest that consumption is really like two illnesses, the infectious disease associated with deprivation which is easily and visibly spread amidst the squalid and overcrowded dwellings of the poor, and the more unexplainable, random condition that mysteriously afflicts members of the affluent classes.

Does this social division of the disease go some way towards explaining the saint/sinner dichotomy the medical profession saw among its sufferers? It is tempting to deduce that the pure and refined consumptive was the upper-class patient and the morally suspect, unhygienic and alcoholic deviant the impoverished worker, but of course this could not be so, for, as Roy Porter has observed, a pathological lifestyle was common to both.[42] For the rich, indulgence in luxuries, unhealthy fashions, idleness – 'exercise is of all means the most beneficial, but patients are usually averse to this', as Alabone observed (p. 70) – and over-participation in society – 'a lady cured of phthisis must not, on returning home, be encouraged to entertain much or shorten her night's sleep by accepting many invitations'[43] – all brought about disease. For the poor, their consumption was heralded by 'constant neglect of rest by working hard during the day, and *taking it out of themselves with pleasure* in the evenings'.[44] A comparison of the two reveals that what the medical profession considered dangerous in both classes was in fact the rejection of those principles central to the bourgeois social ideal: the work ethic and the importance of the family. The lives of consumptives from all classes are pathological because they, in Bennett's words, 'pursue pleasure' (p. 138) outside the home, the affluent in society, the working class seeking what enjoyment they can afford through drinking and frequenting taverns and the music hall. Both sets of lives are hence contrary to the respectable, restrained, domestic existence that was conducive to moral and physical health, for the Victorian home was, after all, a refuge against the contaminating outside world. The political subtext here, then, is that both groups are demonised for failing to emulate the bourgeoisie, the class to which most of these physicians belonged. Through social activity the poor have established a separate working-class culture; the wealthy, in their turn, have revealed through their idleness and indulgence in hedonism and fashion their desire to emulate the corrupt aristocracy. Neither model themselves on the respectable sections of the middle classes, and in the eyes of their doctors consumption becomes their punishment.

A PATHOLOGISED FEMININITY

Medical literature on phthisis reveals much about Victorian attitudes to class, but even more about their gender concerns. Victorian art and literature traditionally represented the disease as female, with consumptive characters in novels, for example, being almost always women. There are few male consumptives in nineteenth-century novels and when they do exist they are generally children, like Paul Dombey, or emasculated, sexually unsuccessful men, like Ralph Touchett in *The Portrait of a Lady*, whom I will discuss in Chapter 6. It is interesting to examine how this gendering of consumption by fiction may have affected its medical representation. A number of physicians state that consumption affects more women than men,[45] yet the statistics I have seen do not provide any concrete medical evidence for this.[46] Incidence for men and women varies in different years and for different age groups, and of course statistics cannot always be considered reliable, but it is still not possible to distinguish an overall trend which renders women more likely to suffer from the disease. Yet while a few nineteenth-century physicians do not relate consumption to sex at all, most of them, of which Alabone is once again a good example, believe that it is 'more frequently met with in females than in males'. Alabone cites others who share his view: 'the opinions of a very great number of medical men, all in favour of a greater liability of females to this disease' (p. 26). The only reason he can suggest for this difference, however, is the greater susceptibility of woman to the vice of vanity and the allure of the fashionable life: 'some writers assign the causes to tight lacing, others to exposure of the neck in females, or to deficiency of exercise' (p. 26).

Of course this feminising of the disease has its roots in the eighteenth century: Lawlor has noted the tendency of physicians like John Stephens to perpetuate the myth that 'women, with their womb-driven physiology and psychology, were supposed to be especially susceptible'.[47] By the Victorian period, this seemed to have become more concrete, as consumption appeared to be linked to menstruation and menstrual disorders, and this was treated as further evidence about the essential 'femaleness' of the illness. As Rohden observed, 'it is often the case that symptoms of phthisis accompany uterine disease' (p. 558). Dobell believed that puberty protected young women against consumption owing to an 'excess of carbon in their system at this time',[48] but more commonly, and more accurately, physicians agreed that the onset of menstruation and the draining of strength which accompanied it would make them more vulnerable to disease. So too of course would the demands common to later female life like childbirth and breastfeeding, which take their toll on all female animals: as eminent society physician Sir Richard Thorne wrote, even the 'female cow suffers most from pulmonary tuberculosis, due to the exhausting process involved in the long-sustained production of milk'[!].[49] Moreover, Sir Hugh Beevor had explored the similarities between consumption and another 'female disease' which frequently accompanied menstruation and pregnancy, anaemia. The two illnesses were frequently confused with one another as their symptoms were similar, both causing pallor, weakness and weight loss. Of course, as anaemia frequently resulted in malnourished women who would hence be vulnerable to opportunistic consumption, the link between the two was far from an arbitrary one: 'the anaemia and debility which uterine diseases so constantly produce, through their reaction on the digestive and nutritive functions, create powerful pre-disposing causes of pulmonary consumption'.[50]

The female reproductive system did have a part to play in women's susceptibility to phthisis: menstruation and gestation did take a heavy toll on female nutrition and hence on their resistance to disease. Hard physical labour, longer working hours and increased alcohol use probably created an equivalent drain on male resources, however, and in fact it is likely that the link between consumption and femaleness was actually more symbolic than medical. By this I mean the fact that the menstrual period recalled and resembled the pulmonary haemorrhage which was considered the defining image of phthisis. Bleeding from the lungs had always possessed a good deal of symbolic power – the most famous cultural image of the consumptive being the figure coughing blood into a white handkerchief – for it was considered the moment at which phthisis could be diagnosed without doubt. For instance, John Keats's reaction upon seeing blood on his handkerchief was to exclaim: 'This is arterial blood: I cannot be deceived by its colour. It is my death warrant.'[51] Haemorrhage hence frequently heralded the onset of the disease, and, when severe or prolonged, often ended it as well.[52] Female sexuality and consumption, then, were both symbolically defined by an outpouring of blood. It is hence not surprising that haemorrhages in male consumptives were the subject of speculation and discussion by physicians. Dr R. E. Thompson's 1884 study of consumption and gender, *The Different Aspects of Family Phthisis*, sought to investigate the differing natures of inherited and acquired consumption, and makes some interesting observations about the damaging traits a consumptive mother can pass on to her offspring, and particularly to her sons.

In regard to a large number of male cases, the influence of the mother increases the tendency to bleeding and especially copious bleeding, and these cases appear to be separated from the ordinary cases of phthisis . . .

The influence of the mother not only increases the numbers, but augments the virulence of the disease.[53]

In this analysis the female sex seems to have almost constructed their own strain of the disease with which to infect their male offspring: if the disease is inherited from the mother it will be a more virulent strain and will be tinged with the essence of pathological femininity in the form of 'copious bleeding'.[54] Thompson develops his link between inherited disease and threatening female sexuality further by invoking haemophilia as another example of the maternally transmitted disorders characterised by uncontrollable bleeding. 'The tendency to haemorrhage, which is in a number of cases transmitted by the mother, is analogous to the conditions of haemophilia, which disease is generally transmitted to the male through the mother.'[55] It also worth noting here that Thompson is only concerned with the passage of phthisis from women to their sons, suggesting that masculine health was more important, or else that female offspring were so inherently pathological anyway that methods of transmission were less relevant to them.

Thompson's subject matter is a common one, for questions of gender and the inheritance debate are frequently bound up together in these texts. Increased female susceptibility is used as 'evidence' for, or alternatively against, contagion theory, depending on the beliefs of the writer. Bowditch regards ' . . . the fact that woman is more liable than man to be taken . . . the strongest argument I know against contagion. The really contagious disease spares neither age nor sex.'[56] Conversely, Rohden believed that 'the contagious character of phthisis must decidedly be asserted' because he knows of many cases 'referring to strong men who have never been ill or in feeble conditions of health, who have been infected by their sick wives'.[57] While this does acknowledge that men also get phthisis, it also constructs them as fundamentally healthy whereas their women are inherently sickly, and more importantly, contaminating. In both examples, however, the myth that consumption is a female disease is used as evidence for medical conclusions about the incidence of the disease – a dangerous mix of cultural and literary tropes, and scientific conclusions. In addition, these stereotypes perpetuate others, for Alabone's observation that consumptives are gentle and docile must be linked to his belief that it is a 'woman's disease': the two myths are necessarily dependent on each other.

It should be noted, however, that while the stereotype of the female consumptive may have had a pervasive influence over medical thinking, there is a simple political investment in constructing phthisis as largely female, one too important to be lightly cast aside by the medical profession. The conventional image of the female consumptive, as represented by Pre-Raphaelite artists like Rossetti as well as by novelists like Dickens and George du Maurier, constructs the disease as having a certain aesthetic value, for, as I will discuss in Chapter 4, it creates beautiful, desirable women.[58] As one surgeon declared in 1842, 'some of the most interesting specimens of female beauty, may be seen in the early stage . . . '.[59] Consumptive women are fashionably pale and slender, delicate and refined, because they suffer from a disease which 'throws an ethereal character over the human form'.[60] This image of the beautiful consumptive remained with the medical profession as it did with the public throughout the Victorian era, as indicated by the writings of Dr Alfred Hillier, at the turn of the century. Hillier discusses the appeal of the consumptive beauty as represented by art, mentioning Simonetta Vespucci, the model for Botticelli's Venus: 'a beautiful figure [which] shows strong evidence of the consumptive condition . . . the slight hollowness of the cheek, the long slender neck, the steep sloping shoulders . . . all suggest the probability of phthisis'.[61] He also notes that 'many of Rossetti's more famous pictures have that expression of suffering which is undoubtedly phthisical in origin . . . it is the appealing sadness of disease'. Hillier does not explore or acknowledge the true appeal of this consumptive art, however, which Bram Dijkstra has defined as the fact that it represents a Victorian male fantasy: the image of alluring sexuality on display, but made passive, subservient and manageable by illness.[62] While reined in and controlled by physical weakness the consumptive female was sexually safe, a delicate and desirable 'angel in the house' figure literally confined *to* the house by her illness. Of course there was always the potential for the consumptive female to become threateningly sexual, contaminating and dangerous, and this finds its fullest representation in the literature of the *fin de siècle*. Indeed, in the duality of the consumptive's cultural representation as at once spiritual saint-like figure and socially subversive and sexually deviant contaminant can be read the echo of the dichotomy that surrounded *all* Victorian middle-class women, constructing them as part angel, part whore. In this context it is possible to see that the whole cultural construction of phthisis is of a feminised pathology, for the paradoxes which surrounded it, the split I have examined between the consumptive as deviant and as holy sufferer, are equally applicable to the cultural construction of womanhood as well. Those attitudes which surround this 'female' disease can be considered an extension of those which framed femaleness in general.

This all has disturbing implications for the male consumptive. His body too is reduced and wasted by the disease, but the consequences are different. The results are not fashionably or aesthetically pleasing, and the passive role of self-sacrifice and suffering he as invalid is obliged to take up is the antithesis of all his gender is meant to represent. Health and strength are vital to the Victorian concept of the virile male, and when they are taken away by illness masculinity is compromised. There had been a certain glamour about consumption in men in the Romantic era, when it had been associated with creative genius, but this had now been dissipated by the work ethic in industrialised Britain. There was no useful place in capitalist bourgeois society for the delicate male who was unable to work. His wife's social position might be enhanced by the invalid role which allowed her to function as a symbol of leisured wealth, but the successful middle-class male should be active and industrious. (The important exception to this was the consumptive artist, whose disease was not thought to prevent his remaining economically valid, and hence culturally acceptable. This was because phthisis, and the position of social outsider which accompanied it, were believed to facilitate creativity. The huge number of famous writers and painters who suffered from consumption was considered proof of this theory.) It is not surprising, then, that doctors, novelists and readers alike had an investment in perpetuating the myth that more women then men were consumptive, and that when men did become ill they were likely to have been infected by their wives. If phthisis were acknowledged as afflicting both genders equally, then it would pose a serious threat to the nation's masculinity and thus its self-image, as well as its health.

By the end of the century the medical literature of the time began to indicate a new acceptance among physicians that consumption was not a 'female disease',[63] but sure enough this change in attitudes was paralleled by increasing eugenic fears about the threat tuberculosis posed to the nation. An interesting source on the subject is Josiah Oldfield, a prolific writer on a number of medical issues, whose work was, significantly, directed at the general public rather than at other physicians. Throughout a career of some sixty years he published repeatedly on the links between food and health, and advocated a vegetarian diet as a morally and physically beneficial lifestyle choice.[64] Phthisis becomes part of his discourse in 1897, when he publishes a tract for the British Vegetarian Society entitled *Flesh Eating: A Cause of Consumption* . This pamphlet explores the likelihood of a link between tuberculosis in humans and meat from tuberculous cows, a valuable subject in the context of public health, as this was later proven to be a major cause of the spread of the disease. For my purposes, however, Oldfield's rhetoric is as important as his message. He discusses in highly suggestive language not only the connection between meat-eating and disease, but also the impact phthisis will have on the nation should it continue unchecked, and the social, as well as physical, implications of this impact:

The outlook is a serious one, for a diseased people continuing in the course which caused the disease means a rapidly degenerating people, and though for a time – even for a century – this be averted by intermarriage with other races bringing home fresh blood from other lands, yet none the less the cancer is slowly eating its way to the heart of the nation and the only result can be that modern, civilised races will follow in the wake of preceding civilised races which, losing stamina, have lost the power of progress and even of cohesion, and have been overwhelmed by other races, barbarous indeed, but not *effete*.[65]

Darwinist anxieties about the degeneration of man can clearly be detected here, but Oldfield fears, not that man will return to a primitive animal state, but that he will simply fail to 'progress' further because his civil-isation has been suspended by disease. Oldfield sees phthisis as a force which consumes the nation's 'stamina', resulting in a consumptive peo-ple drained and weakened by disease and unable to compete with more 'barbarous' and vigorous nations. His use of the word 'effete', its cen-tral importance in the passage emphasised by its italics, indicates that the destructive power of this disease is a question of *productivity*, that it will if unchecked leave England barren and infecund. Consumption represents a threat to a country's production on two levels: it creates an economic problem by rendering sections of the population unfit for work and finan-cially dependent on others, and it interferes with a nation's procreativity because of enduring fears that it, or at least its diathesis, might be passed down from parent to child. An 'effete' nation is a weak nation, vulnera-ble to attack by other powers with greater human resources.[66] From the 1870s the British population was increasing more slowly than that of any other European state, and hence the birth rate became of prime importance at this period. At around the same time there had been increased debate about the advisability of consumptives marrying, in case they passed on their disease, but this question was, in the words of one eugenic physician, 'a very delicate one which it is often difficult to approach, and ... must be discreetly and carefully handled'.[67] In this context Oldfield's interesting use of the word 'cohesion' may be illuminating, for this issue, like other debates around the management of tuberculosis, was a highly provocative subject causing social strife and argument. Also, of course, this discour-agement of marriage was a disruption of the unity and social 'cohesion' that marriage and the family structure bring to a society. A diseased nation is a fragmented and separated nation: if consumption is a disease of social isolation and individualism, it is the very antithesis of a strong united state.

It is significant that Oldfield's text is written to encourage the adoption of a vegetarian diet as a means of preventing consumption. Oldfield's rhetoric suggests that it is luxury and self-indulgence rather than just meat-eating which invites phthisis: 'the curse of consumption was so intimately linked with wrong living, and especially wrong eating'.[68] Indeed, 'the case is such a terrible one that none of our cherished habits must be held sacred if they are found to be at the root of the evil'.[69] The implication here seems to be that the 'cherished habit' of eating for pleasure is in fact 'wrong living', and thus pathological, and the repeated use of 'flesh' rather than 'meat' also seems to invoke a subtext about another kind of fleshy indulgence, sexuality, though this is not explicitly acknowledged here. Interestingly, this text is reminiscent of George Cheyne's famous 1733 treatise on the connection between over-indulgence in food and drink and nervous disease, *The English Malady*. Clearly consumption is linked to pre-nineteenth-century fears about the dangers of luxury and extravagance of any kind, not just the gratification of appetite through meat-eating.[70] Indeed, Cheyne's concerns about luxury had been invoked and linked to phthisis much earlier in the Victorian era by a physician who described consumption as 'the English Malady' in 1837.[71] In this context, it is possible to see how consumption may function as a concrete manifestation of the consequences of luxury, as the vague threat which leisure, idleness and excess had long been thought to pose to the strength and virility of nations becomes in the nineteenth century a tangible menace in the form of this disease. Oldfield suggests how the fall of other empires should act as a warning against the current attitudes of Britain: 'the great cause for alarm lies in the slavery of modern appetite, so just as the old Byzantines cared little so long as the corn ships duly arrived, today the cry which rises on all sides is just as foolish'.[72] Consumption is here regarded as a disease with the power to bring down the nation.

It is notable that Victorian fiction once again reflects the same concerns about consumption as medical writing. Oldfield's fear about the national consequences of an idle, luxurious, 'effete' people is pre-empted by two years by H. G. Wells's *The Time Machine*, published in 1895, in which the future human race are rendered weak and infantile by their lack of striving masculinity, and thus can be preyed upon by the primitive, 'barbarous', but physically stronger Morlocks. This novel inserts itself into consumptive discourse through its significant description of the first Eloi the Time Traveller meets, who is phthisical in appearance:

He was a slight creature – perhaps four feet high . . . He struck me as being a very beautiful and graceful creature, but indescribably frail. His flushed face reminded me of the more beautiful kind of consumptive – that hectic beauty of which we used to hear so much. At the sight of him I suddenly regained confidence.[73]

It is important in this context that the Eloi are a unproductive race in both senses of the word. They are idle and without any trace of a work ethic, but are also, significantly, unable to keep up the numbers of their declining population and doomed to eventual extinction as the birth rate fails to compensate for the numbers of them who become the Morlock's prey. The link between evolutionary failure and consumption is clearly established here: these people are no threat to the physically and mentally superior invading force represented by the newly arrived Time Traveller, who 'regains confidence' at the sight of their fragility.

TREATMENTS FOR CONSUMPTION

Any chapter on the medical representation of a disease would be incomplete without a discussion of the means used to treat it, and yet when regarding consumption in the Victorian period it becomes apparent that remedies are one of the less significant aspects of this illness. As I have mentioned, very little scientific progress was made in the search for a cure throughout the nineteenth century. Cod-liver oil, a panacea linked to consumption's identity as a disease of malnutrition, remained a popular prescription until late in the century. The application of various tubercle-consuming chemicals was attempted, but did not appear to bring any success. There were various other quack remedies produced but they were usually just various blends of opium marketed as cures (Wells's *Tono-Bungay* provides an interesting literary commentary on this kind of medical exploitation). Yet the unusual nature of consumption – which often resulted in dramatic, if frequently temporary, remissions and seemingly miraculous 'cures' – was a gold mine for those unscrupulous physicians who could claim any recoveries were the consequence of their treatment and care, when in fact they were actually a feature of the disease and would probably have taken place anyway.

The most enduring medicine for consumption, however, could not be purchased in a bottle, and actually involved a movement away from the administrations of the physician, a fact which made it a site of constant medical tension and debate. It was foreign travel that remained the primary means of treatment for phthisis throughout the disease's long history, and was never more popular than in the nineteenth century, during which almost every famous consumptive, from John Keats to Robert Louis

Stevenson, as well as thousands of the less illustrious, sought health abroad. It is not surprising, then, that almost every Victorian medical text on pulmonary consumption acknowledges the importance of this trend by containing at least a brief discussion of the most beneficial climates or the most favourable means of passage for the consumptive. A number of physicians even take consumptive travel as the primary subject of their work: texts such as S. Dougan Bird's *Australasian climates and their influence on Pulmonary Consumption* are a fascinating hybrid of tourist guide and medical handbook, combing advice about the illness with cultural commentary. (Bird, who had recently moved to Victoria, even included Australian train timetables!) As Maria H. Frawley notes in her exploration of travelling for health in *Invalidism and Identity in Nineteenth-century Britain*, 'the boundaries between texts that functioned as medical science and texts that functioned as travel literature were not clearly drawn'.[74] Medical writing on this topic, however, displays an awareness that to advocate travel is to risk encouraging the patient to give themselves up to nature's healing abilities, hence displacing the physician to some degree. Dr John Parkin's anxiety about this leads him to suggest that the desired results can be achieved without leaving Britain: relocating within one's own country can provide a change of scene without losing the benefits of proximity to an English doctor.[75] Bird in his turn attempts to reclaim authority over the patient and his cure by attempting to comment on and influence his lifestyle abroad, just as all the other physicians I have discussed aim to do at home. His text reveals that there is no aspect of the consumptive's treatment, even if it takes place overseas, about which the doctor cannot claim to be knowledgeable.

This uneasiness about the consumptive invalid's dependence on and desire for a nomadic existence is reflected in a number of texts which are sceptical about the benefits of a change of habitat for the consumptive, even though it was the best hope of a cure for the disease. Even though knowledge about the pathology of phthisis was limited before Koch, it was still apparent to many physicians that a warmer climate could not accomplish miracles. It seemed unlikely that a change in external conditions could exert a significant influence on the internal disease that existed within the body. Thomas Burgess, author of *The Climate of Italy in Relation to Pulmonary Consumption*, was aware of this as early as 1852: 'Change of scene may and does produce good effects in nervous and dyspeptic invalids ... but what benefits it can accomplish in patients with organic disease, like tubercular consumption in an advanced state, I am at a loss to conceive.'[76] Similarly Parkin claimed 'home is the best place for invalids, and more especially for phthisical ones. They can there have more comforts than elsewhere.'[77] So why did many doctors continue to advocate travel as treatment, in the face of scientific scepticism? A possible answer is offered by Bird's text, which refutes Burgess by pointing out that an emotionally uplifting 'change of scene' could benefit consumptives as much as nervous patients, as mental illness and consumption were associated with one another: 'Consumptive persons are very often intensely impressionable to external, moral and intellectual influences; and cheering, hopeful conditions of the country and people amongst whom they live are matters of no small importance.'[78] Hence Australia was advocated by Bird as a good choice of destination, because, unlike Italy and other European destinations, 'where all that meets the eye . . . conduces to sadness and melancholy', Australia is new, 'an unwritten page suggestive of a brilliant future'.[79] (Presumably Bird's having started a medical practice there made it even more beneficial for consumptives!)

Thus the value of travel for the physician lay in its ability to encourage the important emotional wellbeing of the patient. The main reason for its enduring popularity on a general scale, however, lies, rather unusually, with the desires of the patient rather than the wishes of the physician. Doctors were on occasion baffled by their patients' desire to seek health abroad: 'There seems to be a mysterious attraction between hectic patients . . . and various desolate and woe-begone cities in the South of Europe.'[80] In fact travel was, simply, much more attractive to consumptives than any other treatment offered in the disease's history. The traditional methods popular in the past – blood-letting, and a near-starvation diet – had only hastened the course of the disease. The newly emerging modern treatments, like inhalation of antiseptic gas, or, later on, lung surgery, were equally interventionist, painful and unattractive. To be sent abroad on medical advice was a much more pleasant alternative, and perhaps a more successful one, for even if warmer climes failed to provide a cure, sunlight and unpolluted air did usually bring about an improvement by building up the strength and immunity of the patient, and, in addition, balmy weather provided more comfortable surroundings in which to convalesce.

A life abroad appealed to patients for less purely physical reasons as well. Frawley has noted that invalidism is associated with stasis and inertia, and that, in the nineteenth century, the motion and movement of travel seemed to counteract this, providing a psychological if not a physical remedy for the long-term sufferer.[81] Moreover, to travel for health was to travel purely for personal indulgence, to leave behind the demands of business or family, and to pursue only rest, physical ease and a temperate climate. Such a hedonistic lifestyle transgressed against bourgeois values, but was sanctioned by the illness: surely even slothfulness was socially permissible when the goal was to regain one's health. When not undertaken under strict medical advice, however, such a path did not escape medical condemnation, as Burgess indicates through his ambiguous description of Venice, a popular destination for consumptives: 'The climate of Venice and its topography favours a life of indolence and voluptuous ease . . . a life of inertia . . . neither the moral or physical energies are called into activity.'[82] Venice may be an ideal place for the weary invalid to rest, but it is clear that Burgess considers it much less beneficial to their spiritual health, as it encourages morality to relax along with the body. And, as we have seen, if the patient is not morally upright, then their consumption is thought to have little chance of recovery.

Dr Rohden shares Burgess's concerns about travel in general and Italy in particular, believing that the latter 'renders muscular energy and mental powers languid'.[83] His tirade against the behaviour of consumptives abroad is deeply revealing, for it displays that what really disturbs him is the freedom from medical influence that residence in a foreign land allows:

I have also seen much good arise from a residence at the sea . . . but it is only with regard to persons thus under control [of a physician] that a prognosis can with any certainty be expressed. It cannot be so with regard to those left to their own devices at spas and health resorts . . . a revolt against Nice as a place of resort is justified in the case of most phthisical persons because it is impossible to keep the sick there so far under control, and critical patients are occasionally to be seen turning in waltzes or joining in rapid galoppes. Amusements of this kind ought not to exist for phthisical persons, just as they ought not to be exposed in Rome and Venice to unheated galleries and churches. It is necessary to warn consumptive people against careless attendance on service in churches, for we know that many inflammatory attacks are caused by the draughts there . . . A still more injurious custom is that of attending communion on an empty stomach . . . (pp. 526–47)

Rohden makes sure to emphasise here that it is only under the advice and 'control' of a doctor that a consumptive may benefit from a residence abroad: those who travel independently are risking their health. He also sets out to pathologise both religious and social activity, seemingly in order to undermine anything which might distract from the pursuit of a cure and challenge the authority of the physician. The repeated condemnation of attendance in church is particularly suggestive, as it invokes a long-lived struggle between medicine and religion for influence over the sick. Rohden here indicates his anxiety over the possibility that anything might rival the physician's power, and so recommends that even the Church be cast aside if its worship intervenes in the treatment of the patient. Indeed, this fear that medical authority may be undermined or supplanted is the reason why, in all these texts, the consumptive most likely to die is one who is either too poor to afford the attentions of a physician, or too independent to put themselves in his hands. It seems that the medical profession is especially forceful on this issue in the case of consumption because the nature and progress of the disease make it especially pertinent: 'In acute disease the patient is, so to speak, passive; in chronic disease he thinks and often acts, for himself. This is one of the reasons why these diseases are so difficult to cure.'[84] Behind this statement is a thinly veiled anxiety about the greatest threat to health: 'self assertion': 'one of the noblest attributes of the human mind, but which is only justifiable and useful when measured and limited by real and definite knowledge'[85] – in other words, by medical training. Years of illness, it seems, may mean that the consumptive considers himself an authority on his own disease and 'dubs himself a physician'.[86]

What emerges most vividly from an examination of the treatments discussed in Victorian medical literature about consumption is that the most important single factor in obtaining a cure was the physician. These texts frequently construct the doctor as the patient's only hope of recovery, even though he was hampered at this period by an absence of scientific knowledge about phthisis. It is significant, too, that just as the personality of the consumptive is responsible for their disease, the personality of the doctor dictates whether or not they will be cured. To be a successful physician, the doctor must impose 'his personal qualities [on] the sick person, who often becomes impatient from long illness and vain attempts at recovery and has lost the habit of obeying the physician' (p. 595). It is as though control over the patient's mind results in control over their diseased body, as though force of will alone is sometimes enough to heal. This idea is clearly linked to consumption's pervasive identification with mental illness and hysteria, though it also indicates that being under strict medical control means one is prevented from indulging in dissipated or transgressive behaviour which is inherently pathological. This in turn assumes that the physician is himself morally irreproachable and hence worthy to be a spiritual guide for the patient.

It is understandable that this body of literature written by medical men should advocate the supremacy of doctors, but even more interesting is the repetition of this idea in one of the few consumptive texts written by a patient, *The Crusade Against Phthisis*, by A. B. de Guerville, who describes the importance of his sanatorium doctor to his recovery:

But air, exercise, rest, extra feeding, all that will effect nothing without a doctor at once capable, honest, conscientious and giving himself heart and soul to his work . . . Dr Otto Walther is adored by all his patients. Gifted with a will of iron and hiding under a manner somewhat brusque, a heart of gold, sympathetic and kind, the confidence which he inspires is immeasurable . . . At home [the patient] will do what he wishes to do, whereas I am convinced that one of the conditions . . . of recovery is to do what the doctor wishes.[87]

This text seems to be a genuine, if somewhat gushing, personal account of a recovery from consumption, but even if it is in reality only propaganda for the regime at Nordrach, it is no less useful for my purpose. The author's objective is to encourage his consumptive readers to become patients of Dr Walther, so they may be cured by him as de Guerville has been. Significantly, the work makes apparent that it is the character of the physician which is most important to prospective patients, for that is the focus of the argument, and the readers are presumed to share de Guerville's belief that food, climate and facilities are less important than the powerful personality of the man in charge. The treatment offered here is of secondary importance to the individual that offers it. If consumption is a feminising disease, then the antidote would appear to be the masculine influence of that most virile of patriarchs, the strong-willed and charismatic physician, whose authority and determination alone can cure the weak, the effeminate and the deviant.

This situation reveals the importance of the role played by consumption in the rise to power of the medical profession. As a slow, gradual disease – a 'way of death' – it allowed a long-term relationship to be built between consumptives and their doctors in a way that few other illnesses did: 'it need scarcely be added that no disease could have been selected for the prognosis in which the physician is so often appealed to'.[88] This was a symbiotic relationship that was sometimes dependent, as de Guerville illustrates, and sometimes a struggle for autonomy, as John Hughes Bennett and others display. It was also frequently cynical and distrustful because of the money involved: 'people need to think for themselves . . . they begin to see that doctors as a profession *live* by *disease* and not by health', an inflammatory pamphlet by the British College of Health pointed out in 1868.[89] Most of all, however, it was marked by hope and disappointment, strife, resentment and frustration, as patients and doctors battled with the same inexorable foe. It is also true that the patient was perhaps not the only victim of consumption, for the young medical profession struggling to consolidate themselves in the nineteenth century were also ravaged by this disease which was 'recognised by the public as incurable, and yet exhorts blame, censure and unkind feeling to those who have to treat it'.[90] In this chapter I have been exploring the ways in which physicians viewed and coped with this situation by creating exploratory dialogues around the disease, investigating, rejecting and validating literary and cultural fictions and attempting to claim consumptive discourse as their own. In the chapters to come I will be examining how the Victorian novelist viewed and used these representations and how medicine was in turn 'written' into literary fiction.

CHAPTER 2

Consuming the family economy: disease and capitalism in Charles Dickens's Dombey and Son and Elizabeth Gaskell's North and South

Disease forms an integral part of any social commentary novel written or set in the 'hungry forties', sickness of one kind or another being the perpetual accompaniment of the living conditions of the poorer classes in this era. Industrialisation, urbanisation and the population explosion combined to produce overcrowded housing, inadequate food, contaminated water and unhealthy factory conditions, namely perfect breeding conditions for infectious illness. Fever in its various forms is ever-present in the pages of the 'Condition of England' novels, for example, but tuberculosis is also never far away. An opportunistic disease known to take advantage of any mass decrease in immunity, whether caused by war or food shortage or by the ravages of another illness, consumption asserts itself as the ultimate consequence of deprivation, the lingering, long-term, historical cousin of the newly prevalent industrial illnesses, cholera and typhus. Like these, tuberculosis thrived in the industrial city: unlike them, it did not respond to government interventions, like the sanitary improvements implemented by the end of the century. It endured long past the nineteenth century as a signifier of industrialisation, rather than of simple poverty; as I intend to show, it had an impact not only on the Victorian working population but on capitalism in general.

This impact finds its most apparent manifestation through the challenge tuberculosis represented to authoritative nineteenth-century thinking on the economic effects of disease within society. In his *Essay on the Principle of Population* Thomas Malthus represents disease as a 'positive check to population', in that along with war and famine, it is the main method of thinning out and thus preventing further expansion of a community which has outgrown its means of subsistence.[1] Certainly as one of the biggest killers in the Victorian era tuberculosis seems to fulfil this role, as it was responsible for removing huge numbers of people and of course frequently struck hardest in the most overpopulated areas. Its way of doing this was not an economically helpful or efficient one, however, as tuberculosis often created a very slow and gradual decline. 'Galloping' consumption could kill in perhaps four months, but most forms of the disease took a lot longer to achieve the desired Malthusian end: 'Informed opinion – that is standard textbooks – reckoned that it was fatal in eighty percent of cases in five to fifteen years.'[2] Tuberculosis might eventually contribute to the restoration of a demographic equilibrium and thus to economic health, but in fact while doing so it caused a further drain on society's resources. In the process of limiting population growth tuberculosis actually created a population of unproductive invalids who were physically unable to partake in the workings of capitalist society and were thus a further burden on an already struggling community. I will address later in this chapter the figure of Bessy Higgins in *North and South*, who forms a classic example of this kind of consumptive, as her slowly progressive disease renders her dependent on others for long-term support.

Through her pre-illness existence as a nineteen-year-old factory worker Bessy is also valuable in indicating how tuberculosis resists Darwinian principles of natural selection as well. Unlike other diseases which target a community's more vulnerable members, tuberculosis 'owes its horror particularly to its occurring at the prime of a man's life – from 20–25 years of age – when he should be at the height of his wage-earning capacity'[3] Burton-Fanning notes: and hence it '... crushed breadwinners ... and bereaved young families'.[4] In other words it consumed the bodies and devastated the potential of the most productive section of the population, rather than targeting society's weakest and most economically redundant, those rendered more expendable by age or infirmity. This undermining of the whole concept of 'survival of the fittest' emphasises the subversive abilities of this illness: when Malthusian and Darwinian systems of thought are rendered irrelevant in this way disease becomes a destructive force for which no rational explanation can be provided. In this sense tuberculosis cannot be at all redeemed, as other diseases are, by a sense of its social benevolence in the long term, and it is apparent that, rather than being any kind of solution to economic problems, this disease has always represented an obstacle to the success of the economy.

At the same time, however, this definition is complicated by tuberculosis's age-old link with consumerism, which is represented in the two novels under investigation here. As indicated by its common identification as 'consumption', tuberculosis is semiotically associated with the compulsive desire to purchase and possess commodities. This was, as McKendrick and Brewer have pointed out, thought of as a sickness in the eighteenth century, a time when the buying of goods such as crockery had reached epidemic proportions.[5] There were ambiguous anxieties surrounding this copious spending, for it was at once beneficial to the flourishing economy, 'vital for life giving commerce', yet could also have a harmful effect upon the country's capital reserves. As Roy Porter asks, 'What was spending but the dissipation of accumulated resources leading to economic entropy?'[6] Foreign trade was a particular source of concern: Christopher J. Berry has discussed how imported luxuries from the East – and as we shall see this is especially relevant to the concerns of *Dombey and Son* and *North and South* – were potentially damaging to the economy. 'There is no market for British goods in the Orient, [so] these luxuries must be paid for in bullion . . . The balance is, therefore, "down", which means Britain is in debt . . . Debt would produce, variously, unemployment, a fall in land values and a consequent upsurge in vagrancy with all its associated moral ills.'[7] Consumerism and over-consumption, in other words, could easily lead to debt and deprivation.

In this context we can see how phthisis can function as a cultural metaphor for this kind of economic process, for tuberculosis's gradual wasting and using up of the body's resources of flesh and strength clearly made it a perfect signifier for the dangers of excess and consumerism on the body politic. George Cheyne had linked consumption very literally with luxury as early as 1733, when arguing in *The English Malady* that certain diseases – namely phthisis, cancer and gout – were a direct consequence of over-indulgence in the upper classes:

almost all acute Diftempers . . . happen only to the *Rich*, the *Lazy*, the *Luxurious*, and the *Unactive*, thofe who fare daintily and live voluptuoufly, thofe who are furnifhed with the rareft Delicacies, the richeft Foods, and the moft generous Wines, fuch as can provoke the Appetites, Senfes and Paffions in the moft exquifite and voluptuous Manner: to thofe who leave no Defire or Degree of Appetite unfatistifed.[8]

This was a typical eighteenth-century construction of the pathological nature of wealth and mercantilism, but such a view of consumption persisted throughout the nineteenth century, rather strangely given that we now know it to be a disease of low immunity, in complete contrast to the other diseases mentioned by Cheyne which *were*, and are still, associated with the indulgent lifestyle which accompanies affluence. Consumption, in contrast, is a disease of deprivation, and nineteenth-century medical thinking accepted it is a consequence of industrialisation in general, and the factory system in particular. However, as I indicated in the previous chapter, tuberculosis has long had a dual identity as a disease both 'of the rich and of the poor',[9] and within this identification lies its usefulness as a symbol of both aspects of capitalism, excess as well as deprivation. As Dr John Murray, writing about consumption in 1830, indicated, it was believed that it was 'excess, and the ideal creation of luxuries, which consume our vitals and destroys us'.[10] This is why for every nineteenth-century physician who recommends a nourishing, plentiful diet as a treatment for consumption, there is another who warns against any kind of rich or animal food and lays down strict rules about the necessity of skipping lunch if one has breakfasted late, to avoid overindulgence.[11] Wine, sugar and other luxury foodstuffs were always considered dangerous for consumptives and best avoided. Clearly doctors considered tuberculosis bound up with the process of industrialisation in more complex ways than as a simple result of poverty: even after the turn of the twentieth century physicians Latham and Garland, for example, offer a vague but fascinating description of tuberculosis, 'in all its forms', as 'a direct product of civilisation . . . the disease does not exist in uncivilised countries'.[12] (We might recall similar rhetoric being used by Josiah Oldfield some decades earlier.) The medical reasoning behind this is unclear, but it seems that consumption is being constructed as the price a society has to pay for economic and social progression and development: it is a disease of the western world,[13] and hence seems to be bound up with western capitalism – even though, within the factory system, it consumes productivity alongside flesh.

The destructive economic impact of tuberculosis forms a central concern in *Dombey and Son*, Dickens's moral fable of consumer society in which the progress of capitalism is disrupted by the consumptive illness which kills the heir to the family firm. Consumption is an appropriate disease for Dickens's purposes because it was widely believed to afflict valuable, beloved children like Paul Dombey, being an ailment which cuts down 'that child of hope, for whom in the future . . . imagination has pencilled out a brilliant destiny; that only son, of high promise'.[14] Given this cultural resonance, it is an appropriate affliction to carry off the heir to Dombey and Son, who does indeed have a 'brilliant destiny' carved out for him by his father, except that death intervenes. Even more significantly, however, Paul's illness is represented in the novel as a result of the capitalist way of life, and hence functions as a condemnation of consumerism, as well as an indication of its physical dangers. This text has been described as 'the first of Dickens's novels which can be said without qualification to be a social novel, in that its primary goal is to directly depict society and social relations'.[15] It is thus appropriate that it takes as its main metaphor the 'social diseases', most directly tuberculosis, but also syphilis, which forms a subtle subtext to the Dombey marriage plot.[16] The plot depicts the transgression, downfall and eventual redemption of wealthy businessman Paul Dombey, who functions in the novel as the father of mercantilism and is used by Dickens as a means of exploring and exposing the sickness at the heart of the world of trade. I should add at this point that the model of pathologised consumerism through which *Dombey and Son* will be read here is essentially an eighteenth-century dialogue, but this somewhat anachronistic approach is in fact rather relevant to Dickens's novel, if we bear in mind F. S. Schwarzbach's argument that Dombey himself is something of a 'a relic of the past'. As the owner of a family shipping company, his fortune has been made in eighteenth-century mercantilism, and thus, as a symbol of capitalism, he looks backward rather than forward.[17] By the 1840s 'stewardship of the economy has passed from the hands of [Dombey's] class into those of the great industrial entrepreneurs'.[18] As Schwarzbach observes, the true epitome of modernity is the heavy industry owner of *Hard Times*, who deals in steel or coal, the commodities of the future, and whose new importance in society is indicated in *Dombey* by the pervasive presence of the railways. This casting of Dombey and Son as a mercantile rather than industrial firm is a significant one, however, as it enters the text into the ethical debates I have mentioned surrounding the consumption of the goods and luxuries produced by trade. Dombey supplies commodities for people, not materials for transport or building, and thus is held responsible by Dickens for the social and moral consequences of consumer capitalism, an 'economic doctrine that strips relations . . . to an assertion of monetary power'.[19] Within the world of the novel, those consequences are pathological, and of course take the form of the 'disease of consumer society', tuberculosis.

The book's preoccupation with illness is introduced in the second chapter, when capitalist patriarchy as epitomised by the firm of Dombey and Son is initially perpetuated by the birth of the long-awaited heir, little Paul, then seemingly threatened by the subsequent death of his mother and the need to provide him with a wet nurse. The presentation of Polly Toodle as a likely candidate for the job is accompanied by a policing of her health and that of her family in an attempt to assess the risk of contamination she poses to the baby:[20]

'How do you do Polly?'
'I'm pretty well, I thank you ma'am,' said Polly . . .
'I'm glad to hear it,' said Miss Tox. 'I hope you'll keep so. Five children. Youngest six weeks. The fine little boy with the blister on his nose is the

eldest. The blister, I believe,' said Miss Tox, looking around upon the family,
'is *not constitutional, but accidental?*'
The apple faced man was understood to growl, 'Flat iron.'
'. . . Oh yes,' said Miss Tox. 'Yes! Quite true. I forgot. The little creature,
in his mother's absence, smelt a warm flat iron. You're quite right, You were
going to have the goodness to inform me when we arrived at the door, that
you were by trade a—'
'Stoker,' said the man.
'A choker!' said Miss Tox, quite aghast.
'Stoker,' said the man. 'Steam engine.'
'Oh-h! Yes,' returned Miss Tox . . .
'And how do you like it, sir? . . . '
'Oh! Pretty well, mum. The ashes sometimes gets in here;' touching his chest:
'and makes a man speak gruff, as at the present time. But *it is ashes mum, not
crustiness.*' (pp. 64–5, italics mine)

That this examination of Polly calls upon the bodies of her children to act
as evidence makes apparent that it is physicality and potential pathogenicity which are under examination here. Consequently communicable disease is identified as the main challenge to the prosperity of little Paul and the
capitalist future he represents. Even more significantly, however, the interro-
gation invokes syphilis and tuberculosis in particular as the most important
threats against which the family must be on their guard – reassurance must
be offered regarding any potential pustule or wheeze. This locates the novel
within a discourse of politicised disease, for as Lynda Nead has pointed
out,[21] wet-nursing existed as a site of much tension and controversy regarding possible disease transmission to – and also from – middle-class children,
and became a metaphor for all bourgeois fears of cross-class contamination.

The whole section of the plot concerned with the Toodle family can thus
be read as an exploration of these kinds of anxieties, and, significantly, offers
a resistance to the accepted view of the proletariat as pathologised. Any
illness in the book is of bourgeois rather than lower-class origin. The Toodles
represent an idealised, almost pastoral vision of the working-class family:
against all expectations and despite their living conditions they are the
very essence of health. Identified throughout the text with apples, they are
'plump, rosy-cheeked [and] wholesome' (p. 63), as far as possible removed
from the pallid, fragile and malnourished creatures whom we might expect
to find as the only specimens of the urban poor in the novel. The apple
metaphor associated with them does, however, suggest that they function
as a source of anxiety in a different sense, one equally pertinent in terms
of bourgeois fears of the multiplying masses. The Toodles are like fruit or
seeds, constantly and successfully fertile and reproductive, as Mr Dombey

bitterly notes when contemplating them and contrasting his own family and posterity with that of Mr Toodle: 'an ignorant Hind who has been working "mostly underground" all his life, and yet at whose door Death had never knocked, and at whose table four sons daily sit' (p. 71). With the later death of little Paul this observation becomes even more poignant, as Mr Dombey is left without issue and is finally rendered effectively sterile by his failed second marriage, yet the Toodles continue to produce 'numbers of new babies' (p. 292). This aspect of the plot creates an important tension between Mrs Dombey and her more biologically successful lower-class double, Polly Toodle. The fragile Mrs Dombey, who dies giving birth to Paul, is a typical example of the sickly bourgeois female whose reproductive shortcomings – the heir she finally produces is as delicate as herself – contrasts markedly with the fecundity of Polly, whose milk sustains Paul throughout his infancy; of course Paul only begins to deteriorate into consumptive delicacy after Polly's beneficial breast is taken away from him.[22] Health and fertility, it seems, are denied to the higher classes in the novel, and both are vital to economic success. As Marx has discussed, progeny are essential to the progress of capitalism:

The owner of labour power is mortal. If then his appearance in the market is to be continuous, and the continuous conversion of money into capital assumes this, the seller of labour-power must perpetuate himself 'in the way that every living individual must perpetuate himself, by procreation'. The labour power withdrawn from the market by wear and tear and death must be continually replaced by, at the very least, an equal amount of fresh labour power . . . ie children [*sic*].[23]

With this in mind it is possible to suggest a more cynical or mercenary interpretation of Mr Toodle's response to Mr Dombey's observation that five children must be something of a financial drain:

'You have a son I believe?' said Mr Dombey.
'Four on 'em, sir. Four hims and a her. All alive!'
'Why, it's as much as you can afford to keep them!' said Mr Dombey.
'I could hardly afford but one thing in the world less, sir.'
'What is that?'
'To lose 'em, sir.' (p. 69)

On one level this is a natural and touching expression of love for one's children, which forms an effective contrast between the attitude of Toodle and that of Mr Dombey himself. The language used here, however, hints at a financial context behind this: Toodle cannot 'afford to lose' his offspring as they are all potential sources of labour, productivity, and hence of capital. They are in fact the only commodity, outside his own ability to work, that

Mr Toodle has to offer. This need to 'perpetuate' oneself is not confined to the worker, however, but also applies to the capitalist. Without an heir and successor for Mr Dombey, his firm is without a future, as the unfolding of the plot displays. The 'great failure' of Dombey and Son is the inevitable result of the breakdown of patriarchal inheritance caused by the death of little Paul from tuberculosis (p. 908). Paul's physical 'decline' foreshadows the financial decay of the firm, and as the Dombey empire is symbolic of the whole economic world – 'The earth was made for Dombey and Son to trade in, and the sun and moon were made to give them light' (p. 50) – this can be read as an assessment of the ability of disease to disrupt, thwart and 'consume' the powers and progress of capitalism.

This kind of disruption finds its most suggestive manifestation in the ability of tuberculosis to consume time. Clocks and timekeeping form a pervasive presence throughout the novel. The only place of trade actually represented in the text is Sol Gills's shop which makes shipping chronometers. Mr Dombey himself is at moments reduced to the symbol of his pocket watch, so bound up together are he and it: 'a pair of creaking boots, and a very loud ticking watch, embodied [Florence's] idea of a father' (p. 51). Paul's time at the Blimbers' being schooled for future success is monitored and overseen by the watchful grandfather clock there. Timepieces have a clear role as the heralds of the modern industrial world,[24] in which time is precious and vital – as Nina Auerbach points out, 'the new reliance on watches…was a reality in the 1840s and 1850s: England was in the process of attuning itself to the railroad and its schedule'.[25] Control over the temporal is power, representing control over life, and this is of course frequently a medical power; doctors in the novel are always associated with the ticking of their watches (p. 294). Auerbach has identified time as masculine and has mentioned the significance of the first Mrs Dombey's deathbed scene, which is accompanied by 'the loud ticking of Mr Dombey's watch and Dr Peps's watch, which seemed in the silence to be running a race' (p. 59). This scene can be read as the attempts of modernity (as represented by these two scientific patriarchs) to impose order and control over the sickbed and its feminine occupant, to 'race' medical and economic power against natural illness and death – a race they ultimately lose when Mrs Dombey, in her only gesture of resistance, 'cuts herself loose from time'.[26]

Dombey and Son represents death as the only way of finally escaping from the demands of mechanical time and the capitalist world it represents, then, but illness, more specifically tuberculosis, also offers a means of resisting time in life. The slow, gradual progression of consumption famously renders it as much a way of life as it is a way of death. Little Paul's future is seemingly mapped out for him by the position and system into which he has been born, and requires only the inexorable passage of the years before his father can bring these plans to fruition. In Paul's life Mr Dombey has harnessed time for his own ends – he wishes, in fact, to be its master altogether and bend it to his will:

[Dombey] . . . comforted himself with the reflection that there was another mile-stone passed upon that road, and that the great end of his journey lay so much the nearer. For the feeling uppermost in his mind now, and constantly intensifying and increasing in it as Paul grew older, was impatience. Impatience for the time to come, when his visions of their united consequence and grandeur would be triumphantly realised.

. . . he was impatient to advance into the future, and to hurry over the intervening passages of [Paul's] history. (pp. 150–1)

In fact Paul's 'constitutional weakness' creates its own history, that of an invalid, which differs dramatically from the narrative that Mr Dombey had 'prepared and marked out for him before he existed' (p. 204), and it grants him the ability to resist time. This is indicated by the descriptions of his delicate, worn appearance: 'he looked (and talked) like one of those terrible little Beings in the Fairy tales, who at a hundred and fifty or two hundred years of age, fantastically represent the children for which they have been substituted' (p. 151). Clearly a physical manifestation of his disease (though interestingly the aged and wizened appearance of children is more commonly associated with congenital syphilis than tuberculosis, a point I will return to later), this also suggests that he has been spiritually removed from the normal time span of childhood growth. Spiritually he is already old, but physically he remains small and childlike, destined never to mature. His tubercular decline is presented as a triumph, over society's attempts to assimilate him into the capitalist world, and his father's impatient desire to see him grown up, for Paul wishes to resist both:

'Ha!' said Dr Blimber. 'Shall we make a man of him?'
'Do you hear Paul?' added Mr Dombey; Paul being silent.
'Shall we make a man of him?' repeated the Doctor.
'I had rather be a child,' replied Paul. (p. 210)
. . .
'And you'll try and learn a good deal here, and be a clever man,' said Mr Dombey; 'won't you?'
'I'll try,' returned the child wearily.
'And you'll soon be grown up now!' said Mr Dombey.

'Oh! Very soon!' replied the child. Once more the old, old look passed rapidly across his features like a strange light. (p. 214)

This attempt to 'make a man of' Paul through an intensive, disciplined timetable of schooling seems to be successful until pulmonary symptoms begin to manifest themselves: 'some bird of prey got into his throat instead of the thrush' (p. 149). He is then liberated from the system – 'Paul was such a privileged pupil as had never been seen in that house before' (p. 265) – and takes to his bed. There, of course, he exists outside and beyond everyday time, observing its passage with the detachment of the invalid who has only the schedule of illness to follow:

He lay there, listening to the noises in the street, quite tranquilly; not caring much how the time went, but watching it and watching everything around him with observing eyes.
    How many times the golden water danced upon the wall; how many nights the dark, dark river rolled towards the sea in spite of him; Paul never counted, never sought to know . . . whether there were many days or few, appeared of little moment now (p. 295)

Dickens displays very effectively, in death scenes which are among his most critically acclaimed, the power of tuberculosis to render time meaningless, and to consume youth, growth and future promise.

The perception that tuberculosis was a spiritual disease, traditionally considered an affliction of the pure, the innocent and the young, renders it useful to Dickens in this novel. Sontag suggests that this identification came about partly because tuberculosis breaks down flesh into water and air, a process which can be viewed as the lightening and dissipation of the earthly, corrupt and corporeal into the spirit.[27] This association between the disease and water is reflected by the quote above in which the 'golden water' and 'dark river' form the symbols of Paul's final days. All this makes tuberculosis a useful literary means of countering the terrestrial, materialistic world of capitalism, with its crude dependence on the corporeal – the physicality of labour and the need for strength encapsulated within it – and on the tangible: commodities and objects. As we have seen, health is an essential requirement for participation in capitalism, for those that are healthy labour more effectively, produce more, and consume voraciously, all to satisfy the ever-increasing desires of their hungry bodies. The tuberculosis victim is not only physically unable to labour, but also traditionally thought to be spiritually heightened by their disease so as to be above such earthly, mundane concerns as the desire to consume. (Of course commodities could also seem irrelevant and redundant to the suffering and wasting bodies of the seriously ill.) In nineteenth-century artistic circles, health was undesirable because it was the normal state of common beings entrenched in their bodies, and this was not the expected position of the true genius. The unhealthy were so because they considered their bodies of less importance than their minds and abilities, and treated them as such, and thus the artistic self embraced both creativity and the consumption that eventually became its signifier. These kinds of discourses of disease are pervasively at work throughout the the novel. We can see how Dickens, as a creative genius not unused to hardship, might come to share the Romantic view of ill health as the most productive state of the impoverished and unappreciated but talented artist. His personal struggles in earlier life had after all formed much of the inspiration for the fiction which had brought about his later success: it was his own experience of suffering, and his compassionate observation of the suffering of others, that made his work what it was. In this context, poverty and illness are clearly identified with the artist and the individual – those who resist and protest against the strength and power of capitalism.

If we consider that capitalism requires health to function successfully, then, it becomes apparent that tuberculosis has a powerful ability to act as a metaphorical disrupter of the industrial world. Its intervention in the progress of the Dombey empire can clearly be read as a triumph of the soulful over the materialistic and the individual over the institution. Tuberculosis is a 'disease of individuals'[28] after all, and its victim, Paul, is a small single entity against a huge economic system which he has no desire to become part of, but which he can only escape by becoming ill. (It can also be considered the triumph of artistic creativity over pragmatic finance, something that might be a personal concern of Dickens as an author who spent his early years struggling against poverty.)[29] The romanticised figure of this innocent afflicted child, who displays throughout his final illness his altruistic concern for others and his loyalty to his family and friends, is the antithesis of the mercenary modern way of life. Paul, however diminutive, is the true hero of the book because of his consumption, which may destroy his body, but saves his pure and angelic soul from the truly pathological force in this novel – mercantilism.

Dombey and Son has frequently been read by critics as delineating capitalism and trade as the disease of modern society, as its corrupter and destroyer.[30] Certain passages within the text bear out this analysis; disease becomes a metaphor for all that is wrong about the 'unnatural', capitalist world:

Was Mr Dombey's master vice, that rules him so inexorably, an unnatural characteristic?

... Alas! are there so few things in the world around us, most unnatural, and yet most natural in being so? ... Look around upon the world of odious sights – millions of immortal creatures have no other world on earth ... Breathe the polluted air, foul with every impurity that is poisonous to health and life; and have every sense, conferred upon our race, for its delight and happiness, offended, sickened and disgusted, and made a channel by which misery and death alone shall enter ... Then should we stand appalled to know, that where we generate disease to strike our children down and entail itself on unborn generations, there also we breed, by the same certain process, infancy that knows no innocence, youth without modesty or shame, maturity that is mature in nothing but in suffering and guilt ... (p. 737)

This extract is interesting not merely because it represents disease as a metaphor for social evil, a not uncommon usage of the pathological, but because it depicts the illness which 'strike[s] our children down' – in this novel, tuberculosis – as something created by society, 'generated' by man's avarice and pride. As Dickens's novel is, as Michael Goldberg has said, a 'sustained and powerful attack on Victorian Mammonism', it is perfectly plausible that we are meant to see Paul's affliction as a consequence of, or punishment for, his father's wealth, and all the more tragic and poignant because the child himself is undeserving of it. Clearly, it is the next generation, and the individual – Paul being representative of both – who will pay the price for society's greed.[31] Dickens seems to be suggesting here that consumption is not only a symbolic means of resisting and thwarting the progress of capitalism, but a curse upon the offspring of those who reap its financial rewards.

Of course this construction of consumption as a product of wealth seems to be ignoring the social reality of a disease which was rife amongst the urban poor. Within the context of the novel tuberculosis does not function as the working-class killer which it undoubtedly was in reality. As I have noted, the lower-class Toodles are untouched by disease: instead tuberculosis is represented here as a threat to the bourgeoisie. Paul is not only middle class, but indulged and pampered from an early age in all the ways wealth can pamper him, from the provision of a wet nurse, as we have seen, to the tiny carriage which carries him even onto the beach so he doesn't have to walk, to his 'very expensive' school. Paul's illness is certainly not caused by physical deprivation, but is it, then, caused by prosperity? Tuberculosis has a long history of association with mental illness, which according to Sontag is because they are both 'diseases of higher consciousness', but I would like to suggest that this link is founded in their similar eighteenth-century existence as diseases of affluence; that, as I have indicated, tuberculosis can be considered, like hysteria, 'an English Malady . . . a disease of civilisation resulting from the consumption of too many luxuries'.[32] Certainly consumption's linguistic link with consumerism does cast it, symbolically speaking, as a disease of luxury: in physical terms also it certainly seems an appropriate punishment for over-indulgence, as excess consumption results in the self being consumed. Roy Porter's exploration of the long history of the connection between consumerism and disease in *Consumption and the World of Goods*, quotes 'radical, yet fashionable' late-eighteenth-century physician Thomas Beddoes's identification of the potentially pathogenic consequences of the consumer revolution in Georgian England. Beddoes describes those most at risk from tuberculosis as, significantly, those 'men who abandoned physical hard labour, allured by good money in "the almost feminine occupations of the cloathing manufacture" [who] became "frequently consumptive"'.[33] (It is interesting to note here that the adoption of more 'feminine' trades renders men susceptible to tuberculosis.) The movement from agricultural work to the production of consumer goods invites disease in general and consumption in particular, it seems, and the 'allure of good money' implies that Mammonism once again is to blame. Porter goes on to delineate the effects upon the upper classes, pointing out that the lifestyle changes caused by 'England's singular economic success' in the eighteenth century were frequently far from healthy; it was not only the new trade itself that was pathogenic but also the affluence that accompanied that trade.[34] The effect of this affluence most relevant to Paul's consumption in *Dombey and Son* is the modern bourgeois 'preoccupation with the child's future and his or her standing in society' – a preoccupation motivated by the greater survival rate of children from the eighteenth century onward, but facilitated by increasing surplus income from this period.[35] These altering objectives and fashions of education demanded a rigid new approach to middle-class schooling:

Seduced by the new sensibility, parents pushed their infants into study, music and fine accomplishments. Even girls were now packed off to be 'poor prisoners' in draughty boarding schools. Adolescents, 'weak with excess of sensibility', were then allowed to loaf around on sofas, reading improving literature and 'melting love stories, related in novels' . . . Not surprisingly, thanks to this 'fatal indolence', 'the springs of their constitution have lost their force from disuse'. All such Lydia Languishes live under 'hazard of consumption', triggered by no more than cold or chlorosis.[36]

Dickens had famously strong views on education, and it is clearly apparent that Paul's schooling is central to the child's decline. Boarding schools for children were perfect breeding grounds for infection, as the Brontës could testify (Lowood in *Jane Eyre* is a good example) and the sedentary academic routine advocated by those who prioritised intellectual achievement over physical activity outdoors contributed to decreased immunity. This is clearly represented in the part of the plot which deals with the Blimbers' establishment, which prides itself on its production of the capitalists of the future, something it manages by strictly enforcing bourgeois ethics of application and industry amongst its pupils. This system has disastrous effects upon the minds and bodies of the young, however:

In fact Doctor Blimber's establishment was a great hothouse, in which there was a forcing apparatus incessantly at work. All the boys blew before their time. Mental green peas were produced at Christmas, and intellectual asparagus all the year round . . . Nature was of no consequence at all . . . This was all very pleasant and ingenious, but the system of forcing was attended with its usual disadvantages. There was not the right taste about the premature productions, and they didn't keep well.

Unlike Jane Eyre or Nicholas Nickleby, Paul is well fed and physically well cared for at his luxurious school, but despite this, a regime in which 'nature is no consequence at all' aggregates his already fragile body, which soon manifests consumptive symptoms. Dickens's anxieties about the consumptive consequences of such systems for the young was shared by the physicians of the period: Dr George Congreve, for example, uses the same gardening rhetoric to express his belief that education methods like those advocated by the Blimbers were a direct cause of consumption in the offspring of the upper classes. 'I have known many children of the affluent brought up like greenhouse plants . . . no wonder that, so educated, they become peculiarly susceptible to diseases of the lungs.'[37] Mr Dombey's eagerness to make a successful capitalist out of his son has disastrous consequences, as the boy, like a plant forced to mature too soon, cannot survive.

The plot of *Dombey and Son* raises questions around the fundamental unhealthiness of consumerism, luxury and excess in other ways, too, most notably in connection with the marriage of Mr Dombey and Edith Granger. The moral sickness which surrounds this union seems to demonstrate the ways in which conspicuous consumerism can become pathologically consumptive, and ultimately almost fatal to those involved. Dombey in fact becomes a testimony to the worst effects of luxurious indulgence, for it can be held responsible for the loss of masculinity that brings about his downfall. Christopher J. Berry has identified the classical definition of luxury as a creator of effeminacy; as he points out, Plato considered it a threat to virility because an indulgent lifestyle was not conducive to male strength or power, and compromised the abilities of a warrior:

Those individuals whose lives are given over to a soft, luxurious life are, as we have seen, incapable of defending themselves; they are naturally unfit to be auxiliaries. They are effeminate because it is of the essence not of humanity but rather of masculinity to fight, to risk death.[38]

Prior to his second marriage Dombey lives in comparative austerity, as after the death of his first wife most of his house is shut up, and he, 'like a lone prisoner in a cell', occupies only three rooms which are characterised by their coldness and masculine lack of adornment (p. 76). He is noticeably also at this time the epitome of masculinity, as is made apparent by Miss Tox's gushing first reaction to him: 'His presence! His dignity!... Something so stately, you know: so uncompromising: so very wide across the chest: so upright! A pecuniary Duke of York, my love, and nothing short of it!' (p. 58). After he purchases Edith, however, Dombey gives himself up to luxury; his house is literally rebuilt as a shrine to trade, wealth and display; a 'perfect palace' in which 'no expense has been spared' (p. 583). Edith likewise is associated with 'luxuries of dress ... Chaplets of flowers, plumes of feathers, jewels, laces, silks and satins ...' which are exhibited upon her body as signs of both her husband's great wealth and her own willingness to be bought by it (pp. 650–1). This indulgence in a life of opulence sets Dombey on the path to illness, suffering and financial ruin; he is, like the Platonic view of the 'soft' inefficient soldier, incapable of defending himself against the predatory masculinity of his traitorous assistant, Carker. Thus by the end of the novel he has become totally emasculated, his reason, judgement and business sense compromised, and he is dependent upon his daughter for salvation. It is not until he is stripped of the signs and accumulations of affluence – house, furniture and belongings – that he can begin his return to psychological and physical health, can enjoy a peaceful though feeble old age as a man no longer 'troubled by ambitious projects' of capital and commodity, whose 'only pride is in his daughter and her husband' (p. 970).

Economic principles are therefore the symbolic and actual source of Mr Dombey's illness as they are of his son's. No simple dichotomy of capitalism as health and tuberculosis as resistance to capitalism can be established here, then. Disease is as much the product of the capitalist system as it is a threat to that system. Its representation in the novel is therefore necessarily complex and problematic, and deliberately so. The model it creates is particularly simple, however: if industrialism and capitalism, as consequence of their inherent pathogenicity, produce tuberculosis, and tuberculosis interrupts and undermines the system, then society is, of course, the agent of its own destruction. Its desire to produce and consume despite the physical cost to the masses, and the moral and psychological cost to the upper classes – as represented by Mr Dombey – results in society's own consumption by disease.

There seems an obvious parallel here between this model of the workings of tuberculosis in society and the preoccupation with syphilis and sexuality that was so central to mid-Victorian social consciousness. The difference is that it was not consumerism but sexuality which was seen as the pathological agent that damaged society. Prostitution was thought of as the natural consequence of ungovernable, deviant sexuality and innate vice; it was held responsible for the rampant spread of syphilis, a disease as incurable as tuberculosis but much more stigmatised. The epidemic was of most significance when it affected the navy and the upper classes, thus creating anxieties about the threat to the country's political power. England's military abilities became undermined by her syphilitic forces, and her political and social leaders were equally compromised in strength and sanity by the ravages of disease. In other words, society's illicit appetites produced disease which had far-reaching and damaging effects. The link with consumption is quite clear, and suggests that perhaps Dickens was appropriating the kinds of discourses which led up to the Contagious Diseases Acts of the 1860s, and utilising them, within the context of a different disease, for his own political ends.

That Dickens was at some level concerned with syphilis as well as consumption is made apparent by several aspects of the plot. I have already mentioned Paul's resemblance to the syphilitic child, his aged appearance being a classic sign of congenital syphilis. This would of course suggest his disease had been inherited from his parents, something which works effectively enough within the symbolic context of the novel, as it would reinforce the idea of Mr Dombey's responsibility for his son's death. It is also not beyond the realms of possibility within the actuality of the plot as well, however. Mr Dombey's madness and illness following his 'ruin' and the 'stain of his domestic shame for which there was no purification' (p. 935), and the way in which his fate, that of his friend Carker and particularly that of his wife are all linked with the prostitute Alice – herself finally the victim of an unnamed disease – all suggest support for the possibility of a syphilitic subtext within the novel. This is also relevant to the capitalism plot, as the agent of syphilisation, the prostitute, is as Lynda Nead has pointed out the clearest and most condemning metaphor for capitalism.[39] She encompasses every aspect of economic exchange, being at once producer, supplier and marketer of the commodity that is her own body, a commodity which, when consumed, frequently produced venereal disease. She is in this respect Dickens's model of pathological capitalism summed up in one body. This link between carnality and finance is suggestive in terms of Mr Dombey's downfall too. William Acton's influential paradigm of sexual economics can clearly be related to the novel. Acton likens orgasm to 'spending of the self', so that a period of sexual indulgence becomes a time of inflation followed by a depression brought on by venereal disease.[40] Dombey 'spends' too much on his 'too expensive' young wife during their marriage, and after she leaves him he descends into a bankruptcy both financial and physical; he emerges emasculated, a 'feeble semblance of a man' (p. 958). The syphilitic implications here suggest that sexual overconsumption is as threatening to health as any other indulgence.

We have seen how Dickens uses disease in the novel as a means of exploring and in part condemning the capitalist system it is a product of, and metaphor for. The whole process is, however, complicated by Dickens's own complicity in the capitalism he criticises. As one of the most popular and successful authors of his time, or indeed of any time, Dickens is perhaps the Mr Dombey of the literary world. He was certainly an industrious capitalist in terms of literary production, publishing prolifically and making a substantial amount of money in the process. *Dombey and Son* was, especially, written at the point at which Dickens was emerging into real affluence: Peter Ackroyd suggests that 'from the sales of all his books during the last six months of the previous year he earned altogether more than £3000' and that 'his financial anxieties, at least, were coming to an end'.[41] This would not have have been an insignificant occurrence for Dickens, a man to whom money was important and who worked hard to ensure financial security for himself and his family.[42] It is therefore impossible to separate *Dombey and Son*'s function as a political treatise against capitalism from its existence as a commodity of some financial worth to its author. The system of production and consumption Dickens was critiquing and condemning was the same one his novel had been entered into, and which he was benefiting from. While he could not go along with Marxism owing to his own complicity in capitalism, Dickens was not prepared to accept Adam Smith's doctrine of self-interest either, however. It is thus interesting to speculate upon Dickens's possible guilt about his newly secure position in this economic world. The association he had forged between disease

and capitalism can even, I suggest, be considered responsible for the illness he suffered during the writing of the later parts of *Dombey and Son*,
an illness which seemed to be of largely psychological origin. It included
among its symptoms a kind of 'nervous seizure in the throat', a sensation
of choking, which forges an interesting link between Dickens and his small
consumptive hero, Paul Dombey.[43]

If *Dombey and Son* is concerned with representing the effects of consumption on the affluent middle class, then Elizabeth Gaskell's *North and
South* explores the other side of the question, its impact upon the labouring
population. Gaskell's second industrial novel, like her first, abounds with
various diseases and deaths, to the extent that the author herself said that
'a better title than "North and South" would have been "Death and Varia-
tions"! There are five deaths, each beautifully suited to the character of the
individual . . .'.[44] And of course they are, from the fevers that plague the
unfortunate Bouchers to the more bourgeois illnesses that kill Mr and Mrs
Hale – heart disease and cancer respectively. As always, tuberculosis occupies its own, significant place in the text, however, as the affliction which
incapacitates and finally brings about the death of young Bessy Higgins,
one of the two main working-class figures in the novel (the other is her
father, Nicholas). Through Bessy's existence as an invalided former factory hand, consumption and capitalism are textually drawn together and
become part of the narrative of industrial society that Gaskell is concerned
with constructing.

The capitalist narrative inherent in *North and South* has been the subject
of some critical discussion over the years; perhaps most significantly it
has caught the attention of Marxist critics like Raymond Williams and
Arnold Kettle, who have explored the master/worker relationship and the
opposition between paternalism and laissez-faire that they represent. The
character of Bessy Higgins seems to have been surprisingly overlooked,
however, as any critical study which mentions her has focused upon her
religious beliefs, not her illness.[45] The only exception I have yet found is
Coral Lansbury, who in her book *Elizabeth Gaskell: The Novel of Social Crisis*
briefly draws upon Bessy's function as indicator of the 'insidious malady in
industrial society', but the social disease Lansbury identifies is alcoholism,
not consumption, and the victim is Bessy's father.[46] Lansbury delineates
how Bessy links her father's affliction to its social context, describing how
the hardships of working-class life can be held responsible for this condition.
She thus considers Bessy a spokesperson for the industry-induced sickness
of her class, but does not take this to its logical conclusion by exploring how
Bessy herself functions as model of pathologised capitalism, as I will do.

Tuberculosis functions as a signifier for capitalism in *North and South* as it does in *Dombey and Son*, but in a simpler, more direct way in Gaskell's text. Bessy Higgins's consumption is directly caused by her work in the poorly ventilated cotton factories. She speaks of it as the likely but avoidable consequence of industrial production, rendered inevitable by the nature of the capitalist system which encourages the greed of manufacturers:

'. . . the fluff got into my lungs, and poisoned me . . . They say it winds up our lungs, and tightens them up. Anyhow, there's many a one as works in a carding room, that falls into a waste, coughing and spitting blood, because they're just poisoned by the fluff.'
'But can't it be helped?' asked Margaret.
'I dunno. Some folk have a great wheel at one end of their carding rooms to make a draught, and carry off the dust; but that wheel costs a deal of money – five or six hundred pound, maybe, and brings in no profit, so it's but a few of the masters as will put them up . . .'.[47]

It is worth noting here that Bessy (and presumably Gaskell) believe that her disease is caused by the inhalation of dust and fibre at the factory, rather than by infection. Cause and effect here are clearly apparent; it is common knowledge that factories produce disease along with cotton. With hindsight, we can surmise that Bessy may actually be suffering from occupational emphysema or lung cancer, as consumption, owing to the ambiguity of its symptoms, often acted as a blanket term in the nineteenth century for these and other pulmonary disorders which were unrecognised at the time. Tuberculosis was in actual terms just as much a product of the factory system as those diseases were, however, for poor ventilation in the workplace was largely to blame for the breathing in of both fluff and bacteria.

Bessy's illness is not just a symbolic disruption of capitalism, as Paul's is, but a real one. She has previously sold her labour to provide essential financial support for her family, until her disease intervenes and removes her from the system of production:

And I did na like to be reckoned nesh and soft, and Mary's schooling were to be kept up, mother said, and father he were always liking to buy books, and go to lectures o' one kind or another – all of which took money – so I just worked on till I shall ne'er get the whirr out o' my ears, or the fluff out of my throat i' this world. That's all. (p. 119)

Thus the ways in which capitalism falls down through the intervention of disease are epitomised in Bessy, who is transformed from labourer and breadwinner into an invalid who is a financial burden on her already impoverished family. This makes it necessary for her younger sister to go out to work – 'I were loth to let her go, but somehow we must live' – and thus potentially perpetuates the cycle of illness and poverty that dogs the lower classes in the novel (p. 162). Like little Paul she has become spiritualised and even intellectualised by her removal from health: in the classic tradition of the consumptive she becomes an observer and a philosopher of the religious and metaphysical aspects of the life that is passing her by, and which is to come, rather than a partaker in the petty concerns and demands of the industrial world. She no longer has any interest in its workings and struggles – 'I could have wished to have other talk about me in my later days, than just the clashing ... and clattering that has wearied me a' my life long, about work and wages, and masters, and hands, and knobsticks' (p. 160). Even amid the harsh realities of suffering which are represented in Gaskell's novel, this traditional association between consumption and an elevated, soulful mental state can never quite be abandoned. Bessy is all the more 'ladylike', it seems, from being divorced from the world of trade and health, certainly when compared with her 'taller and stronger' but clumsy and 'slatternly' younger sister (p. 104). There is still a sense here of tuberculosis as an upper-class illness, which seems to bring traces of nobility even to its poorest sufferers. It has the means, then, of making Bessy more significant and worthy of more textual space than Gaskell's other working-class invalids, as well as rendering her a spokesperson for the sickness of her world, and a mediator between it and the middle-class Margaret – whom she originally becomes friendly with, after all, because of Margaret's philanthropic feeling towards an invalid. Bessy is no longer a useful part of the capitalist system, but by being outside it functions all the more effectively as an observer and textual guide whose disease lends her authority. Through her divorce from economic production she can become a literary figure; a narrator.

It is interesting to note that Bessy's illness removes her not only from the world of industrial manufacture, however, but also from the world of commodities and purchasing; as she is no longer able to produce, it seems she is no longer allowed to consume. Bessy is visited by Margaret on six separate occasions, but is never seen eating, taking medicine, or drinking anything but the odd sip of water. She is also, despite being almost the sole object of her father's affection and concern, devoid of any of the sorts of luxurious commodities which might ease the path of her illness. This can of course be viewed as a traditional representation of the dying as casting aside the corporeal and terrestrial desires which preoccupy the healthy. However, the austerity that accompanies Bessy's affliction becomes of more political significance when contrasted with the position of the other invalid in the novel. Mrs Hale's disease seems to produce a whole industry of its own, so many commodities of illness does it necessitate. The 'nourishing and digestible diet' which must be provided for her, the 'medicine and treatments' (p. 179) the doctor prescribes, the water bed which the Hales get to improve her restless sleep, the presents of fine fruit and other delicacies which Mr Thornton makes to tempt her appetite – all contribute to a picture of illness very far from that of Bessy Higgins. It may be a gesture of social realism to acknowledge that the working classes cannot afford medicine or doctor's visits – though the Higginses are not 'very poor' (p. 186), and in fact the Hales are not a great deal more affluent themselves. The other tangible trappings of illness in the Higginses' home are conspicuous by their absence, however. Even the usual charitable help given to the sickly or impoverished – that of sending gifts of food or little luxuries – is ultimately denied Bessy, even though her needs are discussed by Margaret and her mother:

'But it must be very sad to be ill in one of those little back streets.' (Her kindly nature prevailing, and old thoughts of Helstone returning.) 'It's bad enough here. What could you do for her, Margaret? Mr Thornton has sent me some of his old port wine since you went out. Would a bottle of that do her good, think you?'
  'No, Mamma! I don't believe they are very poor – at least, they don't speak as if they were; and at any rate, *Bessy's disease is consumption – she won't want wine.* Perhaps I might take her a little preserve, made of our dear Helstone fruit. No! there's another family to whom I should like to give . . .'
  It distressed Mrs Hale excessively. It made her restlessly irritated until she could do something. She directed Margaret to pack up a basket in the very drawing room, to be sent then and there to the family . . . (p. 186, italics mine)

Thus 'another family', the admittedly needy but noticeably non-consumptive Bouchers, are the recipients of the Hales' philanthropic gifts and Bessy only benefits from Margaret's company and sympathy, not from anything more substantial. The only tangible present Margaret gives her is an old night-cap, and that is, significantly, after she has died.

  This inflicted abstemiousness does not seem dismissible as merely a casual overlooking of Bessy's plight, which Margaret is after all so responsive to in every other way. Bessy is treated differently from other invalids specif-ically because her 'disease is consumption', so therefore she 'won't want' the commodities which are usually deemed appropriate for invalids, and which Mrs Hale consumes in such quantities. It is possible to consider this a deliberate recognition and reinforcement of the idea of tuberculosis as a disease of luxury and over-consumption – in a metaphorical sense, of course, as even before her illness Bessy is clearly unable to approach the extravagance and opulence of a Mr Dombey. Bessy's disease, unlike Paul's, is a consequence of the low immunity which accompanies deprivation and the factory system, but Gaskell's text denies the possibility that it could be improved by little luxuries and a rich nourishing diet, even while recognising the benefit of these for the other invalids in the novel. There is an interesting correlation here between the austere response to Bessy's illness and that advocated by the Victorian physicians who considered consumption a disease of over-indulgence. Within the symbolic world of the novel, tuberculosis sufferers cannot be assisted or comforted by luxury goods, for as victims of capitalism, any interaction with symbols of conspicuous consumerism must do more harm than good. This theory is significant when taken alongside the foreign trade theme which *North and South* offers as a kind of backdrop to its industrial concerns. References to imported goods, mostly articles of clothing such as 'printed calicos' or 'Indian shawls', are repeated throughout the novel (p. 4); Mr Thornton's business is bothered by competition from foreign trade; Frederick Hale becomes a merchant in Spain. This engagement with importation casts interesting light on the questions of working-class consumption which surround Bessy. It is possible that Gaskell denies Bessy luxuries because it is the consumption of 'luxury' goods that has contributed to her disease. There was a belief at this period that the consumption of 'tropical produce', namely sugar, was an important cause of phthisis. For example, *The Use of Sugar: The Primary Cause of Pulmonary Consumption*, published six years after *North and South,* suggested that 'sugar is the primary cause of pulmonary diseases and diseases of the respiratory organs in Great Britain'.[48] This was because such 'unnatural' food led to imbalance in the body's levels of oxygen, carbon and nitrogen, and tuberculosis was the inevitable outcome of this.[49] This theory reveals the extent of the anxiety that surrounded luxury goods, and while its science is not supported with medical evidence, the reasoning behind the argument is sound enough. Tuberculosis is well known to seek out those with low immunity from any class, and the commonest cause of this lack of resistance was inadequate diet. Charlotte Sussman has discussed the impact of colonial trade upon English consumption habits, and has identified the importation of 'sugar and other drug foods' – tobacco, tea, coffee, opium – as responsible for a national decline in nutrition values.[50] These were widely used by the working classes because they acted as appetite suppressors – sugar in particular was desirable because it made unappetising food palatable and provided an inexpensive form of energy, though one which was of course lacking in nutritional worth. Through her mission work Gaskell clearly was made aware of the temptations presented by these kinds of commodities:

There are days wi' you as wi' other folk, I suppose, when yo' get up and go through th' hours, just longing for a bit of a change – a bit of a fillip, as it were. I know I ha' gone and bought a four-pounder out o' another baker's shop to common on such days, just because I sickened at the thought of going on for ever wi' the same sight in my eyes and the same sound in my ears and the same taste i' my mouth, and the same thought (or no thought, for that matter) in my head, day after day, for ever. (p. 160)

Bessy's consumption of sweet pastries here, in an attempt to 'sweeten' an otherwise drab existence, seems just an example of the kind of working-class purchasing which had such damaging effects upon the health of the masses: 'buns, confectionery etc, probably composed of the most dele-terious ingredients . . . is a prolific cause of [consumption]'.[51] Gaskell has already dwelt upon these issues in more detail in *Mary Barton*, in which John Barton spends money on opium rather than food and Mary carefully allots part of her already meagre household budget for luxuries like sugar and tea.

In this respect it is possible to see how tuberculosis can be at once a disease of luxury and consumerism and also of deprivation. Attractive imported goods were essentially superfluous to health but were consumed as if they were necessities, which was damaging because they lacked sustenance, and reduced the desire for more wholesome foodstuffs, as well as reducing the money available to purchase them. This made a not insignificant contribu-tion to the nutritional deprivation of the masses, and thus to the endemic existence of tuberculosis. Issues of gender as well as class become important in this context, as female consumptives were symbolically complicit in their own illness because of the age-old identification between femaleness and consumerism. As Victoria de Grazia reiterates, 'acts of exchange and con-sumption have long been obsessively gendered, usually as female'.[52] The desire for and purchase of luxury goods – food, clothing and furnishings – were 'pivoted around the feminised world of the home', and were hence very much the domain of the wife, mother, or in Bessy's case, daughter. By implication, if women are largely responsible for consumerism, they are also producers of its ills, namely tuberculosis. Bessy is not entirely an innocent victim of her disease, then; her illness signals that she is at once a suffering martyr and an agent of self-inflicted contagion, her consumption the product of a society she has helped create.

North and South offers a kind of alternative 'form' of consumption to that represented in *Dombey and Son*, a form which can be most simply described as the working-class version of the disease. It is interesting to compare Bessy Higgins's illness with Paul's, especially in the context of Logan's exploration of the difference between working- and middle-class pathological bodies.[53] Logan identifies diseases of wealth as nervous complaints – hypochondria, hysteria, melancholia – and discusses how the bourgeois nervous body was 'highly responsive to cultural conditions' and therefore a perfect vehicle for social criticism.[54] We can see how this could refer to Paul Dombey, whose disease of civilisation is certainly linked to psychological factors: his refusal to 'make an effort' to get well in the Dombey fashion, his desire not to grow up, his tendency to think too much which makes him prematurely old – 'his mind is too much for him. His soul is a great deal too large for his frame' (p. 155). This all suggests that he functions as a nervous body, and as such is a perfect site for the social purpose of the novel to be manifested upon. But what, then, of the lower-class body, which deprivation has rendered less susceptible to nervous illness but more prone to consumption? Bessy Higgins represents the 'real' diseased body, one which is not a symbolic but an actual casualty of capitalism, its deprivations and even perhaps its luxuries. Tuberculosis functions in these novels as a disease of multiple cultural meanings: it is a consequence of social and economic over-consumption and thus a punishment for capitalist greed; yet also a symbol of the capitalist exploitation of working-class labour; a disease at once of luxury and deprivation. The juxtaposition of Bessy and Paul through sickness reveals the ability of tuberculosis to function as a powerful leveller of class, for Paul's bourgeois body is consumed by the same capitalist system that has been designed to fuel itself upon the labour and strength of the masses. Consumption thus defeats capitalism in another sense too; health is the one commodity that cannot be bought, even by Mr Dombey. As Paul points out; '[money] can't make me strong and quite well either, Papa; can it?' (p. 154).

CHAPTER 3

The consumptive diathesis and the Victorian invalid in Mrs Humphry Ward's Eleanor

One of the predominating images of the bourgeois consumptive is that of the invalid abroad, the nomadic traveller who wanders to sunnier parts of Europe and beyond in pursuit of that elusive ideal climate with the right 'air' to restore, heal and invigorate weary, diseased bodies.[1] Italy was one of the most popular destinations with the well-to-do invalid, its cultural, historical and artistic attractions especially desirable for those interested in treating their intellect along with their lungs, a place where physical suffering might be temporarily assuaged through indulgence in aesthetic pleasures. For this reason it was frequently used as a setting for literary representations of invalidism: as Italy is the site where illness meets art, it facilitates a movement for authors like Henry James to the portrayal of that illness *as* art.

James links Italy and consumption in the subject of my final chapter, *The Portrait of a Lady*, in which the dying Ralph Touchett travels all over Europe in search of health, but repeatedly returns to Rome where much of the latter half of the novel is set. Similarly, Venice is James's chosen background for the story of one of literature's most famous invalids, Milly Theale in *The Wings of the Dove*. I have not included Milly in this study because her illness is deliberately kept mysterious and consciously never named by James: its identity is even debated by Kate and Densher at one point in the novel.[2] This is probably because Milly is too ethereal to be confined to the indignities of a specific ailment, for her desirability, which is essential to the plot, might be compromised if she were actually and specifically 'diseased' rather than vaguely and generally 'ill'. Her malady may well be phthisis, however, as she certainly has the appearance of a consumptive, being 'slim, constantly pale, delicately haggard' with 'exceptionally red' hair,[3] the whole picture reminiscent of famous Pre-Raphaelite consumptive muse Elizabeth Siddal. However, perhaps the most suggestive evidence to support this diagnosis is revealed through an exploration of what I suggest was an important source for James's book, a novel written by a close friend of James's, the best-selling author Mrs Humphry Ward. *Eleanor*, published in 1900, is also set in Italy and has a number of significant points of similarity with *The Wings of the Dove*. James had been staying with Ward in Italy while *Eleanor* was being written, and when he read it later it inspired some of his best criticism on 'the novel' – on 'point of view'. His reservations about the approach and scope of *Eleanor* may well have been the impetus for the arguably more complex portrait of female illness which he went on to represent in Milly Theale. In a letter to Ward about her novel, James says he 'can't "criticise" – though I *could* (that is I did – but can't do it again) . . . re-write',[4] and I suggest that in fact he did go on to 're-write' Eleanor, in the form of *Wings*. Like James's later work, Ward's is a representation of a pathological love triangle, and follows the lives of two women, one healthy and one ill, who are both attached to the same man. The consumptive, Eleanor Burgoyne, is unsuccessful in her pursuit and dies at the end of the novel, and in this regard both she and Milly seem to evoke the love-melancholic consumptive whose cultural significance in the long eighteenth century has been discussed by Clark Lawlor. That Eleanor and Milly share the fate of earlier lovelorn heroines like Richardson's Clarissa and Smollett's Monimia perpetuates the notion of consumption as a illness of sensibility and thwarted desire: 'when love goes wrong for a woman, she has no alternative but disease and ultimately death – preferably a beautiful one from consumption'.[5] Eleanor's disease is, however, much more than a straightforward cultural signifier, for it is as much about self-fashioning and female power as it is about romantic love. Hence, despite her socially marginalised status as rejected lover, she remains the undisputed heroine and the dominant emotional and spiritual force in the book. And, unlike the betrayed Milly, Eleanor refuses to simply 'turn her face to the wall', instead using phthisis to construct a form of revenge.[6]

William S. Peterson suggests that the twentieth-century view of Ward's work was that it was lacking in imagination, because it drew too heavily on 'real-life' events, and was too directly a simple reflection, rather than an interpretation, of the social, moral and political concerns of its day. After all, 'no novelist wishes to think of himself as merely the author of a series of valuable historical documents'.[7] Thus her novels, which seemed to possess observational intelligence rather than the universal relevance of literary genius, seemed to become dated and ideologically redundant very rapidly. This is considered one of the main reasons why, despite Ward's status as one of the most popular writers of the late nineteenth century, her novels have been largely critically neglected by twentieth-century scholars, and why she remains widely unread today and is no longer in print. The few recent studies of her, most noticeably John Sutherland's *Mrs Humphry Ward: Eminent Victorian, Pre-Eminent Edwardian*, have placed their emphasis very much on her remarkable literary life rather than her work. Yet this realism, the most condemned aspect of her novels, also renders them of substantial use to this study, for they are, in Peterson's words, 'the most complete literary record of late Victorian and Edwardian life'.[8] *Eleanor* is particularly useful to any exploration of consumption, given that its invalid figure is the central character, rather than a marginal one as in many fictional plots, and consequently it allows a much more detailed exploration of the complex cultural metaphors which surround this disease. Ward utilises accepted tubercular stereotypes – primarily this disease's ability to function as a spiritualising illness which purifies the soul of those it afflicts – but also reveals some of the contradictory, even paradoxical, beliefs about the consumptive which are captured by the medical writing of the period but not usually explored in such depth in fiction. Like all her works, this novel closely reflects the religious, metaphysical and scientific themes which preoccupied the author, but, most importantly in the context of this study, it reveals Ward's intense personal interest in illness and in the figure of the invalid, and her self-taught but wideranging and well-informed knowledge of late Victorian medicine.

Sutherland has discussed the chronic ill health which plagued Ward throughout her life, suggesting that 'One could write her biography as a sixty-nine-year medical case report or an anthology of the age's female invalidisms . . . over the years she was racked by a baffling array of chronic, acute, subacute, psychosomatic and organic ailments.'[9] Such experience of suffering clearly has an autobiographical impact on *Eleanor*, a novel which displays, in Vineta Colby's words, 'an obsession with disease',[10] and which sets out to examine the spiritual growth which may be the positive outcome of physical pain. Ward's interest in medicine far exceeded that of a passive patient, however. She was also a 'homoeopath'[11] with an 'instinct for self-doctoring' and an 'extraordinary skill in the use of these little drugs'.[12] Ward did have a personal interest in tuberculosis, for her sister, Ethel Arnold, who was staying with the Ward family while *Eleanor* was being written, was consumptive, and so the book must be considered a record of the suffering – emotional as well as physical – which Ward witnessed on a day-to-day basis. Her exploration of consumption stems from motives more political than personal, however. Ward utilises both the medical concerns and the cultural myths which surrounded this disease in order to engage her novel in discourse about some of the most important issues of the day. Phthisis's reputation as an inherited, spiritual and female disease rendered it an ideal medium through which to discuss eugenics, religious doubt and the position of women, which are all central concerns in *Eleanor*. Of all the diseases with which the medically interested Ward is familiar, consumption is the one most suited to her purposes.

Ward's novel, which is based on the real-life relationship between Chateaubriand and his consumptive lover Pauline de Beaumont,[13] is at once a travel narrative and a chronicle of illness, as it records both the movement of the heroine through Italy and the progression of the disease within her body. Like many real-life consumptives, Eleanor Burgoyne travels abroad in pursuit of the right climate for her lungs. Her search for physical strength and vigour is ultimately doomed to failure, but it becomes in the course of the novel subsumed by a much more essential pilgrimage for mental and spiritual health. Of course the two are inseparable from one another, for *Eleanor* constructs consumption as the physical symptom of emotional unhappiness, and through this representation its heroine's illness is viewed as a product of the mind as much as an affliction of the body. As Lawlor has indicated, this juxtaposition of consumption and emotional wellbeing has always been one of the most enduring myths which surround phthisis, and one which was held true in medical science as well as popular opinion.[14] Dr Thomas Gurney, for example, lists 'grief, sorrow and mental depression' as important causes of consumption.[15] However, this belief was also extremely useful to authors of fiction, who used it as a textual device to heighten the drama in the plot. At the beginning of the novel Eleanor is fashionably delicate in appearance but nonetheless in relatively good health, her phthisis temporarily in recession, it seems, because she is happy and content. She has been 'on the road to death' prior to her arrival in Rome but coming abroad has altered the direction of her path and given her 'a new reason for living'.[16] This is because she becomes intellectually and emotionally fulfilled by her relationship with her author cousin Manisty, whom she works as muse for and secretary to and with whom she is in love. It is important to note that in this consumption/emotion paradigm simply wishing to live enables life to continue, for if the 'depressing passions' of unrequited love bring about the disease, optimism and joy can cure it. There is a clear parallel between Eleanor and Milly Theale here, for Milly is told she will live if she wishes to do so, is encouraged to marry for her health, and her death takes the form not of a worsening of her illness but of mental capitulation to it: she is 'living by will', but when she hears the truth about Densher and Kate 'she turned her face to the wall'.[17]

Eleanor's return to health is destined to be a temporary one explicitly because of her 'depressing passions', for the 'healing' happiness she experiences is short-lived (p. 40). Manisty is content to exploit her artistic abilities in assistance for his book, but does not return her feelings, finding the possibility of her emotional attachment something of a nuisance: 'He had been a brute, an ungrateful brute! . . . But still her claim had wearied him; and he had brushed it aside' (p. 290). Here Eleanor's vulnerability is revealed, for despite her seemingly privileged position as an attractive, educated and intellectual upper-class widow, she is necessarily confined by convention to a very passive and feminine role in her relations with the opposite sex. She thus remains a metaphorically silenced but hopeful and patient angel in the house until a fresh young American relation, Lucy Foster, comes to stay and becomes the object of Manisty's desire instead. It is at this point that Eleanor's jealous resentment awakens and so too does her disease. The two are associated throughout the novel, to the point that it is difficult to tell which of the two is racking her body: 'Gentleness turned to hate and violence – was it of that in truth, and not of that heart mischief to which doctors gave long names, that Eleanor Burgoyne was dying?' (p. 349).

This illness that is both mental and physical, then, becomes the catalyst for the emergence of Eleanor's passionate private self from behind her reserved and proper public persona. As a healthy woman she endures in silence for the sake of propriety, but as a consumptive invalid she has no such reservations. From this point the novel becomes a chronicle of her struggle not to be 'in-valid' to the man she loves. She rejects the 'old inexorable compulsion that lies upon the decent woman, who can only play the game as the man chooses to set it' (p. 197), and instead makes her feelings known, subtly to Manisty but directly and openly to Lucy, in the hope of persuading her to end her blossoming romance with him:

And then – in painful gasps – the physical situation had been revealed to her – the return of old symptoms and the reappearance of arrested disease. The fear of the physical organism alternating with the despair of the lonely and abandoned soul – never could Lucy forget the horror of that hour's talk . . . the floodgates of personality and of grief were opened before her. (p. 345)

This unexpected confession, this opening of the 'floodgates of personality', marks Eleanor's transformation from self-sacrificing 'decent woman' who suffers in feminine silence, to the subversive tragic heroine who dominates the rest of the book. Such an exposing of the self is clearly socially transgressive because it 'revealed what no woman should reveal' (p. 360), and is represented as a verbal 'fall' which she afterwards longs to retract. 'There is one hour yesterday which I wish to cancel – to take back. I gave up everything – everything' (p. 310). It is significant, however, that such a fall is rendered more acceptable and understandable, and less of a 'sin', because Eleanor's physical health is equated with and dependent on her emotional wellbeing:

I came to Rome in a strange state – as one looks at things and loves them for the last time, before a journey. And then – well, then it all began! – new life for me, new health. The only happiness . . . that had ever come my way. (p. 282)

Hence her confession and her appeal to her rival's generosity is not mere caprice but a form of self-defence, a plea not just for her love affair but for her whole continued existence – 'Why shouldn't one try to save oneself? It's the natural law. There's only the one life' (p. 276). Within the discourse of illness in the novel this claim is accepted by Lucy as valid and there is no questioning of the assertion that they who are responsible for Eleanor's unhappiness may also be held accountable for her eventual death. Illness gives her the right to prioritise her needs over Lucy's, simply because Lucy is healthy, with 'all her powers and chances before her. What would kill me would only anticipate – for her – a day that must come' (p. 437). In contrast, Eleanor's chance of happiness with Manisty represents her 'last hope' (p. 281). Illness does not merely prompt unwomanly behaviour, it seems, it can also potentially legitimise it, and thus the invalid is set apart from the conventions and expectations of bourgeois society. Her consumption allows Eleanor freedom to pursue her desires in a way that the more virtuous, passive and healthy Lucy cannot.

The power that illness wields over the healthy is made clearly apparent here. The mix of pity, admiration and guilt Eleanor's suffering commands means that she is able to manipulate the other characters into fulfilling her wishes and carrying out her plans. Her revenge on Manisty is achieved by separating him and Lucy, whose guilty sympathy with the suffering woman leads her to agree to Eleanor's proposal that the two women hide from him and disappear together into the isolated mountains of rural Italy. This journey is deliberately disguised by Eleanor and Lucy so it appears to others as another leg of the consumptive's conventional journey in search of health, but is clearly indicative of the subversive invalid's attempt to 'escape' the restrictions and expectations of the civilised world, to indulge her own whims outside the society she, as a pathological, fallen woman, has become marginalised from. Hence an isolated rural retreat is Eleanor's chosen destination, and the excursion becomes a spiritual pilgrimage into a 'wilderness' (p. 437) both literal and metaphorical, in which Eleanor's soul is tempted and tested. Restraining social expectations and mores can never be entirely left behind, however. Under the influence of Catholic priest Father Benecke, and the aristocratic Italian Contessa Guerrini, and after a period of struggle between will and conscience, the true selfish tyranny of Eleanor's own behaviour is revealed to her. After this social and spiritual awakening, and as her disease worsens, Eleanor repents and brings about the meeting of Manisty and Lucy, but her power over others remains absolute and she merely exchanges one form of autocracy for another. She has become so 'entrenched . . . in Lucy's heart' (p. 360) that the girl refuses Manisty's proposal and it is left to Eleanor to persuade her and manage their final reconciliation:

'But I leave it all in your hands. What else can I do?' 'No', she said calmly. 'There is nothing else for you to do.' [Manisty] felt a tremor of revolt, so quick and strange was her assumption of power over both his destiny and Lucy's. (p. 509)

In the disrupted family unit that comes together at the close of the novel, it is the invalid who has control, not the patriarch, for the previously forceful and dynamic Manisty is rendered impotent as he waits for Eleanor to exert her influence over Lucy, and her pleas eventually succeed where his have failed. Even the domestic details of their departure for England are settled by Eleanor's wishes. In a reversal of her previous position as Manisty's subservient, undervalued assistant, she becomes by the end of the book the undisputed head of a household that frequently contains three men – a Catholic priest, a British government official, and a landowner and political writer. Each is representative of a patriarchal power – the Church, the State, inheritance law and literary authorship – and yet they all bend to Eleanor's wishes, for the combination of her inexorable strength of will and pitiable weakness of body 'made mock of their opposition' (p. 558). This must be one of the most autobiographical aspects of the text, for Eleanor's authority over her friends is evocative of that exerted by her creator. Ward's daughter suggests that the 'physical ailments of [her mother's] heroines' expressed 'only too deep an experience of [Ward's] own, since never, in all the years that she was writing, did she know what it was to have a day of ordinary physical strength'.[18] It is undeniable that Ward's life was, like her heroines', blighted by suffering, but, as John Sutherland has suggested, she was also very aware that sickness had its compensations. Autonomy and influence were the more appealing 'side effects' of ill-health: 'The life-threatening nature of her ailments gave her . . . a power of passive domination over her family. They (particularly Humphry) never questioned anything that was good for her.'[19] It is notable here that Mrs Ward's husband was especially willing to let her have her own way: her illness, as well as the strength of her personality, had eroded patriarchal control in this household.

It is clear that many of the multiple meanings and paradoxes associated with the nineteenth-century invalid are neatly captured by Mrs Ward's portrayal of Eleanor, who is less a literary creation than a hybrid of the stereotypes and cultural myths that surrounded illness in general and the consumptive in particular. As I have discussed, Victorian medical discourse was frequently preoccupied with and disturbed by consumption's ability to 'single out' members of the population, leaving others unscathed. The need among doctors to scientifically explain this seemingly random distribution of victims led to the identification of a tubercular 'diathesis', which was a 'habit of body so liable to consumption that the popular opinion in England associates consumption almost exclusively with it'.[20] This image of a specific physical specimen which would be recognisably vulnerable to phthisis was a seductive one for a medical profession constantly baffled by this disease, and it remained persuasive throughout the century. In this way, then, the popular culture stereotypes which accompany any illness became for phthisis reinforced and validated by the beliefs of the medical profession. Of course, this consequently meant that any sufferer could become a signifier for certain associated traits. Eleanor is a good example of this kind of cultural coding at work, for she neatly matches in body and character what phthisis specialist S. Dougan Bird identified in 1863 as the classic consumptive 'type':

This type . . . has usually remarkable beauty of person and brilliancy of intellect – a through-bred look, which in our national pride we associate with the British aristocracy . . . slender, graceful figures . . . narrow chests, harmonious and delicate features, full and expressive eyes . . . all their senses are highly developed and they almost always have a high appreciation of the high arts. They are . . . 'too good to live'.[21]

Eleanor's intelligence, charm and sophistication – which far exceed the attributes of the other, healthy female characters – are emphasised throughout the book. Her artistic observations 'were the comments of taste and knowledge' (p. 171), and she also 'had a voice, a hand, a carriage that lovelier women had often envied, discerning in them those *subtleties of race and personality which are not to be had for the asking*' (p. 14, italics mine). She possesses too the 'delicate', 'thorough-bred' consumptive appearance described above: as Manisty notes, 'It was the perfection which was characteristic.

So too was the faded fairness of hair and skin, the frail distinguished look'
(p. 60). Eleanor's physical frailty is desirable, even admirable – a sign of
womanly 'perfection' – and is also a sign of her social standing. We can
see how the medical identification of an association between phthisis and
the upper classes, like that suggested by Bird above, is perpetuated by this
novel, whose consumptive heroine is 'naturally at home in the fashionable
world, with connections in half the great families' (p. 270). Her disease is
further associated with her refinement and breeding when an acquaintance
observes 'how ill she is . . . and how distinguished!' (p. 408), making clear
that the latter is a direct consequence of the former.

Bird's description of an aristocratic consumptive diathesis is important,
for it suggests the potential of this disease to undermine the health and
strength of the Victorian upper classes. Of course syphilis, which was
known to be congenital and which caused a high infant mortality rate,
represented the main eugenic threat to the bloodline of old families, but
Eleanor displays how consumption also worked in this role. Even after
Koch identified the tuberculosis bacillus and proved phthisis was infectious, debates about whether it was hereditary still continued. As late as
1907, a huge statistical study in London was still preoccupied with trying
to trace consumption in families.[22] By the end of the century fears about
the germ's ability to pass directly from parent to foetus had been subdued,
but concerns remained as to whether a predisposition to the disease might
run in families, or, in other words, whether a consumptive diathesis might
be inherited even if consumption itself could not be. The contagion theory
simply did not explain why only some of those who had the bacillus in
their bodies went on to develop the disease, and so there seemed to be
another factor which determined susceptibility. Moreover, this seemed to
be a predominantly upper-class phenomenon, for 'among the poor, pulmonary tuberculosis is a strictly infectious disorder but . . . it attacks the
well-to-do classes more or less sporadically'.[23] It was clearly apparent to all
how the consumption could be spread by infection among the working
classes, for overcrowded, ill-ventilated homes and factories were known
to be a perfect breeding ground for contagious disease, and inadequate
diet further encouraged the poor to succumb. The more intermittent and
random appearance of consumption among the upper classes was a different matter, however, as their more healthy lifestyles meant that they
did not live and work at close quarters with the germs of dozens of sickly
people. Thus when a wealthy individual contracted phthisis it still remained
something of a mystery to their doctors, and other possible reasons for
their illness were considered. An 'unhealthy condition of the constitution'

which was 'often, doubtless, congenital and hereditary' was a popular candidate.[24]

All this has consequences for the inbred world of the aristocracy, in which heredity was so important. *Eleanor* is preoccupied with questions of breeding and inheritance: with the significant exception of Lucy, all the six central characters belong to the same old, 'distinguished' family, whose 'connections in half the great houses' of England are at once the source of their power and, potentially, their undoing. The head of the clan, Manisty, is particularly troubled by his ancestry, for he is under pressure from his relatives to return to England and take up the social role that awaits him, but has spent his life avoiding his family home and his responsibility as its patriarch.

> What have I to go home for? . . . I hate my old house . . . Its memories are intoler-able . . . My mother died there – of an illness it is appalling to think of. No, no, not – Alice's illness! – not that. And now, Alice – I should see her ghost at every corner! (p. 321)

It is significant that it is not only 'memories' but a more tangible threat, in the form of pathological contamination, that prevents Manisty returning home and fulfilling his obligations there, particularly as the most pressing of these duties is the need to perpetuate the family line:

> he knew very well that . . . it was his duty to marry and marry soon . . . What did he want with a wife – still more, with a son? The thought of his own life continued in another's filled him with a shock of repulsion. *Where was the sense of infusing into another being the black drop that poisoned his own?* A daughter perhaps – with the eyes of his mad sister Alice? (pp. 66–7, italics mine)

It seems that the continuity of the whole clan is threatened by Manisty's anxiety about hereditary disease, his fear of the continuing taint of the mysterious illnesses of mother and sister. This idea is reinforced by the gradual change of his position, when he begins to consider the youthful and healthy Lucy as a potential wife:

> But now . . . he began to think with a new tolerance of the English *cadre* and the English life. He remembered all those illustrious or comely husbands and wives, his forebears, whose portraits hung on the walls of his neglected house. For the first time it thrilled him to imagine a new mistress of the house – young, graceful, noble – moving about below them. And even – for the first time – there gleamed out from the future the dim features of a son, and he did not recoil. (p. 289)

Lucy may be, as regards 'family and position . . . no fitting match for Edward Manisty' (p. 344), but actually she is a more suitable mate than Eleanor, who is his family's preferred choice. As an outsider, an American, Lucy is a symbol of fresh new blood, the offspring of a 'new money' family without past and tradition, and is consequently 'as strong as Samson'. She therefore brings a needed and healthy change to the 'great clan with innumerable memories and traditions' (p. 270) that is the Manisty family, who are at the end of the novel preserved into posterity by a marriage with strong stock, rather than contaminated by the taint of the well-bred but consumptive Eleanor. Thus eugenic principles might well inform the central plot of the novel – Manisty's choice of bride – for by rejecting Eleanor he is adhering to Victorian medical advice:

> doubtless in view of the certain fact of inherited bodily qualities and the possible transmission of the disease congenitally, it is highly important to do what lies in our power to deter consumptive persons from marriage . . . all these things have combined to make the heads of families cautious in sanctioning marriages with individuals suspected of having a tuberculous ancestry.[25]

In this context it is possible to see a different dimension to Eleanor's 'fall', as her desire to marry and possibly reproduce even though she is diseased is a socially disruptive act, a selfish impulse with potentially dangerous consequences for her bloodline. As I will discuss further with reference to *The Portrait of a Lady*, self-sacrificial celibacy was a more appropriate and desirable path for the consumptive invalid, and one which, by 'giving' Manisty to Lucy, Eleanor does finally take – though still with subversive implications, as we shall see. Yet Eleanor cannot really be held responsible for her behaviour, for the unregulated and possibly contaminating desire she feels can also be considered a direct consequence of her particular disease. There was a widely held belief in the association between consumption and heightened sensibility and sensitivity, and this was frequently interpreted as a sign of refinement, of belonging to a certain social class. The associations that consumption has with heightened emotional state also links it to heightened physicality, however: from the time of the Romantic poets onward it has been associated with sensuality and sexuality. This of course has disturbing moral implications for female consumptives, especially in the Victorian era. Of course, all invalids were frequently considered socially transgressive because they were not economically productive, but with phthisis this transgression takes on a sexual dimension as well. Once again we see the inseparability of emotions and consumption, for Eleanor's emotional state may cause her relapse into illness, but her underlying disease is also responsible for her unfeminine excess of feeling, as she experiences 'all-consuming' love and jealousy. It is apparent that Eleanor metaphorically 'falls' by going against sexual etiquette through her unwomanly confession of her feelings to Lucy and Manisty, but this is really only a symptom of an underlying malady, passionate love. The novel frames desire as an emotion which, for women, is a disease in itself. Eleanor is frequently made feverish by her unrequited longing, is 'like a person in a delirium' (p. 513), 'conscious of a certain terror of herself, of this fury in the veins, so strange, so alien, so debasing' (p. 331). Significantly, through the experience of desire she undergoes a spiritual metamorphosis which evokes the physical changes brought about by consumption; 'a hardness, almost a ferocity of determination, which was stiffening and transforming the whole soul' (p. 331). The language used here creates an interesting parallel between the consequences of passion and of tubercle, both of which harden and transform the body, for it was widely known by 1900 that pulmonary tuberculosis created rigid calcified cavities and deposits in the lungs, and that it gradually colonised, altered and stiffened living tissue.[26] Sexuality in women is clearly pathological and destructive, and hence consumption is the perfect metaphor through which to express this in fiction.[27]

The extent of Eleanor's sexual 'fall' is indicated by the unnatural lack of proper maternal feeling and care she demonstrates for much of the novel. It is a source of shame to her that her romantic love for Manisty comes to replace and overwhelm the purer love and grief which she feels for her own dead son – 'She felt herself a hypocrite. In thought and imagination her boy now was but a hovering shadow compared to Manisty. It was not this sacred mother-love that was destroying her own life' (p. 420). This desire also renders her unable to behave as she should towards Lucy, who is young, far from home and grieving for her own mother, and thus vulnerable and in need of Eleanor's care rather than her envy: 'You who are older, and better able to control passion, ought you not to feel towards her as a tender older sister – a mother – rather than a rival?' (p. 439). Instead Eleanor's illness brings about a reversal of the natural order, as Lucy is forced to take on the supportive role. 'Lucy, with the maternal tenderness that should have been Eleanor's, pressed her lips on the hot brow that lay upon her breast, murmuring words of promise, of consolation, of self-reproach . . .' (p. 283). Similarly, it is Lucy who, despite her youth and inexperience, must become 'the guardian of the whole party, and . . . [is] conscious of a tender and anxious responsibility' during their journey into the wilderness (p. 343). Thus Eleanor has become the antithesis of the ideal domestic angel, demanding from others the love, comfort and reassurance she herself should be dispensing. Yet at the same time the childishness and vulnerable dependence on others her illness facilitates are, as Bram

Dijkstra has suggested, among the most desirable of female traits.[28] Ward is concerned here with revealing the paradoxes associated with the Victorian invalid, who is at once the epitome of delicate femininity and the antithesis of it: admirably self-sacrificing in her suffering and yet subversive and even unnatural in her desires. She is powerful yet powerless, her indomitable will controlling and manipulating her family, but her weak body always dependent on their aid.

By the final chapters of the novel, however, the paradoxes that surround Eleanor have been resolved by the progression of her disease. She remains femininely fragile and dependent, requiring practical assistance from all the members of her household, but has mastered her inappropriate emotions of love and jealousy. Her final elevation from fallen woman to spiritual angel is symbolised by her return to proper maternal feeling: 'with the tender dignity of a mother rejoicing over her child Eleanor received . . . [Lucy] on her breast' (p. 571). This transformation is not an arbitrary one, but is constructed as a direct consequence of Eleanor's movement from merely being ill to actually dying, and as such serves as an important comment on mortality and the possibility of redemption from sin. As an invalid Eleanor is an emotional 'tyrant' (p. 482), made selfish, vengeful and demanding by her body, its diseased physicality causing her to be socially and sexually transgressive. By the closing chapters, however, Eleanor's illness has worsened, and here we can see how Dijkstra's observation that once a woman is dead she becomes 'a figure of heroic proportions'[29] is also true of those approaching death. Eleanor does become a 'heroic' figure, moving into an elevated state in which she exchanges revenge and desire for the more hallowed joys of self-sacrifice and forgiveness, a 'state which held [her priest] often spell-bound before her, so consonant was it to the mystical instincts of his own life' (p. 551). Her closeness to death separates her from and elevates her above the other characters, for in her 'certainty of the spirit' (p. 558) she 'stood alone – aloof from them all' (p. 546). She becomes, in other words, the personification of virtuous Victorian womanhood: asexual, altruistic and incorporeal.[30]

Importantly, Ward constructs this final transformation as being facilitated by the weakening and wasting away of Eleanor's body. Her physicality is consumed by her disease, allowing her soul to be liberated. There is of course a classic, centuries-old association between heightened spirituality and weight loss: ever since Socrates' identification of the separation and opposition of the body and the soul,[31] the physical self has been perceived as fighting the intellectual and moral self for control. Refusal of food seems to resolve this division, as by starving oneself an individual can reduce, confine, control and 'escape her body'[32] and thwart its base, earthly desires. As Joan Jacobs Brumberg has pointed out in *Fasting Girls*, her important study of anorexia, 'such a rejection of appetite can be interpreted as the transcendence of the true self, whether conceptualised as soul or mind, over the corrupt and temporal body'.[33] A slight form was thus a visible symbol of this triumph of spirituality, and hence thinness has long been linked to purity and self-sacrifice, just as fleshiness has been with sensuality and self-indulgence. Jacobs Brumberg makes clear that this cultural myth never has greater resonance than in the Victorian era, when slenderness became a desirable state demanded from all women:

> The woman who put soul over body was the ideal of Victorian femininity. The genteel woman responded not to the lower senses of taste and smell but to the highest senses – sight and hearing – which were used for moral and aesthetic purposes. One of the most convincing demonstrations of a spiritual orientation was a thin body – that is, a physique that symbolised rejection of all carnal appetites.[34]

This cultural coding of body size goes some way towards explaining phthisis's traditional construction as a spiritual illness, for extreme emaciation is of course the defining feature of the disease, and thus the consumptive is a highly visible symbol of the body made penance. Flesh and the corporeal sins it encompasses are eaten away by the disease. Ward displays this very effectively in *Eleanor*, for in what Vineta Colby has described as Ward's 'own version of Gothic horror'[35] Eleanor's consumed body is uncovered and revealed to Lucy and the reader as a symbol of her new etherealness and her laying aside of earthly desires. This dramatic display seems designed to shock the viewer into acknowledgement of this new spiritual status:

> She let the wrapper slip from her shoulders. She showed the dark hollows under the wasted collar-bones, the knife-like shoulders, the absolute disappearance of all that had once made the difference between grace and emaciation. She held up her hands before the girl's terrified eyes. The skin was still white and smooth, otherwise they were the hands of a skeleton.
>
> 'You can look at that' she said fiercely . . . 'and then insult me by refusing to marry the man you love, because you choose to remember that I was once in love with him! *It is an outrage to associate such thoughts with me* – as though one should make a rival of some one in her shroud.' (p. 561, italics mine)

This scene is not only the climax of Eleanor's illness – the point at which her true physical state is revealed rather than camouflaged by clothes and disguised by hope of recovery – but also the climax of the plot: it is the moment when Lucy is persuaded to marry Manisty, only because Eleanor's emaciation provides evidence to convince her. Now that she has witnessed the undeniable 'proof' that is Eleanor's body, Lucy is convinced by her assertion that she has progressed to a stage where corporeal desires are left behind. Through the wasting of her physicality, Eleanor has finally been liberated from the subversive passions which prompted her decline in the first place. 'All my dreams and disappointments and foolish woman's notions have vanished from me like smoke. There isn't one of them left. What has a woman in my condition to do with such things?' (p. 562).

It is apparent that a whole historical tradition of self-starvation is being invoked here by Ward, who enhances the cultural cadence of phthisis in her novel by linking it with questions about appetite, hunger and fasting. Eleanor's loss of flesh both facilitates and indicates her spiritual readiness for the 'good death'[36] she finally makes. It is a symbol of her regained purity and her willingness to give up earthly bonds and pleasures and replace them with the sanctioned ecstasy of self-sacrifice, as she concerns herself with Manisty and Lucy's happiness at the expense of her own. This association between lightness of body and strength of soul does assume that weight loss is self-induced, though: Eleanor's wasting is only valid as a symbol of heightened spirituality if it is brought about by her own desire to reject the corporeal by rejecting the food that sustains and nourishes physicality. Can Eleanor really be viewed as this kind of 'holy anorexic',[37] given that her emaciation is not voluntary but a direct consequence of her disease? An examination of nineteenth-century medical tracts reveals the historical reasoning behind Ward's representation, however. The Victorian medical profession did in fact believe that emaciation was a *cause* as well as a symptom of consumption. As Dr Rohden pointed out in 1875, 'thinness in itself [is] a condition which is disposed to develop or continue phthisis (p. 544), this idea being made evident by the fact that 'the loss of flesh precedes all the other symptoms'.[38] Hence the 'bad and capricious appetites [and] anorexia . . . which accompany phthisis throughout its progress'[39] can be considered a major reason for the incidence of the disease in well-to-do, fashionable patients.

It is thus significant that the affluent Eleanor's body is always defined by its exceptional slenderness even prior to the return of her illness. From her first appearance in the novel her appearance is distinguished by 'the great thinness of the temples and cheeks, together with the emaciation of the whole delicate frame' (p. 14) and Ward makes repeated references throughout the narrative to her 'graceful' frailty. Her weight is not only a symptom of consumption but a pre-existing factor which invites it. If Eleanor's thinness is self induced, however, then so by implication is the illness which it is

'disposed to develop into', and this in turn has consequences for her perceived status as spiritual angel. The malnutrition which 'accompanied the
progress' of phthisis – because it rendered individuals susceptible to the disease – was thought an unavoidable consequence of inadequate diet among
the poor, but in the wealthy classes thinness and its accompanying risks
were usually the direct consequence of the voluntary refusal of food. This
refusal could be the result of 'capacious appetites', or a capitulation to the
demands of fashion, a topic discussed in more detail in Chapter 4. Perhaps
most relevantly to Eleanor, it could also be a means of empowering the
self through a political or emotional statement: Anna Krugovoy Silver has
pointed out that Victorian females' self-starvation was read as subversive
of the family because it represented a refusal of the sustenance provided by
the patriarch.[40] Whether it took place for vanity, contrariness or protest,
though, failure to eat was usually seen as a deviant act, because it was a
rejection of the principles conducive to health. Thus it is possible to regard
Eleanor as fully responsible for the onset of her own illness, not only because
of the unsuitable passions and accompanying mental anguish she experiences, which put an end to any chance of recovery, but also, more directly,
because of her refusal to nourish her body throughout the novel. Consumption and anorexia, then, are bound up together within these metaphors of
illness.

   A preoccupation with hunger and food resounds throughout Ward's
text. Many of the scenes take place at mealtimes, but Eleanor is never
seen eating. She is of course not unique among the ethereal heroines of
Victorian novels in this, because, as Silver has pointed out, having a delicate
appetite was a textually useful signal of refinement and social status in
women.[41] Yet it is notable that Eleanor crosses the line between eating
moderately and not eating at all, and moreover her appetite does seem
to be subversively 'capricious' rather than appropriately restrained, as she
tells Lucy 'I could not eat at luncheon. The ambassador's new cook did not
tempt me' (p. 310). Ward elsewhere points out that she 'toyed with her food,
ate nothing, and complained of the waits between courses' (p. 270). As her
illness worsens Eleanor only eats to please others, never of her own volition,
and never without surveillance – or with a personal agenda in mind – as
motivation:

Lucy . . . had brought coffee and bread and fruit . . . and had hovered round till
Eleanor had taken at least a cup of coffee and a fraction of roll. (p. 380).
Eleanor must needs eat and drink, to soothe Lucy's anxiety. The *girl watched
her every movement,* and Eleanor dared neither be tired nor dainty, lest for every
mouthful she refused Manisty's chance should be the less. (p. 516, italics mine)

Ward makes clear that Manisty is the main reason for Eleanor's disregard for eating, as it seems her 'perpetual hunger for love' (p. 110) and for him has replaced any healthy appetite for food. Vampire-like, he draws out her remaining strength. 'Eleanor worked with him or for him for many hours in each day. Her thin pallor became more pronounced. She ate little, and Miss Manisty believed that she slept less' (p. 97). The novel also hints that the origins of this anorexic self-deprivation pre-date Manisty, however, suggesting that they are a consequence of the emotional and sexual famine Eleanor has endured throughout her adult life. Deprived of passion in her first marriage to a husband who 'hadn't made her at all happy' (p. 79), she has by her own admission been 'hungry and starving for years' and it is only her relationship with Manisty that offers the possibility that she 'might still feast and be satisfied' (p. 277). This gives a different perspective to the novel's repeated references to her physical emaciation, which becomes not just a manifestation of her illness, but also a sign of the socially enforced denial of her physical appetites.

In her emotional decline, Eleanor is reminiscent of Caroline Helstone in Charlotte Brontë's *Shirley*, whose wasting body forms a symbol of her emotional starvation. This was very probably a deliberate reference, for Mrs Ward was an avid admirer of the Brontës and among her most critically respected and acclaimed work were her introductions to the Haworth editions of their novels, which were written in 1898, just before she began *Eleanor*. Certainly a link between a Brontë heroine and Ward's would not be unique in this novel: as Ward critic William S. Peterson has pointed out, she borrows other aspects of *Eleanor*'s plot from the Brontës' work, *Jane Eyre* in particular. (Peterson argues that Ward based the character of Manisty on Mr Rochester, and also draws attention to the violent bedroom confrontation between Lucy and Manisty's mentally ill sister Alice, which bears a striking resemblance to the scene in which Bertha enters Jane Eyre's room.)[42] Ward's literary use of consumption may well also have its roots in her interest in the lives of the Brontë sisters, as they represented the juxtaposition of consumption, anorexia and personal frustration. Like *Shirley*'s Caroline, Eleanor's partly self-induced wasting away can be read as silent protest against her futile, sterile position. The decline of both women is the consequence of their unrequited love for an unsympathetic male, and of the social conditioning that expects them to silently and passively endure their suffering. Unlike Caroline, however, Eleanor's increasing emaciation exerts power and control not only over her own body but, as we have seen, over those around her. Her thinness is not just a means of articulating her repression but a means of resisting it. It also brings her finally to an exultant spiritual state where the corrupting need for physical love is conquered and left behind, a state which elevates her over the other characters who are still enslaved by earthly desires. Through suffering, self-denial and anorexic behaviour she moves closer to a spiritual ideal, and indeed by the end of the novel, when close to death, she has become like a female saint.

This saintly construction of the dying Eleanor fits in with the traditional view of the consumptive as 'too good to live', but it also signals the text's other main concern – the important religious subtext which is bound up with the consumption plot. Ward's first and most famous novel, *Robert Elsmere*, was an enormously popular exploration of Victorian religious scepticism and dissent, which revealed the author's own growing ideological separation from the orthodox church. This thematic preoccupation remained with Ward throughout her life, and is brought to the fore again in *Eleanor*, in which there is a theological struggle between Catholicism and agnosticism, and Eleanor herself functions as the site at which these two meet. She is in fact an ideal focus for this kind of debate: because she is dying questions of faith become all the more poignant for her, because she is consumptive she is considered to be blessed with a innate spirituality, and as an intelligent, educated woman she functions as an autobiographical figure who represents many of the author's personal fears and doubts. In this context, then, it is significant that a parallel is drawn between Eleanor's suffering and that endured by the elderly Father Benecke, who is excommunicated by his Church after the writing of a controversial book. He represents his worst punishment – being no longer able to partake in Holy Communion – as a kind of famine of the spirit, and his description of it recalls the emotional hunger and longing expressed by Eleanor earlier in the novel:

'Madame, you see a man dying of hunger and thirst! He cannot cheat himself with fine words. He starves! . . . For forty-two years,' he said, in a low pathetic voice, 'have I received my Lord – day after day – without a break. And now "they have taken Him away – and I know not where they have laid him!"'

Nothing could be more desolate than tone and look. Eleanor understood. She had seen this hunger before. She remembered a convent in Rome where on Good Fridays some of the nuns were often ill with restlessness and longing, because for twenty-four hours the Sacrament was not upon the altar. (pp. 389–90)

That Eleanor understands his torment and has 'seen this hunger before' can be read as an identification of her position with his, especially as she goes on to mentally compare and contrast the causes of their shared starvation.

He, tortured by the martyrdom of thought, by the loss of Christian fellowship! –
She, scorched and consumed by a passion that was perfectly ready to feed itself
on the pain and injury of the beloved, or the innocent, as soon as its own selfish
satisfaction was denied it! There was a moment when she felt herself unworthy to
breathe the same air as him. (p. 390)

Even though Eleanor feels herself 'unworthy' by comparison because Father
Benecke's suffering is of holy origin, it seems that her vampiric passion functions as its secular double. His hunger arises because he is deprived of the
sustenance of Christ's body; hers because she is deprived of Manisty's. This
metaphorical affiliation between religious and earthly love is a suggestive
one, because it functions both to indicate Eleanor's spiritual status and,
through association with the pure priest, lessens the moral taint left upon
her by her forbidden desires. It also, of course, narrows the gap between
the Church and the individual, as Eleanor and Father Benecke are both
revealed as unfulfilled mortals hungry for spiritual nourishment. Eleanor
may be an erring woman who has sinned, but she has the capacity to achieve
a kind of priestly saintliness nonetheless. By the end of the novel she is not
only the epitome of purity and self-sacrifice, but is further strengthened
and empowered by her renewal of religious faith. The ensuing radiance
of her increased spirituality is such, indeed, that she becomes a 'light', a
'divine message' to guide the lost, troubled Father Benecke back to 'the sure
ground of spiritual hope' (p. 552) he has wandered from. This influence over
the priest must surely be another, final 'victory' (p. 558) of her femaleness
over the patriarchal powers she has struggled with. And of course it is her
disease that has made this possible: closeness to death, and her physical
frailty and emaciation, have given her a 'mystical intensity' (p. 555) which
makes her an example for others to follow. Even the feverish delirium that
accompanies her consumption has enabled her to become a kind of vision-
ary, as in her pyretic dreams she receives a vision of the Crucifixion which
the priest identifies as 'an omen of peace' (p. 553). In this sense she is indeed
sought out and blessed as a religious messenger. It is very significant that she
reaches this sublime state alone, that it is achieved through the purging and
purifying penance that is her illness, her own suffering and sacrifice, and
it is independent of the intervention and influence of the Church, whose
claim over her soul she has always resisted:

'As to what may be *true*, Father – you can't be certain any more than I! but at least
our dreams are true – to *us* ' ...
   'It is all true my friend,' he said, bending over her – 'the gospel of Christ. You
would be happier if you could accept it simply.'

She opened her eyes, smiling, but she did not reply. She was always eager that he should read and talk to her, and she rarely argued. But he never felt that intellectually he had much hold upon her. Her mind seemed to him to be moving elusively in a sphere remote and characteristic, where he could seldom follow. (pp. 553–4, italics Ward's)

Eleanor's faith is introspective and individual, and does not need a priest to act as medium. As a dying consumptive she has become privileged, and is able to communicate more directly with God. She views him not as something remote or distant from her own humanity, but as a personal, internalised force within herself. "Don't quarrel with me – with my poor words. He is there – *there!*" she said, under her breath. And he saw the motion of her white fingers towards her breast' (p. 556, italics Ward's). This is of course a suggestive, ironic moment in the text, for if God, the source of Eleanor's salvation, is present within her breast, then so is the source of her destruction, consumption. The presence of the former, it seems, has made possible the entrance of the latter.

This internalisation of faith – bringing of Christ inside the body and casting aside of the intervention of the Church – is very suggestive when taken alongside Eleanor's anorexic behaviour patterns and the extreme purity of her final persona. In creating her spiritual heroine it seems Ward is invoking a much older form of female religious mysticism, for Eleanor can be closely identified with historical saints. The definition of canonised holy women offered by Walter Vandereycken and Ron van Deth in *From Fasting Saints to Anorexic Girls* seems to fit the dying Eleanor exactly. Catherine of Siena and others 'were God's chosen ones, with whom He communicated, to whom He expressed His will by means of visions and to whom He entrusted supernatural powers and signs'.[43] And of course it is through fasting and denial that this communion with God is achieved, for 'holy fasts were signs of His attendance',[44] and allowed the sufferer to share Christ's suffering on the cross. Starvation traditionally empowered the individual, enabling the fasting one to obtain freedom from the patriarchy that attempts to impose itself between the holy anorexic and her god: 'To be the servant of God is to be the servant of no man. To obliterate every human feeling of pain, fatigue, sexual desire and hunger is to be the master of oneself.'[45] Through hunger and suffering, Eleanor too achieves personal autonomy and becomes worthy to be the 'servant of God' rather than of the priest or the patriarch.

This ability to bypass the authority of the Church and render the individual responsible for their own faith must have been an attractive prospect for Ward, whose religious life was marred by a lifelong struggle with strict orthodoxy. Her cynicism about certain symbolisms made her an outsider in a Church that demanded complete compliance in its believers, a demand she considered a tyranny, as she explained in a letter to her friend Bishop Creighton in 1898:

If only the orthodox churchmen would allow us on our side a little more free-dom . . . Every year I live I more and more resent the injustice which excludes those who hold certain historical and critical opinions from full membership in the National Church, above all from participation in the Lord's Supper . . . Nothing honestly remains to them but exclusion, and hunger . . . [46]

The 'exclusion and hunger' experienced by religious dissenters like Ward suggests how autobiographical *Eleanor* actually is. The possibility of a con-nection between Ward and the character of Father Benecke is touched upon by William S. Peterson in his book *Victorian Heretic*, but Peterson, who ignores the hunger motif which links them and does not acknowledge the importance of the novel's schismatic heroine, deeply underestimates the political implications of this text. In fact the novel uses the consumptive Eleanor as a means of working out an alternative form of religiosity, rep-resenting a faith which is within rather than without, private rather than public, individual rather than sacerdotal. This religion does not depend on the Church as a place of worship because it transforms the body into a temple, a receptacle for Christ, as Eleanor herself indicates: 'He is there! – *there!*' (p. 556). Yet Eleanor is a problematic messiah because it is consump-tion which has literally as well as spiritually carved out the room for faith in her breast. The religion she represents has pathological origins and carries a heavy price. Eleanor's physical existence, at least, is cut off in its prime, and unlike the vigorous Lucy who will transform Manisty's life, she will not fulfil a social purpose, will not have a useful productive future. The altru-istic potential of her newly found emotional superiority is, from a social point of view, wasted. This brings us back to the troubling paradox which is central to Eleanor's character as it is to the representation of all literary invalids: is her partly self-induced disease really an admirable embracement of a purifying ritual which cleanses the soul through Christlike bodily suf-fering, or is it a socially subversive rejection of the principles conducive to maintaining God's greatest gift, a healthy, useful body?

It appears that Ward herself may be undecided about this, for the novel represents a constant shifting between alternative means of viewing the invalid figure and the paradoxes which surround her. Ward's own feelings on the subject are illuminated by a letter she wrote to her father, shortly before *Eleanor* was written, about the Catholic literature she had been studying. As this letter discusses her feelings about the physically destructive asceticism of saints it makes an interesting companion piece to the novel in which her central character achieves saintly qualities through mortification of the flesh, and hence it seems worth quoting at some length:

> One of the main impressions of this Catholic literature . . . has been to fill me with a perfect horror of asceticism, or rather of the austerities – or most of them – which are indispensable to the Catholic ideal of a saint. We must talk this over, for of course I realise that there is much to be said on the other side. But the simple and rigid living which I have seen in friends of my own . . . seems to me both religious and reasonable, while I cannot for the life of me see anything in the austerities, say, of the Blessed Mary Alacoque, but hysteria and self-murder. The Divine Power occupies itself for age on age in the development of all the fine nerve-processes of the body, with their infinite potencies for good or evil. And instead of using them for good, the Catholic mystic destroys them, injures her digestion and her brain, and is then tortured by terrible diseases which she attributes to every cause but the true one – her own deliberate act – and for which her companions glorify her, instead of regarding them as what – surely – they truly are, God's punishment. No doubt directors are more careful nowadays than they were in the seventeenth century, but her life is still published by authority and the ideal it contains is still held up to young nuns.[47]

It is clearly fasting that Ward is here condemning as 'hysteria and self-murder', and it is a surprising judgement when one considers how Ward uses Eleanor's bodily wasting to facilitate her increased spirituality. It is significant that Eleanor's illness matches what Ward considers the causes of the saint's asceticism, for it is initially brought about by her mental and emotional distress, as we have seen, and in this respect her consumption is in the novel condemned, initially at least, as a form of self-induced, deadly 'hysteria'. Yet Ward's text does not rewrite the saint's narrative, and indeed she perpetuates it by allowing her heroine's behaviour to be read as self-sacrifice rather than self-destruction. Like her canonised sisters, Eleanor too is ultimately 'glorified' by her actions in the opinions of her 'companions'. She must suffer in atonement for her previous sins but once the penance has been paid she becomes undeniably holy, finally making a good death, and remaining 'through all the the years that followed, the more passionately, the more tragically beloved' (p. 572) by those she leaves behind.

Consumption, as an illness known to be a result of deprivation, must surely be included among the 'terrible diseases' which Ward mentions as afflicting the saints, and should indeed be thought of as 'God's punishment' for the arrogance and carelessness of asceticism. Yet in this heavily romanticised representation in her novel Ward constructs it much more like a gift, a means of dying which first actually enhances life. The gradual, gentle nature of the illness allows Eleanor time to prepare her soul and repair her past mistakes, so she may be ready for the end, and able to leave life in the best Victorian fashion. Ward here implies that dying of this disease has its own rewards, and this whole aspect of the plot must be intended as a comfort for real-life consumptive readers. Ward may condemn as irresponsible the Catholic 'ideal' epitomised by the lives of the Saints, but in fact in *Eleanor* she promoted and 'published' her own, very similar Protestant version. By using the powerful mythology that surrounds phthisis Ward is able to construct Eleanor as a contemporary saint. Consumption is her vehicle of penance, the modern alternative to the hair shirt, and yet the increased spirituality and good death it ushers in is the ascetic's ultimate reward. And of course in this final guise Eleanor satisfies the popular concept of the consumptive expected by the Victorian public, being flawed, even sinning, yet always finally redeemed to purity and imbued with the radiance of the chosen one who is set apart from others. Through its association with hyper-sexuality, consumption may undermine her angel status, but it can also restore it tenfold. Yet like the Catholic saint she resembles, Eleanor is no docile, passive pilgrim. Her spiritual journey is a constant struggle with patriarchal power, with socially unacceptable passions, with her conscience, and of course with her disease. The ambivalence with which her character is treated by Ward is symbolic of the ambiguity that surrounds the Victorian invalid in real life: it is impossible for the strong and well to decide whether she should be pitied for her suffering, admired for her forbearance, or feared for the potential subversiveness signalled by her existence as an *un*-healthy member of society, and hence as Other.

CHAPTER 4

'There is beauty in woman's decay': the rise of the tubercular aesthetic

One of the characteristic aspects of consumption, a feature which separates it from other serious illnesses of the modern era, is its association with fragile loveliness and sexual attractiveness. Other important diseases like syphilis or leprosy were associated with physical disfigurement; those less so, like cancer and gout, with age. Yet the stereotypical image of the consumptive from the Enlightenment onwards is, as Lawlor suggests, one of delicate yet desirable youth: 'By the end of the eighteenth century, consumption is not only the symbolic disease of the lover or a desired condition for the dying Christian, but also the glamorous sign of female beauty.' This picture is clearly a product of the belief in a tubercular diathesis, which, as I have previously discussed, held that consumption usually affected the most physically attractive members of the population; that the young and were in some inexplicable way more susceptible to it. This age-old consumptive myth survived despite changing medical opinions about the disease, and was accepted and reinforced by the Victorian medical profession, as well as the general public, as revealed by the comments of Dr Sealy in 1837:

Phthisis Pulmonalis is characterised in the earlier stages of life, by a peculiar diathesis or external manifestation of constitution. Those indications are a peculiar delicacy of texture and colour of skin, a precocity of intellect, a clear brilliancy of eye and a graceful tenuity of figure, forming in all the most attractive appearance of the human youth of both sexes.[1]

Such a belief in the 'external manifestation' of the disease remained an important feature of the approach to, and diagnosis of, consumption throughout the century. In 1884 a Dr Mahomed undertook a study, later published in Guy's Hospital Reports, which attempted 'to obtain a portrait of the phthisical contour, or rather of the facial expression in phthisis, through photography'.[2] This project involved the photographing of a number of randomly selected hospital patients in order to produce an image of the 'the typical phthisical face'. Though its results 'were not entirely satisfactory', they still suggested that specific consumptive types existed, namely 'the dark, forbidding and phlegmatic temperament', and, the one most commonly associated with consumption, the 'fair, delicate and often graceful sanguine temperament'.[3] More significantly, that such a study took place at all reveals the extent of the medical fascination with the external appearance of the consumptive and the strength of the belief that phthisis affected those with certain, usually aesthetically pleasing, facial characteristics. Consumption can never quite escape its reputation as a disease which afflicts the physically attractive. Its perceived aesthetic appeal did not only lie with the innate beauty of its pre-ordained victims, however, for, most interestingly, phthisis itself was in fact thought to enhance that beauty, in complex cultural ways, and it is this intriguing 'side effect' of the disease which I wish to explore in this chapter.

The whole phenomenon of admiration for the consumptive appearance cannot be isolated from the specific cultural milieu of the eighteenth and nineteenth century which embraced it. This provides an insight not only into the way the disease was perceived but also into the aesthetic and sexual preoccupations of an age. Consumption both created and facilitated an ideal of predominately, but not exclusively, female attractiveness which was in a sense the antithesis of traditional standards of beauty, which were associated with the appearance of good health. Lawlor has quoted Dr Edward Barry's description of the diathesis in 1726, which reveals the potential for glamour inherent in the disease: 'a long neck . . . a clear florid Complexion, the Cheeks and lips painted with the purest red, the Caruncle in the Corner of the Eye, from its intense Colour, appears like *Coral,* and all the vessels are so fine, as to appear almost *diaphanous* . . .'.[4] As Lawlor notes, here 'consumption seems to be a kind of natural cosmetic', painting the face with desirable colour. In the eighteenth century, the consumptive appearance – dramatically pale and ethereally thin with the red cheeks and bright eyes of fever – became the defining, fashionable look of the time. Of course this fashion was not simply a matter of appearance which could be lightly cast off, but became a whole way of life, a way of being rather than a way of looking, with damaging implications for women's physical and mental health and for their social roles.

Rather incongruously, the consumptive fashion was consolidated for the Victorian period by male sufferers, for it was probably Romanticism which brought tubercular glamour into the new century. An enduring bond was forged between this disease and the poets, artists and musicians of the late eighteenth and early nineteenth centuries. Phthisis not only killed John Keats, but functioned for his contemporaries and followers as the physical manifestation of his all-consuming intellect.[5] It was also believed to be stalking Shelley, except that his boating accident intervened; famous European consumptives included Friedrich Von Schiller and Adalbert von Chamisso. Through these gifted sufferers, the disease became identified with youth, genius and tragedy, and glamorised by these associations. The whole Romantic ethos was designed to change the dominant cultural view of disease, however, as Mario Praz has argued in *The Romantic Agony*:

> For the Romantics beauty was enhanced by exactly those qualities which seem to deny it, by those objects which produce horror . . . there is no end to the examples which might be quoted from the Romantic and Decadent writers on the subject of the indissoluble union of the beautiful and the sad, on the supreme beauty of that beauty which is accursed.
>
> In fact, to such an extent were Beauty and Death looked upon as sisters by the Romantics that they became fused into a sort of two-faced herm filled with corruption and melancholy and fatal in its beauty.[6]

Hence Romantic poetry sought to find beauty in the 'horror' and 'melancholy' of consumption: Shelley's 'Ode to the West Wind' and Keats's 'Ode to a Nightingale' are good examples of this process at work. Romanticism was also preoccupied by the liberation of the mind and spirit from the corporeal shackle that was the human body. Illness was hence viewed as the means by which flawed physicality could be left behind and the creative soul freed: the true artist was weak in body because he was strong in mind. Good health began to be considered earthly, prosaic, even vulgar. Byron was clearly aware that his rather corpulent figure as a young man was not only distasteful to him, but unsuitable for his career as a poet, and was so pleased with his newly fragile appearance following a dangerous illness that he declared to Lord Sligo: ' "How pale I look! – I should like, I think, to die of a consumption." "Why a consumption?" asked his friend. "Because then" (he answered) "the women would all say 'See that poor Byron – how interesting he looks in dying'."[7] Byron consequently spent most of his adult life on a stringent diet, exercise and bathing regime in order to emulate the consumptive appearance of his desirably delicate fellow poets Keats and Shelley. In doing so he foreshadowed a major trend among Victorian women, who later in the century would stoop to drastic measures, from tight lacing to vinegar drinking, in order to resemble the ethereal consumptive.

With the passing of Romanticism the pursuit of a tubercular aesthetic became a female concern and remained so. It was now more than a desire to appear 'interesting', spiritual and poetic, and became formative of female identity, as part of what Dijkstra calls the 'cult of invalidism', a phenomenon which transformed the lives of middle- and upper-class women in the second half of the nineteenth century. In *Idols of Perversity* Dijkstra identifies the ways in which Victorian literature and art 'exploit[ed] and romanticise[d] the notion of woman as a permanent, a necessary, even a "natural" invalid'.[8] He discusses the economic reasons which lay behind this enthusiasm for the sickly female, namely the need for the bourgeois capitalist to display his financial success by sustaining a wife who was able to lead a leisured, unproductive existence. Invalidism in women became fashionable partly because it represented the ultimate exhibition of unproductivity, for a sick wife was an incapacitated wife unable to play any part in the household finances, except as a drain upon them, and was hence a testament to the patriarch's monetary value and power.

As well as her function as the personification of idle wealth, the middle-class wife had another duty, as keeper and preserver of the masculine soul. As Dijkstra explains, capitalist society was thought to have a damaging effect on the morality of the men who struggled for money and power within it; a wife, however, 'could, by staying at home – a place unblemished by sin and unsullied by labour – protect her husband's soul from permanent damage; the very intensity of her purity and devotion would regenerate, as it were, its war-scarred tissue ... '.[9] Separation from worldly concerns or bodily desires was essential for the virtuous wife if she were to be an effective angel in the house and an efficient guardian of her husband's morality, and of course invalidism functioned as perfect expression of this, for no one was further from worldliness, sin or lustful corporeality than the incapacitated, resignedly suffering woman confined to her sickroom.

There was, therefore, a clear social investment in this advocacy of ill health, and one which can be held partially responsible for the prevalence of female illness in the nineteenth century. Invalidism became a way of life for women because it was a means of demonstrating the most desirable female characteristics, namely purity, passivity and a willingness to sacrifice oneself for others, especially men. The invalid woman's weakness of body meant that she was entirely and suitably dependent on others for physical, emotional and financial support, and yet her patient endurance of pain proved her strength of soul. Hence sickness came to signify virtue, and the sickly woman became the ideal woman. This cult of invalidism was developed and consolidated by Victorian art, which reveals the aesthetic potential of suffering, saintly femininity: many nineteenth-century painters were concerned with seeking out the physical as well as spiritual beauty of the invalid. Through this process, ill health itself begins to become glamorised, in that it is associated with the type of femininity which men wish to paint and women aspire to have. Here we can see the tubercular aesthetic beginning to emerge, for it is important to note that wasting disease, most likely in the form of phthisis, is the predominant cause of this aesthetic ill health. Many of the ill, dead or dying women in paintings like those by Alfred-Philippe Roll, Carl Larsson and Louis Ridel resemble the archetypal consumptive, with their emaciated bodies, pale, sharply defined faces and feverish eyes. When they are covered they are clad in what Dijkstra identifies as 'the loose-fitting clothing of the terminal consumptive',[10] but it is when phthisical women are drawn naked that the most sinister sexual implications of the disease are made apparent. Romaine Brook's 'Dead Woman' and Albert von Keller's 'Study of a Dead Woman' reflect a preoccupation with woman's internal body, by which I mean not the internal organs but the skeleton. The consumed flesh of the consumptive allows the bones to be clearly outlined, and they are portrayed in great detail with almost fetishised attention by the artists. Significantly, this sexualised interest in the phthisical female skeleton is used as a symbol of predatory masculinity in *Trilby*, as I will discuss later. Certainly its representation in art was a contributing factor in consumption's erotic appeal.

The artist perhaps most associated with the aestheticisation of phthisis was the Pre-Raphaelite star Dante Gabriel Rossetti, who is famous for his portraits of beautiful women, a number of which were of his 'consumptive' lover and later wife Elizabeth Siddal. Siddal's history has passed into glamorous legend and is a fascinating real-life testament to the transforming power of the consumptive aesthetic. As a case study her life forms a suggestive dialogue with the consumptive heroine of fiction, and so bears exploring in some detail here. The daughter of a shopkeeper, Siddal was working as a dressmaker before she was discovered by the Pre-Raphaelites in 1849, recruited as a model for, initially, Walter Deverell, and then Holman Hunt and John Millais, and gradually drawn into their middle-class, artistic circle, later becoming an artist and poet herself. Siddal's foremost biographer, Jan Marsh, has suggested that in her early days of work with the Brotherhood Siddal 'was not then renowned for her beauty', indeed 'rather the reverse, because it was for her plainness that she was originally picked as a model'.[11] Early paintings of her by Deverell and Hunt certainly reinforce this view. Her colouring was unfashionable, for she had bright red hair and freckles, both of which were considered ugly at this time. Her appearance was at the most striking and unusual rather than pleasing to the eye; as poet William Allingham, who had known her in the early

1850s, recalled, 'Her pale face, abundant red hair and long thin limbs were strange and affecting – never beautiful in my eyes.'[12] Yet over the years that followed she came to be considered one of the most famous beauties of the Pre-Raphaelite movement, as well as becoming the wife of Rossetti, arguably its most important member. This social and physical transformation is important in the context of this study, for I suggest it was facilitated to a large degree by Siddal's consumption-like illness, which manifested itself in 1854 and remained with her for the rest of her life.

I am wary of identifying this disease as definitely phthisis, as there seems to have been some medical ambivalence about its diagnosis,[13] probably because some of her symptoms – her extreme lack of appetite for instance, which might today be classified as anorexia nervosa – may have been at least partly psychological. Georgie Burne-Jones, a close friend of Siddal's, recorded in her memoirs that 'her long years of ill-health have often puzzled me, as to how it was possible for her to suffer so much without ever developing a specific disease'.[14] Implicit here is the question of whether Siddal's vague illness may in fact have been mental in origin. Jan Marsh notes that her sickness did not prevent her participation in things she wanted to do, like travelling, painting or socialising, though 'she was frequently unwell when it came to irksome duties such as writing a thank-you note to her mother-in-law for a dinner invitation she was sufficiently fit to accept'.[15] Of course, even if Siddal did suffer from a form of hysteria, it does not rule out the presence of organic phthisical disease as well, but it makes it difficult to separate the fact from the fiction. A study of Gabriel Rossetti's personal letters reveals that Siddal's main symptoms were bodily wasting, weakness and unspecified pain, and occasionally vomiting (the latter possibly from laudanum abuse) but there was no mention of a cough or pulmonary haemorrhage, the most defining symptoms of consumption.[16] Yet she was confidently identified as a consumptive, rather than a hysteric, by many of her friends and contemporaries, as well as by biographers past and present. Most notable of these is the most important biographer of the Pre-Raphaelite movement, Gabriel Rossetti's brother William, who in his memoirs identified Siddal's illness as a 'phthisis, with the accompaniment of . . . wearing neuralgia'.[17] Other biographers such as Violet Hunt have followed this early example and reinforced the view of Siddal as consumptive: Hunt described her as 'long legs, long fingers, long throat, dullish prominent eyes, luxuriant hair – all characteristic of one type of what we now colloquially call TB'.[18]

In the private sphere, Ruskin (at one time a patron of Siddal's) was convinced that she suffered from phthisis, encouraging her to winter in the

South of France, and to stay near a 'cattleshed' – the breath of oxen being a traditional cure for consumption.[19] As regards Gabriel Rossetti, those personal letters which discuss Siddal's illness – and it is worth noting that almost every mention of her in his correspondence is accompanied by some sort of report on her health, as though she were only defined by her illness – describe her as being in a 'decline', an accepted term for wasting specifically due to consumption. Indeed so enduring has been this view of Siddal that she has become a sort of mascot for the disease, and is mentioned as an example of a famous real-life consumptive even in modern books about its history. Hence it is important to consider not whether Siddal's illness really was consumption, but why it was represented, in both public and private spheres, as though it were. Was there a deliberate attempt to construct her as a consumptive rather than as a hysteric, even though the latter condition matched her symptoms more closely? Could it be that she herself, her friends, and later her biographers, had some sort of political investment in constructing her illness as phthisis? And, if so, what was the nature of this investment?

The answers are revealing not only about Siddal's life but also about the disease itself. The process by which she became identified as consumptive was primarily an acceptance and reinforcement of the tubercular diathesis, for she came to personify this myth both physically and emotionally, as I will discuss. In turn, however, this process had the effect of investing Siddal with the specific attributes of this disease. She came to be considered beautiful, fragile, romantic and even artistically gifted, because of consumption's traditional association with these admirable qualities, as summed up by Dr East:

It is true that there are minds so sensitive and powerful that perfect health . . . may be rare.

A person, once seeing a consumptive face, can never forget it . . . There is frequently a peculiar mental activity; the mind seems developed very early, especially the imaginative facilities. Some of the most interesting specimens of female beauty may be seen in the early stage . . .[20]

Given the desirability of these attributes to an impoverished young woman and aspiring artist, it is possible that Siddal herself encouraged this view of her symptoms, knowing that consumptive illness could function as a means of achieving her aims. For example, it is significant that she first became ill at exactly the time when Rossetti began to introduce her to his family and friends, an event fraught with anxiety because of her humble background and her somewhat dubious prior profession as artist's model. Hence her poor health became a useful tool to assert her gentility and to rectify her inferior social status, for as a physically delicate woman she could embrace the invalid-centric values of the middle class and reject any suggestion of working-class robustness and vigour, as well as remove herself from the taint of sexual immorality associated with models (this was a disreputable profession because it was associated with posing naked and with the clandestine relationships which frequently took place between subject and artist). Consumption, a disease associated with refinement and 'great purity' of mind and body, was the perfect vehicle for her social advancement. Furthermore, the dramatic worsening of her condition in 1860 led to a reunion with Rossetti, who had abandoned her two years earlier, and the guilt he felt at witnessing her physical state became the prime motivation for their sudden marriage a few weeks later.[21]

Illness facilitated Siddal's class mobility even to the extent of its culmination in a socially successful marriage. Correspondingly, it gave her a glamour and desirability which she had lacked as a healthy but humble young model. Her reputation as a fragile and suffering near-invalid romanticised her public image as much as Rossetti's haunting and flattering portraits of her. These paintings suggest that Rossetti too benefited from his wife's consumptive associations and the glamour they lent her, for his work emphasised her delicacy and sickliness as if to exploit the popular appeal of illness. He represents Siddal as possessing the sort of unusual, unearthly beauty which personified the tubercular aesthetic. Her extreme pallor, made more dramatic by her vivid red hair, her delicate, emaciated features, her heavy-lidded eyes, indicative of the drug addict – she was addicted to laudanum, a drug commonly used to control the symptoms of phthisis – and most of all her expression of melancholy and resigned suffering, were all characteristic of the consumptive.

Certainly her poses in the many drawings and watercolours Rossetti has done of her reinforce this sense of invalidism: she is almost always portrayed sitting or reclining as though too exhausted to stand, frequently resting her head on her hand in a gesture of weariness, sometimes asleep. Her hair is almost always worn down, a common feature of Rossetti's paintings which has often been read as as an expression of sexuality in women, but which is equally valid as a symbol of illness, as tightly pinned up hair was unsuitable for invalids, being uncomfortable on a pillow. Siddal in fact started something of a fashion by her loosely pinned, almost unrestrained hair.[22] Within a society which prizes ill health as a signifier of ideal femininity, the physical manifestation of sickness becomes associated with the ideal of feminine beauty, a trend clearly displayed by Siddal, whose attractiveness was inseparable from her perceived consumptive state. Ford Madox Brown noted a meeting with her in 1854, in terms which paid homage to the captivating appeal of her tubercular appearance: 'Called on Dante Rossetti, saw Miss Siddal looking thinner and more deathlike and more beautiful and more ragged than ever, a real artist, a woman without parallel for many a long year'.[23]

Siddal's personality seemed to resemble the tubercular diathesis as much as her physical appearance did. She possessed the heightened sensibility and emotional instability that was associated with phthisis, as well as with artistic genius, and was prone to nervousness and depression which became especially severe after a sad late-term miscarriage which had severe consequences for her mental health.[24] Rossetti's alleged infidelities were thought to have added to her suffering, and shortly after her death she gained a public reputation as wronged lover and wife who had been tortured by the behaviour of her husband as well as by her consumption. This all combined to make her the subject of a romantic legend of tragedy and pain which endured well into the the twentieth century, even though she died in 1862.[25] A good example of the way Siddal's private life became appropriated into popular myth is the story of how she modelled for Millais's drowned *Ophelia* while submerged in a bath. This is one of the most famous anecdotes associated with the whole Pre-Raphaelite movement, and one which came to epitomise the sacrifice of health and comfort for the sake of Art and beauty:

She had to lie in a large bath filled with water, which was kept at an even temperature by lamps placed beneath. One day, just as the picture was nearly finished, the lamps went out unnoticed by the artist, who was so intently absorbed in his work that he thought of nothing else, and the poor lady kept floating in the cold water till she was quite benumbed. She herself never complained of this, but the result was that she contracted a severe cold ...[26]

Jan Marsh has observed that this incident 'came to stand as an emblem or foreshadowing of her fate', and certainly Siddal's public persona was defined by her ability to suffer and endure without complaint: this signified her 'proper' femininity and constituted the source of her enduring appeal. It is important to note that there is always a pathological element to her self-sacrifice, for, as Marsh points out, 'in later accounts, the "severe cold" was sometimes transmuted into pneumonia and other life threatening ailments'. Siddal's romantic aura was created not only by the physical and emotional pain she suffered, but, in an extension of this, by the threat of death which always surrounded her. It seems that her desirability lay in her fragility and that she was special because she always seemed hovering on the verge of death, and looked as though she was not quite of this world.

This is captured by one of Rossetti's most famous paintings, *Beata Beatrix*, which is thought to be the most faithful likeness of her, a belief which further associates Siddal with death because the painting was a posthumous tribute to her begun shortly after she passed away. *Beata Beatrix* is an interesting inclusion into this study, for it is a visual representation of the epitome of the consumptive sublime. In it the moment of death is romanticised and aestheticised, and, as it is the death of a young and beautiful woman, eroticised: Siddal's facial expression is one of almost sexual enthralment and the picture has a sense of 'necrophiliac longing [which] is hard to evade'.[27] She is portrayed in a rapt, trance-like state, welcoming death as though it is a benediction, with her face uplifted, bathed in a radiant aura of light. Its sexual overtones aside, this is the Victorian 'good death' personified,[28] the end of life conceived of as a moment of beauty and tranquillity, but it is a complete rewriting of Siddal's actual end, which was the antithesis of this kind of cultural ideal. The painting transforms the reality of her sudden and undignified death from a laudanum overdose – which, even more subversively, may have been deliberate – to resemble a peaceful passing to a better world. The sundial in the background is important in this context, for it serves as a reminder of the inexorable passage of time which brings death to all. Its presence assists in the painting's construction of Siddal's end as intrinsically natural and inevitable, as well as gradual, the consequence of organic and probably consumptive disease rather than, as it in fact was, an accident, or worse, suicide. An interesting touch is the poppy in the foreground of the picture, which is dropped into her lap by a bird, 'the messenger of death' as Gabriel Rossetti described it. Jan Marsh has suggested that the inclusion of a white poppy, the flower 'from which opium derives', may be symbolic of Siddal's laudanum habit.[29] This is an important observation, but as the poppy is presented to Siddal by an angelic dove, the image appears more like a gift or benediction than a symbol of drug addiction. In this sense it can be read as a blessing which eases her suffering, rather than the cause of it: a means of facilitating the rapt and peaceful end which is pictured here. Of course, when regarded in this light, this detail assists in the construction of her death as phthisis, for opium was indeed a blessing for consumptives as the only way to relieve their symptoms and the means by which consumption became associated with a good death.[30]

Beata Beatrix (oil on canvas) by Dante Charles Gabriel Rossetti (1828–82)
© Birmingham Museums and Art Gallery / The Bridgeman Art Library Nationality /
copyright Status: English / out of copyright

Beata Beatrix can thus be regarded as Gabriel Rossetti's attempt to transform the circumstances of his wife's death. By manipulating her death scene
through art he casts aside the scandalous reality of her laudanum overdose
and suggests a more conventional and natural, as well as more aesthetically

pleasing, end. This famous picture is the definitive symbol by which posterity has come to identify Lizzy Siddal, and hence it has an important part
to play in her representation as a consumptive. By implying her death was
a consequence of disease, it goes some way towards reinforcing the written
accounts of her life which constructed her as a consumptive invalid, and it
silences the parallel narrative which suggests that she was in fact a hysteric
and that in suicide she met a hysteric's end. This is an interpretation which
was damaging to Rossetti's artistic reputation – his work had constructed a
romantic, idealised public image of her throughout their relationship – and
also to Siddal's own. Her phthisis had after all been considered both a sign
of her genius and the reason why this genius never came to fruition, her
art limited and hampered as it was by ill health. Mental illness was a much
less glamorous interpretation of the cause of her decline and death. It also,
of course, carried a social and moral stigma from which Rossetti must have
wished to disassociate his wife's memory, for the sake of his own reputation
as well as hers: 'Suicide was the negation of the good death ... [it] was
traditionally regarded as a form of murder, seen as a felony in criminal law,
and an offence against God.'[31] This alone is motivation enough for the
desire of the Rossetti family and their friends to have Siddal represented as
a consumptive.

Beata Beatrix cements the traditional link between phthisis and beauty,
by pictorially representing the loveliness of the consumptive woman. Along
with Rossetti's many other drawings and paintings of Siddal, it forms the
public face of the consumptive persona, revealing her as fragile and ethereal
but hauntingly unforgettable, strikingly unusual in appearance, spiritual,
and above all, tragic. Siddal's illness utilised already existing stereotypes
about phthisis to produce an image of her as a desirable, refined, artistically
gifted yet passive and feminine woman, a glamorous but socially unthreatening image which was useful not only to her, but to those associated
with her, namely the Rossetti family and the Pre-Raphaelite circle, who
benefited from the presence of a popular romantic legend as their muse.
Yet in turn Siddal's identification as a consumptive shaped and influenced
cultural perceptions about the disease, particularly its aesthetic connotations, as her cultural role was after all primarily to function as a symbol
of female attractiveness. Phthisis was thought to be the reason for her
'unearthly',[32] unusual and newly fashionable beauty, which Rossetti's many
paintings of her made so familiar to Victorian England. Hence her face and
body, as well as her romantic and tragic life, helped to shape phthisis as
a stylish, even desirable illness. Her classically consumptive silhouette –
tall, long limbed and extremely thin – was considered unattractive in the

early 1850s, as Allingham indicated, but would become sought-after later in the century, as we shall see, and continues as an ideal female body type even today. Rossetti himself experimented with the representation of other types of female physicality throughout his career, but it is significant that his 'fleshy' paintings of voluptuous women, mostly inspired by Fanny Cornforth – who became his principal model and sometime mistress in the late 1850s – provoked moral censure by a Victorian public who considered them shockingly and provocatively sexual. David G. Riede indicates how even Rossetti's friends and fellow Pre-Raphaelites were ambivalent about his fleshy portraits: 'Ruskin, like Hunt, responded to this new development in Rossetti's art with a mixture of admiration for the technique and horror at the new "coarseness" that was marking his work "compared to what it used to be – what Fannie's face is to Lizzie's".'[33] Whereas the portrayals of the slender, sickly Lizzie were praised for their ethereal beauty, later paintings such as *Bocca Baciata* and *The Blue Bower*, which represent the healthy, buxom Fanny in vibrant color, were considered titillating but crude. Frail, consumptive beauty was an appropriate, respectable subject for art, but the portrayal of robust, corpulent female sexuality was considered to be dangerously close to pornography.

The consumptive aesthetic Siddal's history epitomised was at the height of its popularity in the 1890s when she became, through her association with beauty and death, a kind of mascot for the Decadent movement, Oscar Wilde being one of her most famous admirers. It seems no coincidence, then, that several important fictional heroines of the *fin de siècle* appear to invoke her image. For example, Milly Theale in Henry James's *The Wings of the Dove*, who is dying of a mysterious, unnamed disease, resembles Siddal physically, being willowy and pale with vivid red hair. It is also significant that this novel and its characters represents Milly as a dove, a symbol which associates her with Lizzy Siddal, for 'dove' was well known to be one of Rossetti's nicknames for his lover, and his letters frequently drew the the symbol of a dove to stand in for Siddal's name. James did not know Siddal, as he only arrived in England several years after her death, but he knew several of her surviving Pre-Raphaelites and was friendly with Sir Edward Burne-Jones, the husband of her close friend, Georgie. Hence it is unlikely that he was unaware of her legend.[34] Another friend and colleague of the Pre-Raphaelites – he had known Rossetti, Millais and Burne-Jones since the 1860s, and remained close friends with Millais until his death[35] – was the artist George Du Maurier, who wrote the best-selling 1895 novel *Trilby*, named for its Siddal-like heroine, who is another tall and slender artist's model afflicted by a wasting disease that transforms her whole life, from her physical appearance to her social status and her marital prospects.

I have suggested that both Siddal and Rossetti manipulated and exploited the transforming power of the consumptive aesthetic for social and even economic ends: Elisabeth Bronfen has, however, a different interpretation of the significance of their artistic relationship. Bronfen suggests that Rossetti's portraits of consumptive beauty were symbolic because they 'signify the virility and immortality of his art and by implication of himself as artist'.[36] In other words, the dying muse serves to indicate the strength of the artist who paints her: in capturing Siddal's wasting physicality Rossetti reminds the viewer of its opposite – his 'masculinity . . . productivity, creativity, health' – which is vital enough to create a work of art which will survive long after its subject is dead.[37] Bronfen's book argues that the dead or dying woman is fetishised in art for psychoanalytic reasons, that witnessing female mortality allows the spectator to defy or triumph over death. Hence Bronfen interprets 'the theme of [Siddal and Rossetti's] artistic relationship as his survival and surveyal of her fading' – an especially helpful reading because it is reminiscent of gender relations in *Trilby* as well.[38] The notion of the male artist as a vampiric figure who 'feeds upon [the] face by day and night' of his wasting lover, as Christina Rossetti's 'In An Artist's Studio' describes it, is central to Du Maurier's representation of art, gender and death, as we shall see.[39]

Trilby is particularly useful as an exploration of the aesthetic associations of consumption because it is a novel preoccupied with the construction and representation of beauty. The Bohemian world described in Du Maurier's novel is primarily concerned with the aesthetic appeal of music and art, but as the novel progresses these pursuits become fused together in, and superseded by, Woman, in the form of Trilby, the muse who inspires and creates both. Trilby begins the story as an artist's model whose body motivates male painters into the production of beauty, then becomes a beautiful and famous opera singer who produces exquisite music, and finally develops, through invalidism, into the personification of the feminine ideal. The three male protagonists begin the novel worshipping Art, but by its end worship only Trilby. Like Elizabeth Siddal, however, she is not fundamentally and naturally desirable: Du Maurier makes it clear that wasting illness is the source of her aesthetic appeal. As I will show, Trilby only becomes truly beautiful and feminine after she enters a 'decline' that culminates in her death. Hence critics have read the novel as a reaffirmation of the cult of invalidism and a somewhat anti-feminist advocation of the aesthetic appeal of the wasting woman.[40] It is certainly true that Du Maurier does not challenge the dominant cultural opinion which holds that only a sickly woman may be truly pure or truly beautiful in body as well as spirit, but the novel has an interesting subtext which is preoccupied with exploring notions of what is considered beautiful and the influence of society in constructing these concepts. The text reveals that beauty is not an innate, stable entity which can transcend time or personal opinion, but rather is a changeable, shifting concept swayed by social and cultural considerations and objectives. In other words, Du Maurier makes the reader aware that feminine ideals are created by fashion and society rather than by nature, and in exploring the current fashion for the tubercular aesthetic he reveals the damaging consequences of these ideals, even while he himself seems to be seduced by them and their representation in his lovely heroine.

Questions about the perception of feminine beauty are introduced on the very first page of the novel by the mention of the Venus de Milo, a small bust of whom is among the clutter in the apartment of the three English friends.[41] The Venus is referred to again at the end of the novel when Du Maurier suggests a comparison between her and Trilby (p. 355). This is a small but important detail, for in the second half of the nineteenth century this work of art became synonymous with debate over what constituted the ideal female figure. This discourse posited the naturally curvaceous body against the very slender, wasp-waisted silhouette so fashionable in the Victorian era, a shape which for most women could only be achieved by the assistance of corsetry. The corset was, however, a highly controversial garment, which many physicians believed was damaging to female health and was responsible for a number of female ailments, including consumption, a very significant point which I shall return to later. Hence as part of the backlash against corsetry the Venus de Milo's voluptuous and unrestrained figure was frequently advocated by physicians, concerned husbands and feminists alike as the healthy ideal which all women should emulate. The Venus represented a natural, classical, artistic aesthetic, an alternative feminine ideal, and the antithesis of the currently fashionable shape. It was also the antithesis of the consumptive aesthetic, as Alfred Hillier pointed out in his book *The Prevention of Consumption*, in which he compares the phthisical appearance of Botticelli's Venus to the 'magnificent proportions of the Venus de Milo, a still more beautiful figure and the embodiment of physical health'.[42] The Venus de Milo thus became an integral part of the discussions about beauty for both tight-lacers and those who advocated dress reform.[43] Thus its inclusion in *Trilby* introduces questions about the changing fashion of body shape, and the social expectation which shaped and influenced such changes, and their potentially pathological consequences. Du Maurier also makes clear that he considers beauty a transient social and cultural construct, in a discussion early in the novel about Trilby's own appearance:

Favourite types of beauty change with each succeeding generation. These were the days of Buckner's aristocratic Album beauties, with lofty foreheads, oval faces, little aquiline noses, heart-shaped little mouths . . . A type that will perhaps come back to us some day. May the present scribe be dead! Trilby's type would be infinitely more admired now than in the fifties. Her photograph would be in the show windows. Sir Edward Burne Jones – if I may make so bold to say so – would perhaps have marked her for his own, in spite of her almost too exuberant joyousness and irrepressible vitality. Rossetti might have evolved another new formula from her; Sir John Millais another old one . . .

Trilby's type was in singular contrast to the type Gavarni had made so popular in the Latin Quarter at the period we are writing of, so that those who fell so readily under her charm were rather apt to wonder why. Moreover, she was thought much too tall for her sex and her day, and her station in life, and especially for the country she lived in . . . (pp. 128–9)

In a way reminiscent of Elizabeth Siddal, Trilby is not initially considered beautiful because her 'type' does not fit the current model of feminine attractiveness, but this is not regarded by Du Maurier as a real comment on her actual appearance. This paragraph reveals, in somewhat ironical terms given its date of publication and its historical perspective, that fashion is fickle and inconstant: if she had lived in the 1890s (when the book was written) instead of the 1850s (when it was set), Trilby's looks would have been in keeping with the ideal of the day and hence widely admired. Yet Du Maurier acknowledges the power of this force which dictated the terms of beauty and controlled the way in which women were perceived by others. His mention of Rossetti and the other Pre-Raphaelites is an important one, for it invokes the part they played in seeking out, representing on canvas and then making fashionable 'new formulas' of female beauty, including of course the tubercular aesthetic. Rossetti's ability to influence public perceptions about ideal femininity through his art made popular the phthisical appearance of Elizabeth Siddal and heralded the rise of the cult of consumptive beauty in whose footsteps Trilby eventually follows. It is significant, however, that Trilby's failings as a mid-century beauty are her 'joyousness and irrepressible vitality' which, along with her 'much too tall' body, are indications of good health and vibrant sexuality (we might here recall Fanny Cornforth, another curvaceous and loose-living 'stunner' whose fleshy beauty was criticised in the 1850s for its coarseness, here). It is this which really renders Trilby's appearance unfashionable, and hence by the end of the novel, when, reincarnated as the passive near-invalid la Svengali, she has neither vitality nor joyousness, she has become a sought-after beauty whose photograph is indeed 'in the shop windows' (p. 354).

The construction and representation of female beauty was of particular interest to Du Maurier, who worked as the principal society illustrator at *Punch* magazine from 1864 until his death in 1896. *Punch* was an 'accurate barometer of the conservative male upper-middle-class view of women's role in society, one of its favourite themes',[44] and hence Du Maurier's popular cartoons frequently featured fashionable women, whose faces, bodies and clothes are captured by him in great detail, and often formed the object of his satire. The latest styles of female clothing which changed, altered or disguised the body were especially sought out for criticism by *Punch*, which campaigned against the use of the corset, in particular, for many years. In this context *Trilby* can be regarded as a literary representation of the concerns about contemporary female beauty expressed by Du Maurier throughout his artistic career. Indeed, when we consider the many illustrations in the novel, all of which were drawn by Du Maurier himself, we get a sense of its preoccupation with the visual expression of life and especially of femininity, and his awareness of the social implications of external appearance.

Trilby at first seems to be a heroine cast in Venus de Milo mould, for her entrance into the novel is accompanied by a both a drawing and a description of her strong, tall body, which clearly rejects the confines of fashion in favour of health and comfort: 'it was the figure of a very tall and fully developed young female. She bore herself with easy, unembarrassed grace like a person whose nerves and muscles are well in tune' (p. 14). Such physical health and ease in a female was the antithesis of the fashionable, bourgeois woman of the day. It is significant too that in her first appearance in the novel she is in a state of undress, fresh from modelling for 'the altogether', so that attention may be drawn to her underclothes, making clear that there is no possibility of a corset among them: she wears a 'military overcoat, and female petticoat, and nothing else!' (p. 17). The health and vigour and 'grace' obtained by wearing unrestrictive clothing mean a sacrifice of respectability, however, for Trilby's scanty and unconventional clothes are representative of her lack of virtue and the resulting ambiguity of her social position. In the Victorian era, to be uncorseted was to be 'loose' in morals as well as clothes. Leigh Summers has discussed how the corset is simultaneously provocative – enhancing woman's curves, drawing attention to her sexuality – and morally restrictive and protective, forming a rigid barrier between flesh and the outside world:

Clothing was, in the mid-to-late nineteenth century, considered to have protective properties. According to the *fin de siècle* psychologist Carl Flugel, these protective properties were commonly extended to apply to the moral as well as the physical sphere. Flugel noted that the symbolic equation of physical stiffness and uprightness was considered integral to moral probity and firmness.

Tightly laced corsetry ... disciplined and contained the 'Western' body and acted as a symbol of civilisation and order ...[45]

Trilby's attire does away with such barriers, implying that she does not need or want moral protection, and yet as she is, despite her disreputable profession, essentially a bourgeois woman – her father was a clergyman and a gentleman – this creates a social problem and patriarchal threat which the male protagonists in the novel set out to resolve.

Du Maurier does not talk specifically about the corset in this novel, for as a woman's undergarment it was unmentionable even in the ostensibly Bohemian world represented there. However, he invokes it through a tirade against the corset's companion in restrictive female fashion, the high heel. As David Kunzle has pointed out, the two have long been associated with one another: 'tight lacing and high heels appear, for a good two centuries, as a kind of inseparable Siamese twins, sustained by the same historical, psychological and perhaps complementary physiological circumstances'.[46] They are certainly linked in both medical and cultural discourse in the nineteenth century. Both were tools of fashion which unnaturally shaped and formed – or deformed – the body to resemble a socially desirable template. Both corset and high heels were invested with similar erotic power yet were the subject of heated debate about their potentially damaging effects on the human body.[47] Du Maurier seems to be rejecting the appeal of fashion in favour of natural beauty, for although he and the male characters fetishise Trilby's 'astonishingly beautiful' (p. 17) feet early in the novel, it is made apparent that their rare perfection is achieved by her refusal to emulate 'civilised adults, who go about in leather boots or shoes'. It is significant here that leather shoes, like certain types of clothing, are associated with 'civilised' or respectable people who contrast with the barefooted and sexually loose Trilby. Clothes and shoes are crucial bourgeois symbols, for they cover and conceal the body, as well as signalling wealth and social status, or its absence. Du Maurier makes explicit the potentially damaging consequences of such signification, however, by indicating that highly desirable and sought-after garments, like fashionable shoes, can corrupt and deform natural beauty: '[the foot] can sometimes be very ugly indeed – the ugliest thing there is, even in the highest and fairest and most gifted of her sex ... And all for the sake of a high heel and a ridiculously pointed toe – mean things, at the best!' (p. 18). There is an interesting question here as to whether *Trilby* is intended as a criticism of fashionable dress, a far from frivolous concern when one considers the extent to which clothing functions as a symbol of society's expectations and conventions, as Sarah Hale, the author of a number of women's conduct books, observed in 1868:

How came the art of dress to be considered a silly, trifling matter, when God's word so clearly reveals its high import?

Dress, then, is something more than the necessity of climate, something better than condition of comfort, something higher than elegance of civilisation. Dress is the index of conscience, the evidence of our emotional nature. It reveals, more clearly than speech exposes, the inner life of heart and soul in a people ... [48]

Through his discussion of fashions of both body and clothing, Du Maurier can be seen to examine the world which dictated these fashions. The unapologetically free-living Trilby initially resists the social restraints symbolised by the corset, high-heeled shoes or stylish dresses. Unlike the ideal of bourgeois femininity, she is not virginal, in fact has had several lovers, and is widely believed to be the mother of the small half-brother she cares for. She is not passive or dependent, for she works to support herself and her brother, and freely walks the streets of Paris unchaperoned. Most importantly, she is not fragile or delicate, but is health and strength personified because she is unrestrained by the shackles of conventional female clothing, as indicated by her unfashionable, slightly masculine clothes and slippers. Early in the novel Svengali mentions her 'beautiful big chest' and 'lungs made of leather' (p. 71), both of which signify that she is the antithesis of the corseted female form, which would be characterised by a reduced chest and restricted lungs which only allowed the shallowest of breaths. As a result of all this her liberated body, instead of being praised as strong and active, is considered to be unfeminine and unladylike, even 'rather grotesque in its mixed attire of military overcoat and female petticoat' (p. 17). The text even stresses her inherent androgyny by commenting that she 'would have made a singularly handsome boy' (p. 16) and that 'it was a real pity she wasn't a boy, she'd have made such a jolly one' (p. 16). Once under the influence of her new middle-class English friends, however, the morality of the world beyond the Bohemian Latin Quarter soon begins to impact upon Trilby, acting like a symbolic corset by shaping her into a more feminine body and confining her within a more respectable soul. This 'strange metamorphosis' into the bourgeois angel (p. 129) is symbolised by her acquisition of the respectable lady's most defining feature – a fashionably slender body and small waist – but is also inevitably accompanied by a fashionable disease, consumption.

Anna Krugovoy Silver has discussed Trilby's transformation from healthy grisette to fragile invalid in *Victorian Literature and the Anorexic Body*, which explores the clear connection the novel establishes between body weight and morality. As I have indicated above, in the early section of the novel the voluptuous Trilby is the picture of physical health: 'a tall, straight, flat-backed, deep-chested, full-bosomed young grisette' (p. 40). However, this vital corporeality accompanies and symbolises social and moral failings, for Trilby is at this point in the novel working class, and, even worse, 'has all the virtues but one . . . the very one of all that plays the title role' (p. 48). She has been sexually promiscuous – 'she followed love for love's sake only, now and then' (p. 50) and what is perhaps worse, at this stage she is 'absolutely without any kind of shame' (p. 95), as her relaxed willingness to pose naked reveals. The novel implies that her sexual desires are equivalent to her enthusiastic appetite for food, an appetite unusual in a female character in a Victorian novel. On several occasions in the early chapters she is described eating her lunch, and especially significant is that she does so sitting cross legged on the floor, and 'quite unconcerned' about the effect she is having on the men who watch her eating as though it were a sexual act: 'Gecko . . . stared at her in open-mouthed admiration and delight, as she ate her sandwich.' Du Maurier seems to deliberately play with the erotic overtones of this scene: 'When she had finished she licked the tips of her fingers clean of cheese, and . . . made herself a cigarette . . . inhaling the smoke in large whiffs, filling her lungs with it, and sending it back through her nostrils, with a look of great beatitude' (p. 19). In this passage, Trilby is not simply eating: rather she is consuming and internalising both food and smoke in a way which suggests a powerful, all-engulfing appetite that is a source of both fascination and fear for her male admirers.

Of course these attitudes towards food and sex are inappropriate for a Victorian heroine, and the society of the novel cannot tolerate them for long. Trilby is forced out of innocence and into shame about her behaviour by her three English friends, particularly by the hypocritical Little Billee, who 'adored piety in woman, although he was not pious by any means' (p. 46), and so reacts with horror when he comes upon Trilby posing naked in front of a class he is about to attend. After this incident, Trilby begins to see herself as others see her, and to realise that she is a fallen woman in their eyes. Hence she has a moral awakening and gives up her disreputable profession to become a *blanchisseuse de fin* – as Showalter says, 'as if to signify her own purification and revirginization'.[49] She now embraces respectability, 'so that the dreadful past – never to be forgotten by her – should be so lived down in time, perhaps, to be forgotten by others' (p. 124). And of course this moral change must be accompanied by a physical one:

And week by week the friends noticed a gradual and subtle change in Trilby . . . she grew thinner, especially in the face, where the bones of her cheeks and jaws began to show themselves and these bones were constructed on such right principles . . . that the improvement was astonishing, almost inexplicable. Also, she lost her freckles as the summer waned and she herself went less into the open air . . . And a new soft brightness came into her eyes that no-one had ever seen there before. They were stars, just twin grey stars – or rather planets just thrown off by some new sun, for the steady mellow light they gave out was not entirely their own. (pp. 126–7)

As Silver has pointed out, Trilby's 'fat, symbolising her sensuality, melts away, her thinness indicating that she is now eating less and, metaphorically, denying her body's appetites as she did not do before'.[50] As a further symbol of her self-sacrifice, Trilby from this point on now only prepares food for her friends, is no longer seen eating with them as she had been previously. There are sinister overtones to this transformation, however, when one considers that it marks the beginning of a gradual 'decline' which culminates in Trilby's death. It is not only an 'astonishing improvement' in beauty, purity and femininity which her awakening conscience brings her, but frailty, disease and suffering. Near the end of the novel, Trilby looks back on the invalid existence she has led in recent years: 'I've always been weak and ill, and often so languid that I could hardly walk across the room' (p. 378). So what is this mysterious ailment which slowly saps away her life? Silver has suggested that although Trilby cannot be classed as an anorexic because she does not appear to consciously refuse food or to be 'actively pursuing the goal of thinness' her wasting is nonetheless 'figurative of the logic of anorexia', in that 'Not eating, in *Trilby*, equals virtue, sexual self-control, purity and femininity.'[51] We do not know exactly what causes Trilby's initial weight loss, the first step on her path to invalidism, but it is decidedly the result of her own, deliberate decision to change in body and soul. Trilby is as delighted as her male friends are by her newly fragile physicality: Du Maurier tells us that after her transformation 'she seemed even happier than she had ever seemed before' (p. 126).

There is certainly a suggestion of what we would now define as anorexia about Trilby's wasting, but it alone is not a convincing diagnosis, for her disease is ultimately beyond her control. The final chapters of the book make clear that Trilby has no say in her decline, that she does not want to die, and that to please her villainous husband and mentor Svengali she has tried to 'force' herself to eat food which her body does not want. Du Maurier even tells us that 'her insanity was not enough to account for [her condition]' (p. 387): the mental illness she is believed to suffer from may contribute to her state, but there is a physical cause as well. The novel deliberately does not name her disease, for reasons I will return to. However, the many descriptions of Trilby are strongly suggestive of its diagnosis as consumption. Her first physical transformation, quoted above, dwells upon her increasing thinness, the pallor which replaces her previously healthy colour, and most noticeably the 'new brightness' of her eyes, which give off a light which has its source elsewhere and is not 'entirely their own'. These all recall the traditional appearance of the consumptive, emaciated and ethereal with the unnaturally bright eyes of fever. We learn also that more concrete signs of Trilby's illness begin after a 'three days walk from Vibrate to Paris' which culminates in her catching 'a chill', and we are told that her constitution 'never got over' the effect of this exertion (p. 378). The onset of phthisis was often heralded by cold or 'flu, as the opportunistic disease usually followed in the wake of another less severe ailment which left the body vulnerable to infection.[52] Then the later descriptions of her decaying body elaborate on the same consumptive theme: her 'increasing pallor and emaciation' are stressed, as is the 'pure, white and delicate skin' and her hands 'almost transparent in their waxen whiteness' (p. 383). All these descriptions suggest that she is suffering from the white plague. The use of the word 'decline' (p. 391) to describe her illness is also suggestive, as a term recognised as a description of consumptive wasting. The mental instability characterised by her loss of memory has a long history of association with phthisis. And, of course, the sources for *Trilby* were, according to Du Maurier's foremost biographer Leonee Ormond, *Scènes de la vie de Bohème* by Henri Mürger and *La dame aux camélias* by Alexandre Dumas, and these both have consumptive heroines with promiscuous pasts who are tragically separated from their lovers but reunited on their deathbed, with clear echoes of Trilby herself.[53]

It is no accident that Du Maurier does not explicitly identify Trilby's wasting disease as consumption, however, as his sources do with their heroines. Her diagnosis is deliberately left mysterious to allow a Gothic, almost supernatural interpretation of her illness and death. The novel's ending implies that Svengali's evil hypnotic power, which has been the reason for the previously tone-deaf Trilby's great musical success, and has trapped her into remaining with him for several years, is also responsible for her strange bodily wasting. He has drawn the life out of her and replaced it with his musical ambitions. His sudden death releases her mentally but not physically from his influence, for Trilby continues to fade as though she can no longer survive without his powers sustaining her. His strength even extends beyond the grave, so that when he wishes it Trilby is called to join him in death: his portrait is sent to her, and she becomes hypnotised and then dies suddenly while gazing at it. Silver has observed how Svengali 'is very much within the vampire tradition' because of his supernatural powers of manipulation over young women, and notes how his once-scrawny body grows stout and strong as Trilby's declines, a process reminiscent of a vampire sucking the blood out of a victim.[54] Silver's analysis ignores the fact that Trilby's wasting begins before she falls under Svengali's spell, however, for after her initial hypnosis to take away her neuralgia, she prefers to suffer from her pain for the rest of the early part of the novel, rather than let him repeat his sinister 'cure'. This implies that something other than Svengali has set her on the path to invalidism. Her initial fall into physical delicacy and fragility was in fact a deliberate and self-motivated transformation, but it was prompted by the desire to win the approval and love of Little Billee, whose condemnation of her former self proved the catalyst for change.

This all suggests that the truly pathological force in *Trilby* is in fact hungry masculinity which wishes to consume, possess and transform the beloved object, something which is both achieved through and symbolised by consumptive disease. Both Svengali and Little Billee desire Trilby but wish to change and shape her to meet their needs. Little Billee requires a chaste, pious angel figure for a bride, Svengali is searching for a conduit for his musical talent, and both worship female beauty. Hence her illness facilitates the aims and desires of both men, for her wasting enhances her beauty – 'day by day she grew more beautiful in their eyes, in spite of her increasing pallor and emaciation – her skin was so pure white and delicate, and the bones of her face so admirable!' (p. 391) – and, in true consumptive fashion, simultaneously purifies her soul and raises her social status. As Taffy remarks after her initial transformation, 'I'm blest if Trilby isn't the handsomest woman I know! She looks like a grande dame masquerading as a grisette – almost like a joyful saint at times!' (p. 129). In the guise of 'joyful saint' – something which seems to be becoming a familiar image of the consumptive, if we recall Mrs Ward's *Eleanor* – Trilby has clearly become an ideal Victorian woman and a worthy potential bride, in complete contrast to her subversive earlier self. Along with this new, virtuous femininity, however, goes the physical weakness of disease, and it is this which renders her vulnerable to Svengali and finally delivers her up to him when she returns to Paris exhausted and 'in dreadful pain' after the death of her brother and the loss of Little Billee:

> Then I could stand it no longer, and went to Svengali's . . . I didn't want to a bit, but I couldn't help myself. It was fate, I suppose! He was very kind, and cured me almost directly . . . And I slept for two days and two nights! And then he told me how fond he was of me, and how he would always cure me and take care of me, and marry me, if I would go away with him . . . I stayed with him there a week, never going out or seeing anyone . . . I'd caught a chill. (p. 376)

Consumptive illness first transforms Trilby into an object of men's desire, and then makes her appropriately feminine and helpless and so unable to escape that desire's consuming power. The weakened, wasting and hypnotised Trilby is an empty vessel to be filled by Svengali with his musical genius, is 'just a singing machine – an organ to play upon – an instrument of music . . . a flexible flageolet of flesh and blood' (p. 441). This representation of a consumptive woman as an instrument is an interesting one, for phthisis was known to break down the internal body, namely the chest, transforming fibres into fluid and air, creating cavities in the lungs and reconstructing new, calcified and unnatural walls. Therefore the remodelling of Trilby's body into an 'instrument' can be read as a literal as well as a symbolic process through the action of phthisis, and this is a further manifestation of the ways in which this disease facilitates Svengali's objectives. In fact disease and male sexuality are repeatedly identified with one another in the text, for both are responsible for Trilby's suffering and eventual death. In this sense her tubercular beauty is fatal in more ways than one. Du Maurier makes explicit the connection between disease, male concupiscence and female beauty in one of Svengali's most sinister speeches to Trilby, soon after her wasting begins to make itself apparent:

> Even Svengali perceived the strange metamorphosis. 'Ach Drilpy', he would say, on a Sunday afternoon, 'how beautiful you are! It drives me mad! I adore you! I like you thinner; you have such beautiful bones . . . We have got a poet too, my Drilpy. His name is Heinrich Heine . . . He adore French grisettes . . . He would adore you too, for your beautiful bones; he would like to count them one by one, for he is very playful, like me. And ach! what a beautiful skeleton you will make! And very soon too, because you do not smile on your madly loving Svengali. You burn his letters without reading them! You shall have a nice little mahogany glass case all to yourself in the museum of the École de Médecine, and Svengali shall come . . . and push the dirty carabins out of the way, and look through the holes of your eyes into your stupid empty skull, and up the nostrils of your high, bony sounding board of a nose without either a tip or lip to it . . . and into the roof of

your big mouth . . . and between your big ribs to your big chest . . . And then he
will look all down your bones to your poor crumbling feet . . . (pp. 129–30)

This is an important passage on many levels. Primarily, it is a foreshadowing
of Trilby's death by the man who will be ultimately responsible for it. In
addition it is a reinforcement of the aesthetic and erotic appeal of the
consumptive appearance, and one which reveals the source of that appeal:
Trilby's wasting enhances her beauty in Svengali's eyes because it displays
more clearly the object of his desire, the fetishised female skeleton. To
Svengali, female flesh is less sexually alluring than 'beautiful bones'. This
is clearly a manifestation of the cult of female invalidism, and can be read
as a symbol of male anxiety about female sexuality. It is after all a rejection
of the healthy female body in favour of what is partially revealed only
by consuming illness, and is fully exposed only by death and decay. This
passage is also a fantasy of the kind of absolute male dominance over the
corporeal which can only be facilitated by death. Svengali imagines himself
examining and desecrating Trilby's fleshless body: 'Svengali shall come . . .
and look through the holes of your eyes . . . and into the roof of your big
mouth . . .'. As Athena Vrettos has noted, here 'Trilby becomes a cadaver
for Svengali's visual experimentation and appropriation. The act of looking
translates into the act of dissection, revealing an imaginative link between
sexuality, spectatorship, and death.'[55] Svengali's desire is reminiscent of the
nineteenth-century physician's delight in the possibilities offered by the
female cadaver, for it is only through death that the mysterious secrets
of the female sex can be truly revealed to the probing and penetrating
male. Svengali is aligning himself here with the inquisitive medical student
who wields a gruesome power over the unclaimed dead body. He is clearly
preoccupied by this image of the dead Trilby displayed to him, for earlier
in the novel he describes in grotesque detail her lying on a mortuary slab:

. . . and one fine day you shall lie asleep on one of those slabs – you, Drilpy, who
would not listen to Svengali, and therefore lost him! . . . And over the middle of
you will be a little leather apron, and over your head a little brass tap, and all day
long and all night the cold water shall trickle, trickle, trickle all the way down
your beautiful white body to your beautiful white feet till they turn green . . . And
people of all sorts, strangers, will stare at you through the big plate-glass window –
Englanders, chiffonniers, painters and sculptors . . . and say, 'Ah! what a beautiful
woman was that! Look at her! She ought to be rolling in her carriage and pair!'
And who just then should come by . . . but Svengali . . . (p. 107)

The speech has the effect of constructing the dead woman as spectacle,
even a work of art, in a way which recalls *Beata Beatrix*. Both Rossetti's

painting and Svengali's depiction reveal the erotic and aesthetic potential of female consumptive death. This is the cult of invalidism taken to its logical conclusion, becoming another disturbing late Victorian obsession: the cult of the dead woman. The fascination with the dead and dying female displayed by so much of the art and literature of the period reveals that, in nineteenth-century consciousness, the invalid woman finds her most passive, pure and unthreatening state when her life expires. As Marsh notes, 'embalmed in death, the beautiful pale woman remains desirable and as it were, still willing, a strange and compelling image of love, sex and loss'.[56] In *Trilby*, Du Maurier implies the misogyny that lies behind this cultural romanticisation of the dead woman, displaying that even in, or especially in, death, beauty is there to be exploited; either by interested passers-by who see Trilby's body as entertainment, or by the 'painters and sculptors' who may reproduce it, Rossetti-like, for profit, but most of all by Svengali's predatory and necrophiliac male gaze.

I have invoked the corset in relation to *Trilby* because this garment seems to bring together all the novel's issues about the perception of female beauty and the demands of fashion and the influence of consumption and masculine desire on both. As I have indicated, the corset was the means by which the majority of Victorian woman could emulate a fashionable and desirable ideal of wasp-waisted femininity. A tiny waist in woman signified ladylike self denial and restrained appetites, as indeed general female thinness did, but in addition was a symbol of virginity and youth, thicker waists being associated with pregnancy and the aftermath of childbirth.[57] The small waist hence became the definitive feature of female beauty, a sought-after status symbol which was eroticised and even fetishised by Victorian culture in the way that, for example, large breasts are today. Of course the waist was not the only part of the body enhanced by the corset, for breasts too were pushed up, reshaped and revealed by its structure, and, as Kunzle has observed, the corset's 'elimination of abdominal in favour of pectoral breathing'[58] created an increase in their movement, rapid shallow breathing inducing the 'heaving bosoms' beloved by fiction and long eroticised by being read as a sign of heightened emotion, or desire.

The corset was, therefore, a highly sexualised garment which shaped the female body so that it signified purity and sexual availability all at once, and so it had a vital part to play in enhancing the attractiveness of its wearer in the eyes of the rest of society. It was also a valuable asset within the marriage market, for it made its wearer more attractive to potential husbands. As a defender of the corset observed in 1865, 'the cultivated eye admires a slender figure in woman because it suggests ideas of culture and refinement; a proper

care of the person, and above all a desire to please. It also suggests the reverse
of masculine muscularity . . . '.[59] This 'desire to please' the opposite sex had
dangerous consequences, however, for when tightly laced – as it must be
to achieve the smallest and most desirable shape – the corset could have
damaging side effects. Tight lacing had an incapacitating effect on those
who wore it, cramping and confining the body, restricting the lungs, and
making it impossible to draw a deep breath.[60] This restricted oxygen intake
from reduced lung capacity made all but the gentlest exercise difficult or
impossible, and in the long term the pressure which the garment exerted
on the internal organs could also permanently deform the body. Muscle
atrophy in the torso was also a problem with prolonged use, when the
body became accustomed to the rigid support and was unable to function
without it. Hence the corset was considered to beget illness, partly because
of the damage it itself could inflict and partly because it encouraged women
to lead a sedentary lifestyle which seemed to invite other ailments. Its use
solidified the connection between illness and the bourgeois woman, and
played an important part in the rise of the cult of invalidism: 'to the fashion
of corset wearing may be attributed many of the weaknesses and ailments
of the feminine gender', as R. B. D. Wells, the author of *Woman and Her
Diseases,* declared in 1880.[61]

Corsetry was therefore a means by which women could signal their
passive, chaste and self-sacrificial femininity through delicate health, as
well as by a slender body. The most significant thing about this garment,
however, was that its side effects created not just a general air of ill-health,
but rather an appearance evocative of one specific disease in particular. Leigh
Summers has observed how the physical effects of a tightly laced corset –
a thin, wasted body, pale complexion from lack of oxygen, shortness of
breath, and extreme fatigue – were in fact the same as the manifestations
of phthisis: 'tightly laced corsetry was in fact integral in the emulation of
consumption's lesser and more appealing symptoms'.[62] In some cases tight
lacing emulated consumption even more, as corsets sometimes damaged the
lungs to the extent that they caused the wearer to cough up blood – always
the defining symbol of phthisis. There is a remarkable affinity here between
consumption, the fashionable disease, and the corset, the garment which
constructed the fashionable figure. This forms a revealing motive for the
enduring appeal of tight lacing, as it becomes a method of constructing or
imitating the tubercular aesthetic through artificial means. Summers argues
that stays enabled women to physically resemble the romantic, ethereal
consumptive persona and to receive the desirable cultural associations that
went along with it, even if they did not actually suffer from the disease.

Corset use did not simply mimic consumption, however, for the Victorian medical profession believed that tight lacing really could be a cause of phthisis. 'Any article of dress which interferes with the free and natural action of the lungs ... may be considered a powerful disposing cause of pulmonary tubercle', argued Alabone in 1880 (p. 27). This was a reiteration of the long-established medical view of corsets – 'Tight stays, while they spoil the female figure by distorting the beauty of nature, are very prejudicial ... [Ladies are] martyrs to an all-destroying fashion', observed Dr Thomas Bartlett in his book about consumption in 1855.[63]

We would expect this consumptive connection to be an effective deterrent against the use of corsets, for vague fears about the possible dangers of confining the body might be one thing, but a link between tight lacing and the most deadly disease of the nineteenth century was quite another. Yet this seems to have had little or no effect on the popularity of tight lacing, which did not really begin to decline until the turn of the century,[64] and was at its peak in the 1860s, two decades before phthisis was identified as an infectious disease and corsetry therefore accepted as less of a threat. It is clear that women continued to tight lace despite of, or perhaps even because of, the link between it and consumption, and that they rejected the widespread medical condemnation of the practice. This can be read as a rejection of the authority of the medical profession by bourgeois women, who resisted patriarchal attempts to exert control over their dress as well as their bodies. Kunzle has identified the continuation of corset use in the face of conservative male disapproval as a feminist 'protest against the total absorption of women into a life of constant child-bearing and rearing, and the limitation of her sexuality to exclusively procreative ends'.[65] It is true that the corset allowed resistance to the women's conventional role as mother, by visibly asserting female sexuality and (as it constricted the womb and could even induce abortion) being antagonistic to child-bearing (another thing it had in common with consumption, of course). In this sense it *was* subversive of the patriarchal values which rendered the medical profession primarily concerned with women's reproductive capacity, but Kunzle's view does not consider tight lacing as a manifestation of the deeply anti-feminist cult of invalidism. Women who tight laced were certainly doing so against the advice of their doctors, but they were in fact merely acquiescing to a different but equally repressive power – the demands of a fashion which championed the consumptive aesthetic. The socially motivated desire to look romantically thin, pale and fragile was so all-consuming that even the threat of severe, potentially fatal illness could not prove a deterrent.

This struggle between fashion and physician finds an interesting fictional representation in Charles Reade's popular 1886 novel *A Simpleton*, which like *Trilby* is a criticism of the pathologising power of fashion, but which unlike *Trilby* is not at all seduced by or complicit in that power, perhaps because Reade has used medical sources for the book – 'the medical truths, both fact and argument, are all from medical books' – and has made his hero a physician.[66] Reade's biographer Elton E. Smith suggests that *A Simpleton* reveals more about 'the author's special interest in doctors and the practice of medicine' than any of his other novels. The 'Simpleton' of the title is the main female character, Rosa, who is represented as a typical middle-class Victorian girl, frivolous, empty-headed and somewhat vain, and preoccupied by dress and keeping up with her friends. Rosa's redeeming feature, however, is her 'dazzling beauty' (p. 15), which unlike Trilby's is natural and healthy and needs no illness to enhance it into appropriate femininity. Indeed, it is defined by a very un-tubercular rosy 'glowing skin, with . . . the rich blood mantling below it' (p. 97) and a curvaceous figure with a 'bosom that would have done honour to Diana' (p. 32). Consumption-like illness, when it comes, is actually a destroyer of beauty. Rosa experiences a 'slight but frequent' haemorrhage of the lungs, which 'weakens her visibly'. 'She began to lose her rich complexion, and sometimes looked almost sallow; and a slight circle showed itself under her eyes' (p. 15). She and her father are concerned that her bleeding is the first signs of phthisis, and the physicians whom they consult are undecided, and experiment with unsuccessful treatments while Rosa gradually becomes a 'ghost' (p. 15) of her former self. Her decline is halted, however, when she requests that her lover, the young and poor but talented Dr Staines, be called in to see her, and he immediately identifies her illness as 'congestion of the lungs' caused by 'tight stays' (p. 21), which will improve as soon as she stops wearing them. Rosa's reaction to this diagnosis is one of outrage: she at first denies that she tight laces, and then when caught out refuses to obey her doctor's request, to 'throw that diabolical machine into the fire' (p. 29). Implicit here is the suggestion that consumption would in fact be a more socially acceptable diagnosis for her. That Staines mentions corsetry at all is thought to be 'rude [and] indelicate' (p. 31) and his insistence that to get rid of her corsets is the only way to be 'healthy and happy' is to her a form of 'tyranny'. Rosa makes clear that clothes are one of the only aspects of female life which are not under male control – 'No English lady would let her husband dictate to her about such a thing' (p. 31) – and so feels justified in denying the authority of her father, her lover and her physician in order to keep her tiny waist. Her father, who had previously had the power to forbid her engagement to Staines, is impotent when it comes to questions of dress. Rosa is even incensed enough by Staines's advice to temporarily break off their engagement, choosing her neat figure over the man she loves. Eventually she does repent, and ceases to tight lace, a change which proves Staines correct, for Rosa swiftly becomes 'a picture of health and bodily vigour' once again (p. 34). After her marriage to Staines, however, Rosa becomes involved in the demands of the Season and in a 'rivalry' with a female acquaintance who represents all the temptations of fashion, the young, rich and pretty Mrs Vivian, who much to Rosa's chagrin possesses 'a waist you could span' (p. 130). Mrs Vivian physically resembles the tubercular aesthetic, 'a skinny woman, with a pretty face' but 'dying eyes', which Rosa considers 'lovely' – 'a bag of bones in a balloon ' (p. 134), as Staines contemptuously describes her. Rosa is torn between the wishes and advice of her physician and the desire to emulate her friends and especially her stylish rival, and so takes up her stays again, unknown to her husband. The medical man cannot be deceived for long, though, for Rosa's body cannot lie, and the consumptive symptoms which soon return make her actions plain to Staines. The exchange which follows his discovery is an important one, for it reveals the pathological tyranny of the fashionable world represented in the novel by Rosa's friends, in which appearance and dress are valued above health:

You dressed to go out; dressed again in stays; dressed again without them; and all to deceive your husband, and kill yourself, at the bidding of two shallow, heartless women, who would dance over your grave without a pang of remorse, or sentiment of any kind, since they live, like midges, *only to dance in the sun, and suck some worker's blood.* (p. 135, italics Reade's)

Fashion, as represented in this passage, is not merely 'shallow' and frivolous, but is a symbolic vampire waiting to 'suck' the 'blood' and consume the bodies of its followers. In this context it is possible to see Rosa's decline as evocative of the illness of those other wasting heroines of the late century, Lucy in *Dracula* and Trilby herself. The use of a vampiric metaphor here has the effect of depicting fashion as a powerfully seductive and influential force, which captivates and controls young women. Like the aristocratic Dracula, it was born of the idle and luxurious upper classes (who are the 'midges' of Staines's speech) and it must be battled with by the bourgeois physician in order to rescue the vulnerable women who are its prey: 'It [the corset] brought you to the edge of the grave. I saved you ... ' (p. 134). Of course they have not only to be saved from the physicality of the corset, but also from their own ignorant worship of it. 'But all you women are monomaniacs; one might as well talk sense to a gorilla', observes Staines in despair (p. 135).

I have previously discussed how phthisis was frequently constructed by the Victorian medical profession as the consequence of a pathological lifestyle and how consumptives were considered to have invited disease through their behaviour. That so many women were willing to sacrifice their health and their lungs for their figures suggests one of the reasons for this kind of medical reasoning. Indeed, that the appearance if not the reality of consumption was actually pursued by tightly laced females displays how they may be regarded as the most socially deviant of all those patients who were believed to be the instigators of their own illness. None of the other lifestyle factors which were considered causes of phthisis, like alcohol abuse or social or sexual excess, were actually undertaken by the individual with a view to emulating the disease: it was, rather, an unfortunate and unforeseen side effect of this behaviour. The explicit aim of those who tight laced, in contrast, was to achieve a fashionably consumptive look. This provides an interesting insight into the reasons why consumption was commonly and inaccurately regarded as a largely female disease. This belief was held for a number of complex social and and cultural reasons, but corsetry undeniably had an important part to play in its construction, by linking the illness to what Charles Reade describes as 'the mania of the sex' – dress (p. 137). Alabone, who adamantly believed that consumption 'was more frequently met with in females than in males', suggests that physicians held the corset largely responsible for this phenomenon: 'writers assign the cause [of increased female susceptibility] to tight lacing and exposure of the neck in females . . . ' (p. 26). Alabone goes on to pathologise fashionable women's clothing in general, observing that 'ladies should cover the chest and neck . . . it is terrible to contemplate the bare chests of ladies who, martyr-like, expose their delicate breasts to the unmerciful changes of temperature. The ballroom and the theatre are, alas, too frequent examples of this folly' (pp. 56–7). Women here are once again represented as 'martyrs' to the cause of a fashion which subverts the basic function of clothing – to cover and protect the body – and which combines flimsy materials, low necklines and tight lacing to render the stylishly dressed woman vulnerable to consumption.

Both *Trilby* and *A Simpleton* are concerned with exploring Victorian fashion's preoccupation with the consumptive aesthetic and the impact this has on the bodies and lives of young women. Their approaches to fashion are interestingly different, however, for Reade represents fashion as a female preoccupation and the phthisical waif as a female ideal. It is the women in his novel who admire the appearance of ill health and who advocate corsets: the men are either ignorant of, and unimpressed by, the effects or appearance of tight lacing, like Rosa's father, or condemnatory of the practice, like Staines. The opinion of other women is what matters in terms of appearance, and masculine approval is not sought. Reade constructs fashion as an issue of class rather than gender, for Rosa dresses to define her social position, tight lacing to imitate her wealthier friends, and is horrified when her maid blurs the boundaries between them by wearing very similar clothes. *A Simpleton* ignores the possibility that the pursuit of a tiny waist or delicate face was spurred on by the need to appear desirable to potential husbands. It in fact reassures its readers that such artifices are unnecessary, for the men in the novel are all drawn to the healthy and vibrant Rosa, as she is when unrestricted by her corset. *Trilby* gives a very different perspective of the fashion for the sickly woman, for in this novel consumptive beauty is worshipped by all the male characters and hence social forces conspire to make the heroine emulate it. Of course Trilby has no need of a corset, for her desirably slender and fragile body, like Elizabeth Siddal's, is achieved 'naturally', through disease. Trilby is hence exonerated from the taint of tight lacing, but she is no less a victim of the demands of fashion and male sexuality. Du Maurier makes his readers aware of the frivolous and transient nature of contemporary ideals of beauty and femininity, but his initially free-spirited heroine is still ultimately a victim of such expectations – expectations which are as inexorably and fatally all-consuming as the disease which so often accompanied them.

CHAPTER 5

Consumption and the Count: the pathological origins of vampirism and Bram Stoker's Dracula

In previous chapters I have examined how the Victorian consumptive was traditionally regarded as being beautiful, spiritual and saintly – 'too good to live' – or, alternatively and paradoxically, as socially subversive and sexually deviant. I am concerned in this section with exploring the possibility that there existed a development of the latter view in which the consumptive was not just considered to be dangerously pathological, but was actually thought of as fitting into a vampiric paradigm. We have seen that both *Trilby* and *A Simpleton* use the vampire motif in connection with consumption, but this is only part of a much bigger picture: nineteenth-century fiction and medical writing seem to conspire together to create this image of the phthisical patient, which is surely the most powerful of all 'metaphors of illness'. This construction of the consumptive does, however, stem from the folkloric origins of vampirism, which date back to the Middle Ages.[1] The history of the vampire myth is, of course, in essence the history of disease itself, for belief in the Undead arose out of a need to explain mysterious or untimely death in past cultures which had little medical understanding and that therefore associated illness with supernatural forces. As Edward Tylor points out in *Primitive Culture*:

Inasmuch as certain patients are seen becoming day by day, without apparent cause, thin, weak and bloodless, savage animism is called upon to produce a satisfactory explanation, and does so in the doctrine that there exist certain demons which eat out the souls or hearts or suck the blood of their victims . . . vampires are not mere creations of groundless fancy, but causes conceived in spiritual form to account for specific facts of wasting disease.[2]

The vampire was held to be the tangible and terrible cause of the human suffering which was actually brought about by wasting disease, and of course these illnesses suggested the presence of a vampire because those afflicted appeared to have something draining the life out of them. Clive Leatherdale's *Dracula: The Novel and the Legend* develops this pathological explanation for vampirism, arguing that the ghastly effects certain illnesses produced on their victims would have been considered indications that demonic forces were at work: 'sufferers of particular rare diseases that produce visually alarming symptoms might easily at one time have been condemned as vampires'.[3] Leatherdale suggests several diseases which may have have been linked to the vampire myth, among them pernicious anaemia and cholera. More convincing in the role is a rare disorder called porphyia, in which, as Leatherdale says, 'the body cannot metabolise iron, and must take it in a readily digestible form – such as drinking blood'.[4] Porphyria sufferers are also extremely sensitive to sunlight, and must avoid garlic as it encourages the breaking down of old blood cells. It therefore has several traits in common with vampirism, but the rarity of its occurrence renders it an unlikely source for a folk belief that existed all over Europe and beyond. Vampirism is simply too widespread a phenomenon to be the consequence of a very unusual disease. Rabies was a more readily identified possibility: physician Juan Gomez-Alonzo has argued that because vampirism is identified with, and perpetuated by, biting, sufferers from rabies – who experience suggestively Undead symptoms like insomnia, hyper-salivation, hallucinations and hydrophobia – were likely to have been considered vampires by other members of their community.[5] Rabies, is, however, not a lingering disease, as death usually occurs within a week of the symptoms appearing,[6] and so does not match the gradual decline associated with vampirism, whose victims waste away slowly.

What is emerging here is the likelihood that over the centuries the vampire myth was formed by social anxieties which accompanied a number of different wasting diseases, and that the elements which constitute this myth – from the vampire's appearance to his behaviour – are compounded from the symptoms of all these illnesses. The vampire, originally thought of as the cause of ill health, never lost his pathological associations, remaining a metaphor for illness even long after medical knowledge had identified the wasting diseases vampirism had been held responsible for. By the end of the eighteenth century the folkloric vampire was beginning to be transcribed and transformed by poetry and prose. The modern vampire represented in Romantic and Victorian fiction, which has remained the enduring image of the Undead ever since, is a rather different creature from the decaying, mindless revenant of most folklore. The nineteenth-century literary vampire, from the Byronic Lord Ruthven of John Polidori's influential *The Vampyre* to Dracula himself, was aristocratic and sophisticated, 'a magnetic figure of sexual power, lordly authority and deep cunning'.[7]

The creature is still identified with disease, but not with the madness of
rabies or the squalor of cholera: instead, I suggest, with a more individualist
and (arguably) upper-class illness, one which was very much at the fore-
front of the nineteenth-century mindset – consumption. Phthisis was the
most common wasting disease in this period, and can of course 'result in
recognisable vampire symptoms: weight loss and fatigue, not to mention
coughing and spitting blood in advanced cases'. In addition 'the disease
has been known to be conveyed by a carrier who is himself immune – an
obvious vampire candidate should his identity be disclosed'.[8] So a symptomatic similarity exists between the two afflictions, but it is likely that
the nineteenth-century vampire became *symbolically* linked to consumption because of this disease's association with Romanticism, which I have
discussed in Chapter 4. It was after all the Romantic poets who really began
the literary tradition of vampirism, in works such as Coleridge's *Christa-
bel*, Shelley's *The Cenci* and Keats's *Lamia* and *La Belle Dame sans Merci*.[9]
The latter uses particularly consumptive imagery to describe its vampire's
victim, the 'haggard', preyed-upon knight:

> I see a lilly on thy brow,
> With anguish moist and fever dew;
> And on thy cheek a fading rose,
> Fast withereth too.[10]

The phthisical symptoms described here by Keats – pallor, feverishness,
the 'fading' flowers metaphor which is habitually and repeatedly used to
describe consumption – are, as we shall see, perpetuated and developed in
fictional portrayals of vampires throughout the century.

It is difficult to say to what extent fictional portrayals of the Undead
influenced cultural beliefs about vampirism, but it is undeniable that this
connection between vampires and phthisis was not confined to the literature
of the period, but also manifested itself in real life. New England folklorist
Dr Michael E. Bell has recently delineated his investigations into the beliefs,
myths and superstitions that surrounded the vampire tradition, in which
he examines the possibility that nineteenth-century consumptives were
believed to be vampires. His book, *Food for the Dead*, examines a number
of folk accounts which describe how the exhumation of the body of a
consumptive and the removal and/or burning of their heart was considered
a cure for those relatives of the dead who were also afflicted with the disease.
Bell cites, among others, the case (also described by Raymond McNally in
his book *A Clutch of Vampires*) of nineteen-year-old Mercy Brown, who died
of consumption – the same disease which had already killed her mother
and older sister – in Exeter, Rhode Island, in January 1892.[11] Mercy was

survived by a brother, Edwin, who also became afflicted with consumption, and was known to be dying by March 1892 when his father and a number of the townspeople attempted to save him by trying an unconventional folk remedy. These people had come to believe that something or someone was preying on the family and drawing the life out of them, that it had been responsible for the previous deaths and was now threatening Edwin's life. In an attempt to locate and put an end to this monster they exhumed the bodies of Edwin's mother and sisters, and found that Mercy's corpse still retained blood. This confirmed their suspicions, for it was considered evidence that Mercy was 'undead' and that she had been sustaining her unnatural life by consuming the blood of her brother. Hence the onlookers removed her heart, burnt it, and fed the ashes to Edwin, believing that this would restore the vitality which had been drained from him. The cure did not succeed, and it was considered that Edwin was just too far gone for any cure to be possible, but the attempt to save him was, nonetheless, validated and officiated when it was reported in the local paper.[12]

The exhumation and desecration of the body of Mercy Brown was not an isolated incident. Bell's book describes around sixteen similar occurrences in North America between 1799 and 1892,[13] all involving men and women who had died of consumption. His research reveals the fascinating possibility that, in certain communities in the nineteenth century, phthisis and vampirism were synonymous. Wasting which was actually consumptive in origin was frequently considered a sign that the afflicted was being preyed upon by a vampire, and it was thought that when that victim passed away he or she, like Mercy Brown, would in turn become a revenant and return to feast on the loved ones left behind. The belief that vampires usually attacked those people who had been close to them when alive – something that Jonathan Harker refers to in *Dracula*: 'I suppose it is thus that in old times one vampire meant many ... the holiest love was the recruiting sergeant for their ghastly ranks'[14] – was considered the explanation for consumption's tendency to run in families.[15]

Bell's research is more or less confined to New England, but he does quote several accounts describing the same practices in the Old World,[16] including a tantalising reference to the subject made in 1893 by folklorist C. A Fraser. Fraser had collected beliefs from third-generation Scottish Highlanders now living in Canada which suggested that vampirism and phthisis had been linked in Britain:

I was a little shocked to hear of a repulsive superstition which I have read of as being peculiar to certain parts of England – I mean a horrible vampire story given in explanation of the ravages often made in a family by consumption. I did not meet this superstition myself, but was told that it was among them. Consumption was rife among them, it seemed to be hereditary. They looked so remarkably robust, and yet fell so easily prey to this disease, and it seldom lingered! ... The matter seemed so hopeless ... I stood by sick-beds with a sore heart, knowing too well that the haste with which a doctor was procured would be fully equalled by the zeal with which his orders would be disregarded. They had faith in the physician, the man, but none whatever in his prescriptions.[17]

The above passage not only indicates that there was a vampiric/consumptive tradition in England as well as in America, but also hints at the explanation for this 'repulsive superstition', which seems to arise out of the inability of nineteenth-century medicine to successfully treat the disease. I have discussed how medical ignorance about phthisis facilitated the flourishing of its myths, fictions and quack remedies, and nowhere is that more apparent than in this instance, which reveals how in the absence of scientific facts even the most sinister and supernatural explanation could be considered. The idea that vampirism could be a cause of consumption was seductive because it offered a definitive course of action: destroy the Undead and the living will be saved. Such an unorthodox treatment was seized upon, even though it necessitated the desecration of the grave and body of a loved one, because it provided a possible cure for a disease considered 'hopeless' by most physicians.

At first consideration the possibility raised by this folk superstition, that consumptive wasting was actually caused by vampirism, seems to bear little resemblance to the real-life pathology of the disease. If vampirism did have a real-life pathological counterpart we would expect it to be transmitted by, or identified with, blood, or other bodily fluids for which blood commonly functions as a metaphor, such as semen. Phthisis, being airborne, does not require the exchange of bodily fluids in order to be passed from one person to another. This is, however, an anachronistic objection that only becomes apparent with hindsight, as for most of the nineteenth century the medical profession simply did not know what caused consumption. Even Koch's identification of tubercle in 1882, which finally confirmed that the disease was contagious, did not yet establish that its most usual means of transmission was through breathing (Koch inoculated his test animals with tubercle, so a transfer of blood *was* involved in the process). The ongoing debate about whether it might be hereditary or congenital, which continued for several years after Koch, reveals that many Victorian physicians thought it could be passed from parent to child through bodily fluids. Even more significantly, a number of them believed that it actually was a *disorder* of the blood. Dr Carl Both suggested in 1868 that phthisis was 'contained in the blood of [consumptive] persons and that it was an 'impurity'.[18] Dr C. W. de Lacy Evans wrote in 1881 that it was 'caused by increased oxidation of the blood',[19] and, perhaps most suggestively, Gowan argued in 1878 that 'the essential principle of causation was ... diminished and retarded supply of blood to the lungs and body generally', and condemned bleeding as a method of treating the disease because 'the consumptive patient has need of every drop of blood in his body'.[20] Gowan's comments are particularly interesting because they create a possible causal link between the consumptive and the vampire's victim, by suggesting that the physical sufferings of both arise for the same reason – lack of blood.

Even if both 'conditions' arise from the same source, however, there is still of course a marked difference in the way this blood loss is effected in their respective victims. The vampire draws blood out of the body by piercing the flesh and drinking, in an external, violent attack which leaves noticeable puncture marks behind. Phthisis, in contrast, works silently and insidiously to consume from within, and, unlike the primary lesion common in syphilis, there is no tangible sign of its entry into the body. However, it should be noted that the vampire attack in both folklore and fiction is rarely characterised by the bite or the action of having blood drained. As J. Gordon Melton points out in his extensive compendium of vampirism, *The Vampire Book*, many mythological vampires 'do not take blood, rather they steal what is thought of as the life force from the victim'.[21] Blood is symbolically important, as the medium in which the life force is carried, but biting is not always central to the image. In nineteenth-century literature, the vampire *is* a blood drinker, defined as such by his long fangs, but his visit usually takes place 'off-stage' (like the numerous attacks on Lucy, in *Dracula*) or is experienced in a dreamlike trance in which the vampire is not seen by the victim and the drawing of blood is defined only by a sensation of pain and weakness of unknown cause (like Laura's experience in Le Fanu's *Carmilla*). The vampire is in this sense as invisible as a disease. Apart from the bite marks, the only tangible evidence that the incident has taken place is usually the bloodstained nightdress or pillowcase,[22] which are, of course, the defining signifiers of consumption in popular culture. That something is draining the life out of the victim only becomes apparent gradually as the nightly visits continue and their health declines. It is this loss of colour, flesh and health which marks the most apparent affinity between the two afflictions, as well as the nocturnal nature of both their sufferings, for, as Bell has pointed out, 'consumption's victims suffer most at night, sweating profusely. They awaken, coughing and in pain.'[23]

Bell's work raises interesting questions about how this vampiric super-stition may have influenced the representation of the consumptive in the Victorian mindset. Some answers are offered by an examination of the most famous and influential of all portraits of vampirism, Bram Stoker's *Dracula*, a novel which is both the cumulation of a century of vampire lore – it brings together elements from earlier vampire literature as well as folklore – and the classic and authoritative model for all subsequent portrayals of the Undead. Like so many vampire texts, *Dracula* is clearly preoccupied by fears about contagious illness, and Clark Lawlor briefly suggests that it can be considered a reflection of 'the contemporary anxi-ety about Koch's discovery that consumption is an infectious germ'.[24] Most other critics have, however, generally assumed that it is venereal disease, not consumption, which is the dominant pathological force in the novel. This theory has its roots in the suggestion made by Stoker's great-nephew and biographer, Daniel Farson, that the author actually died of tertiary syphilis, probably contracted from the prostitutes he visited.[25] The willingness of critics like Elaine Showalter, Robert Tracy and Jeffrey L. Spear to accept this diagnosis reveals how useful it is as a means to read *Dracula*.[26] The fear of female contamination the text displays is illuminated if we can accept that 'Stoker's attitudes are based on personal experience and resentment', resentment directed both at the prostitutes who had infected him and the unsatisfactory wife who, Farson conjectures, had driven him to associate with such women.[27] Within this syphilitic reading the mark the Sacred Wafer leaves on Mina's forehead is evocative of a lesion, and the mouth of the female vampire becomes a 'vagina dentata that is also infected and unclean'.[28] Hence 'the staking of Lucy and the other vampire women are at once fantasies of total sexual power and of sexual revenge', and the final destruction of Dracula and the saving of Mina are indicative of a desire to stamp out the disease.[29] These are persuasive and important readings of the novel, but, as Barbara Belford has pointed out, Farson's belief that the cause of death given on Stoker's death certificate – 'locomotor ataxia six months' – was in fact syphilitic *tabes dorsalis* or GPI is not conclusive evidence that the author was actually afflicted with syphilis: 'Like most middle-class Londoners of his time, he died at home, not in a hospital, so there are no medical records.' Belford cites the opinion of Dr R. B. Gibberd, a neurologist at the Charing Cross and Westminster Medical School, who believes that the death certificate's statement of six months is significant: 'if Stoker had locomotor ataxia for only six months before his death, then it was unlikely to be due to syphilis'.[30] Stoker did suffer from Bright's disease and it seems likely that kidney failure due to this was the actual cause of his death. Paul Murray adds that even if Stoker did have syphilis it was quite possible that he was unaware of it: 'in those days, doctors often took it upon themselves to decide how much they told people'.[31]

All this does not of course mean we can reject the possibility that *Dracula* has a syphilitic subplot. Stoker, a man 'allegedly proud of his reputation as a womaniser' and certainly familiar with the dissolute sex lives of his theatrical friends, must have had concerns about venereal disease, even if he was not personally touched by it.[32] It is, however, reductive to assume that this is the only illness being represented and explored in *Dracula*, a novel filled with all kinds of disease, from Lucy's hysteria to Harker's brain fever and Mrs Westenra's heart failure. Other potential pathological influences on Stoker's work include the mysterious illness which confined him to bed until he was seven years of age, the Sligo cholera epidemic which his mother recounted tales about when he was a child, and the medical writings of a distant relative – a Dr William Stoker – who wrote graphically on wasting diseases and whom Paul Murray suggests may have been read by the young Stoker.[33] It is probable, then, that Stoker is interested not solely in syphilis but in the prevalent and important 'social' diseases of his day. Of these, tuberculosis was not only the biggest killer, but, as a disease associated with emotional instability, the perfect medium through which physical and mental illness, the two sides of Lucy's condition, could be brought together. I will show that consumption therefore *does* have an important part to play in *Dracula*: that the novel's representation of vampirism was influenced and shaped by the myths and images that surrounded the Victorian consumptive, and that a tubercular reading of the plot provides important insights into its thematic concerns.

Consumption had always seemed to Stoker a disease associated with the supernatural and with life after death. Clive Leatherdale suggests that he was 'deeply impressed' by a popular Gothic legend surrounding the famous consumptive who was the subject of my previous chapter: Elizabeth Siddal, the late wife of Stoker's neighbour Dante Gabriel Rossetti.[34] It was reported that when Siddal's coffin was opened in 1869, to retrieve some of Rossetti's poems which had been buried with her, it revealed a still-perfect corpse, whose beautiful hair had continued to grow for the seven years following her death, so that it filled the coffin. This incident became, according to Leatherdale, the inspiration for a Stoker short story, 'The Secret of the Growing Gold', and may well have contributed to the conception of *Dracula*. There is, however, more concrete evidence that consumptives and vampires were linked in Stoker's mind while he was writing the novel. In his collection of Bram Stoker's uncollected works,

Shades of Dracula, Peter Haining reproduces a newspaper article from the *New York World* which, on 2 February 1896, Stoker cut out from the paper and kept among his notes for *Dracula*, which he was writing at the time and which he published the following year. Hainings argues that this article, which was entitled 'Vampires in New England', was an important source for the novel and 'played the role of catalyst to the ideas that had been swimming around in [Stoker's] imagination'.[35] That Stoker did directly draw upon this piece is indicated by an anecdote it contains – about a horse being attacked by a vampire bat in Chile – which as Haining notes is very similar to an experience in the same region described by Quincey in *Dracula*:

One night [Darwin] was camping with a party near Coquimbo in Chile, and it happened that a servant noticed the restlessness of one of the horses. The man went up to the horse and actually caught a bat in the act of sucking blood from the flank . . .[36]

I was on the Pampas and had a mare that I was fond of go to grass in a night. One of those big bats they call vampires had got at her in the night, and what with his gorge and the vein left open, there wasn't enough blood in her to let her stand up . . . (p. 151)

But it is the central subject of the article, which is not discussed by Haining, that I want to examine, for it is concerned with perceptions about real-life consumptives. The 'Vampirism in New England' it describes is 'the ancient vampire superstition [which] still survives . . . The belief entertained . . . that a person who has died of consumption is likely to rise from the grave at night and suck the blood of surviving members of the family, thus dooming them to a similar fate'.[37] The article goes on to list several cases, unnamed but very similar to those described in more detail by Michael Bell, of New England families who responded to the ravages of consumption by exhuming the bodies of those who had already died of the disease and burning their hearts to protect the health of those left behind. The author describes the belief that consumptives were actually the victims of vampirism as a 'frightful superstition', and indicates with incredulity that it was 'not merely the out of the way agricultural folk, but the more intelligent people of the urban communities [who] were strong in their belief in vampirism'.[38] It is important to note, though, that elsewhere the article's tone is ambivalent, particularly regarding the accounts of consumptive death it contains:

An intelligent man, by trade a mason, informed Mr Stetson that he had lost two brothers by consumption. On the death of his second brother, his father was advised to take up the body and burn the heart. He *refused to do so, and consequently he was attacked by the disease.* Finally he died of it. His heart was burned, and *in this way the rest of the family was saved.*[39]

This passage implies a willingness to accept to some degree the belief in vampirism. Even though it, like the rest of the piece, accepts that it is the real 'disease' of consumption which has blighted this family, the writer does not challenge the notion that burning the hearts of the previously afflicted can save those still living, or that 'refusing to do so' may bring about their death. This marks a progression from the idea held by the townspeople who are the subjects of the article – that consumption actually *is* vampirism – but it still seems to be reluctant to completely separate the two conditions. The author does not wish to deny that consumption is actually a disease, but he cannot rescue it from its vampiric associations, and hence the 'cure' for the vampire can still be accepted as a cure for consumption. In this context it is worth mentioning a comment made by Bell, who points out how in certain late-century cases it was the lungs, rather than the hearts, of dead consumptives which were burnt and consumed by their living relatives, and as 'it is in the lungs of consumptives that the disease is located . . . this [could] be considered a rudimentary attempt at inoculation'.[40] This possibility reveals how traditional vampiric folklore and new medical knowledge become merged together by attempts to conquer consumption.

That Stoker not only read this article but cut it out of the paper and retained it among his notes, suggests that he was likely to have considered the possibility of a link between vampirism and consumption. This may well be the reason he represents the illness of Lucy Westenra, one of the most detailed and important accounts of vampiric wasting in literature, in pathological rather than supernatural terms. The section of the novel which deals with Lucy is fundamentally a narrative of illness, and, as William Hughes has observed in his book *Beyond Dracula*, 'Lucy's descent into vampirism is structured as a medical case, the progress of her "illness" being observed and investigated by a variety of participant characters.'[41] Stoker's representation of vampirism as disease invites a consumptive reading of the novel, for as we shall see Lucy's symptoms are concurrent with the effects of phthisis.

Central to Lucy's representation as a consumptive is the novel's implication that she has been physically delicate even before the Count's arrival in England. Mina's journal mentions at the beginning of the Whitby section that Lucy 'has got a beautiful colour since she has been here' (p. 64), a comment which as Hughes says 'conveys a muted suggestion of less robust

health in the past, evidently observed by the diarist herself prior to the
Whitby visit. Lucy's enhanced colour supersedes an unhealthy pallor which
is acknowledged only in its eclipse.'[42] Mina continues to express concern
about her friend's health, almost daily referring to it in her diary in the
weeks prior to Dracula's first attack:

Thank God, Lucy's health keeps up ... Lucy frets at the postponement of seeing
[Arthur] but it does not touch her looks; she is a trifle stouter and her cheeks are
a lovely rose pink. She has lost that anaemic look which she had. I pray it will all
last. (p. 72)

Lucy is asleep and breathing softly. She has more colour in her cheeks than usual
... I am so happy tonight, because dear Lucy seems better. I really believe that she
has turned the corner ... (pp. 88–9)

That Lucy's health is such a ongoing source of anxiety to Mina suggests that
it is somewhat fragile even before she becomes Dracula's prey. Hughes has
suggested that Lucy's sleep-walking and her 'supersensitive' (p. 87) nature
are indicative of hysteria, and that this is symbolically important because
this touch of mental instability renders her receptive to Dracula's call. It is
apparent, however, that Mina, while certainly concerned about her friend's
'restlessness' (p. 87) and low spirits, is actually worried about a physical
rather than a mental disorder. Mina's journal reveals that she is specifically
preoccupied with Lucy's weight and colour, worries repeatedly about her
taking cold – 'I dreaded lest she catch some deadly chill from the night
air' (p. 91, and see also p. 72 and p. 92) – and reports on the sound and
depth of her breathing on several occasions, reassuring herself that it is soft
and regular at the start of Chapter 8 and then observing with alarm the
'striving to get her lungs full at every breath' after Lucy's midnight trip to the
graveyard (p. 91). These things all indicate that it is most likely consumption
which Mina fears for her friend. To be 'delicate' in the Victorian era was, I
suggest, to know oneself to be at risk from phthisis: the disease was known to
be opportunistic and to seize upon any weakening of constitution. Weight
loss was not only an early sign of phthisis, but could also invite it because an
undernourished body did not have the resources to fight off infection. In
addition, as I observed in the previous chapter, it commonly followed in the
wake of a cold, which could well explain Mina's anxiety about 'deadly chills'.
It is in this context interesting to speculate on the Westenras' reason for
coming to Whitby in the first place, for as a bracing seaside resort 'specially
suited for cases of functional debility, general anaemia ... scrofula [and]
phthisis' it may have been chosen to build up Lucy's health.[43] Also, as

Diane Mason notes in her recent Ph.D. thesis, Whitby is very close to Scarborough, which was '*the* recuperation place for consumptives' in the nineteenth century:[44] Anne Brontë, for example, spent her final days there. Hence Dracula may have chosen the North Yorkshire coast as his point of entry into England – an otherwise unusual choice, given its distance from London where he intends to make his home – because it was a likely place to find a delicate woman to prey on.

It is likely, then, that Lucy displays a tubercular diathesis before Dracula's visits begin. Could this be the reason she is chosen to become his victim? As soon as he arrives in England, Dracula seems to have specially sought out Lucy; he does not seem to attack other women in Whitby and he noticeably passes over the healthier Mina, even though she shares a room with Lucy.[45] (He feeds from Mina later in the novel as revenge on those who plot to destroy him, not because she is his first choice of victim: 'you are to be punished for what you have done. You have aided in thwarting me; now you will come to my call' (p. 288).) Certainly Lucy has 'certain traits which presumably attract Dracula from afar',[46] for, as indicated above, critics have supposed that it is her slightly unbalanced psychological state which makes her vulnerable prey for the vampire and that she may also unconsciously invite Dracula's attentions.[47] Her wish that 'a girl could marry three men, or as many as want her' (p. 59) has been read as a manifestation of the kind of deviant sexual appetites which appeal to the Count (appetites which he allows her to realise when his attacks necessitate sexually symbolic blood transfusions with four different men). It is certainly true that her tendency to sleepwalk allows Dracula to exert a power over her and entice her out to the graveyard where he first feeds from her. However, he does not seem to require her somnambulism after she returns to London, when he is repeatedly able to visit her at home, and he needs no similar tendencies in his prey when he places the practical and unhysterical Mina – and indeed, her 'business-like' husband – into a trance at Dr Seward's house. Both easily succumb to his power at this point, even the pious Mina admitting that 'strangely enough, I did not want to hinder him' (p. 287). This considered, is it really Lucy's mental traits which make her an attractive victim for Dracula, or is it possible that it is her physical state which is appealing to him instead? When we consider the likelihood that Stoker did identify consumption with vampirism in *Dracula* we can see that Lucy may well have an affinity with the Count before he arrives in England, for, as a delicate woman, she is an obvious target for his consumptive power. Within a consumptive paradigm, vampirism is, in effect, the logical ending to Lucy's story. It is as if Dracula can sense from afar the physical as well as mental weakness which renders her vulnerable to him. And, of course, she, like the Count, is 'tainted ... with that devil's illness' (p. 355).

More concrete evidence of this connection between consumption and vampirism is revealed when Dracula does begin to drain Lucy's blood, and Mina's fears become realised as previous delicacy is compounded into what closely resembles a consumptive decline :

Lucy seems to be growing weaker ... I do not understand Lucy's fading away as she is doing. She eats well and sleeps well, and enjoys the fresh air; but all the time the roses in her cheeks are fading, and she gets weaker and more languid day by day; *at night I hear her gasping as if for air* ... Last night I found her leaning out when I woke up, and when I tried to wake her I could not; she was in a faint. When I managed to restore her she was as weak as water, and cried silently between *long, painful struggles for breath* ... (p. 95, italics mine)

It is notable here that Stoker depicts painful and difficult breathing as the most concrete symptom of Lucy's wasting, rather than the dizziness and lightheadedness which are also classic accompaniments to blood loss, and that this troubles her most at night when she is in bed, or upon waking, the times when consumptives had the most difficulty with their breathing. This aspect of her illness is stressed again and again throughout the chapters that follow, as Lucy repeatedly 'complains of difficulty in breathing' (p. 111). Her description of her own symptoms is especially insightful: 'This morning I am horribly weak. My face is ghastly pale, and my throat pains me. *It must be something wrong with my lungs*, for I don't seem to ever get air enough' (p. 109, italics mine).

This speech makes apparent that consumption functions, in *Dracula* as in Du Maurier's *Trilby*, as the prosaic, real-life explanation offered by the novel for what is actually a supernatural disorder. Not having medical or occult knowledge, and kept ignorant by her doctors about the true cause of her wasting, Lucy assumes her illness is of the lungs. It is possible that the first Victorian readers of *Dracula* might have come to the same conclusion, for consumption does, after all, fit Lucy's early symptoms perfectly. Even the pain in her throat she describes above, and her inability to talk, which is later noted by Van Helsing – 'she did not speak, even when she wrote that which she wished to be known later' (p. 323) – are evocative of the symptoms of tuberculous laryngitis.[48] Later generations are too familiar with the legend of *Dracula* to fail to identify Lucy's wasting as the consequence of vampirism, but this could not have always been the case. It is likely that Stoker meant the supernatural cause of Lucy's condition to not be immediately obvious to the reader, and so invokes consumption as a possible alternative explanation because, having read the article in the *New York World*, he knew that the two had been confused with one another in real life in the past. At any rate, he is clearly influenced by the symptoms and appearance of phthisis when he comes to describe his vampire victims. Even the excellent physicians in *Dracula*, while acknowledging that Lucy's illness is 'obscure' (p. 111) and thus seemingly far removed from the common diseases of the day, give a description of her condition which tallies exactly with that of the dying consumptive: 'She was ghastly, chalkily pale; the red seemed to have gone even from her lips and gums, and the bones of her face stood out prominently; her breathing was painful to see or hear' (p. 120). It is notable that phthisis-like emaciation described here – 'the bones of her face stood out prominently' – is not actually consistent with blood loss, for the latter could not have affected Lucy's body fat in the short period of time which had elapsed. Stoker seems to here be deliberately invoking the appearance of phthisis as he describes the effects of vampirism. In addition, Lucy's pallid, shrunken gums, which her doctors note on several occasions (p. 153 and p. 159), are a typical symptom of consumption, as Dr Daniel Cullimore indicated in 1880: the phthisical patient's 'gums are pale and often exhibit a festooned appearance toward their dental margins'.[49] When we consider these kinds of symptomatic similarities it is not difficult to see why creating a parallel with the consumptive might be a useful way for a novelist like Stoker to frame his representation of the vampire's prey, just as the vampiric paradigm was an appealing answer to the phthisis problem for some communities in the nineteenth century. Both victims are ravaged by a mysterious force which consumes their blood, their strength, and ultimately their life: in one case this consuming process is external, in the other it is internal, but the effects are the same. By invoking an actual wasting illness which was common in the nineteenth century Stoker makes his supernatural decline all the more realistic and frightening for his Victorian readers.

This comparison between vampirism and phthisis is not a benign or sympathetic one, however, for, as represented in *Dracula*, it is a metaphor which reinforces the old stereotype that consumptives are in some way responsible for their own affliction. Lucy has been read as attracting and inviting Dracula's attention, and hence her eventual death at his hands, through her hysteric behaviour – somnambulism and nervous 'restlessness' – as well as through the transgressive, even pathological sexuality implied by her desire for polygamy. It is no accident that the more emotionally stable and sexually monogamous Mina is finally saved from Lucy's fate. Although she is still a victim to be fought for and pitied by the other characters, Lucy is also a co-conspirator with the Count, whom she is drawn to by the subconscious desires that manifest themselves in her sleep, and therefore she is complicit in her own decline. This has notable resonance within the consumptive plot as well, for those aspects of her personality which render her vulnerable to Dracula are also identified by nineteenth-century medicine as classic causes of consumption. Nervous or highly strung people like Lucy, 'who feels influences more acutely than other people do' (p. 87), were more likely to become consumptive: as Alabone observed, 'Depressing passions and violent emotions of the mind pre-dispose greatly to the production of this disease' (p. 24). Indeed, on the most basic level Lucy's behaviour does invite illness for, by sleepwalking in the middle of the night, clad in only her nightdress – unlike her more respectable father, also a somnambulist but one who always dressed himself after getting up – she recklessly, if unconsciously, exposes her body to the cold. She also risks her reputation by going out alone and scantily clad, and Mina fears for her respectability just as much as for her health (p. 92). Of course, with consumption the two are linked, for transgressive behaviour of any kind was medically believed to render its perpetrator more vulnerable to the disease, and sexual dissolution in particular was considered an invitation for consumption: 'This awful malady is too often the sad end of those who immolate their health and happiness at the accursed shrine of lewdness and unnatural sensuality.'[50] Certainly Lucy's seduction by Dracula constitutes the most 'unnatural' of sexual behaviours, and it does result in a 'an awful malady' and 'a sad end' for her. It is clear that consumption and vampirism are linked causally as well as symptomatically, and that in both conditions the victims are themselves held to blame for their affliction.

The vampiric/consumptive parallel has another, even more disturbing implication. Victorian literature does not only use consumptive imagery to depict the vampire's prey – a likely comparison given the similarities between the victims of both consuming conditions – but it frequently creates an actual affinity between the consumptive and the vampire himself. The Undead in nineteenth-century fiction are inevitably portrayed as cadaverous, pallid and anaemic-looking, classic phthisical traits which are in fact rather incongruous in creatures who subsist entirely on blood. We would expect the slowly drained victims to appear consumptively colourless and wasted but not those who feast on them.[51] Yet even the most well-fed literary vampires display a consumptive appearance, from the central character in James Malcolm Rymer's popular 1847 novel *Varney the Vampyre* – in which

Varney is 'bloodless' and 'utterly destitute of flesh'[52] – to Count Dracula himself. Dracula has 'firm though thin' cheeks and a 'general effect . . . of extraordinary pallor' (p. 18), which is not dissipated by his frequent feasting on Lucy and Mina: he appears temporarily younger-looking after his arrival in London when he is refreshed by plentiful blood, but not actually more healthy, remaining extremely 'thin' and 'waxen' (p. 282 and p. 287) until the end of the novel. Also displaying a consumptive diathesis is Lord Ruthven in John Polidori's *The Vampyre*, the novel which really conceived the modern literary vampire, and the fair, long-limbed and 'very pale' Count Vardalek, in Stanislaus Stenbock's *The Sad Story of a Vampire*.[53] The consumptive appearance of the undead is made even more explicit in Victorian fiction's portrayal of female vampires, for they appear to represent classic examples of the tubercular aesthetic, being defined as they inevitably are by a cadaverous beauty as pathological and fatal as it is irresistible. Good examples of this are the seductresses of Hume Nisbet's vampire stories, like the 'poster-like invalid' Ariadne in *The Vampire Maid*, who at first appears 'half a corpse', so 'lividly white' is she.[54] Similar in appearance is the mesmerising subject of *The Old Portrait*, a female vampire captured – in more ways than one – on canvas, a perfect representation of the pathological woman displayed as a work of art. She is defined by her 'passive pallidity' and 'transparent' body[55] – transparency being traditionally associated with the consumptive look[56] – and her eyes have the power to 'intoxicate' the narrator so that she may leave the painting and drain his life force. It is significant that unlike the male undead, who are permanently sickly in appearance, female vampires are physically transformed from consumptive invalids into sanguine femmes fatales after feeding on their prey. Lucy Westenra is newly 'voluptuous' and 'more radiantly beautiful than ever' when cornered in her tomb by Van Helsing (p. 200). Similarly Nisbet's Ariadne is restored to health and strength after a young man arrives at her home: even as soon as they touch hands her cheeks regain 'a slight glow of colour . . . which improved her so greatly that she appeared younger and almost beautiful'.[57] This process continues over the days that follow, as she is gradually revitalised by his blood: 'She grew stronger every day, while I appeared to be taking her place as the invalid.' The previously 'bloodless' appearance of *The Old Portrait*'s vampire is also transformed after her visit to the entranced narrator:

then consciousness returned and I looked round wildly . . .
    The picture and frame were still on the easel, only as I looked at them the portrait had changed, *a hectic flush was on the cheeks while the eyes glittered with life*

and the sensuous lips were red and ripe-looking with a drop of blood still upon the nether one.[58]

Nisbet's choice of diction here suggests that even in their freshly fed, newly sanguine state the vampire is evocative of the consumptive. As I discussed in the previous chapter, bright, 'glittering' eyes were known to be indicative of the feverishness which habitually accompanied the disease,[59] but a more concrete connection is created through the inclusion of the word 'hectic'. This was a term commonly used in both medical and popular literature to describe phthisis, which was sometimes also known as 'hectic fever'.[60] In fact Nisbet's vampire neatly encapsulates the two different faces of phthisis, for her changing appearance in this story encompasses both the flushed feverishness and the drained and deathly pallor which were both commonly experienced by the disease's sufferers. Periods of feverish excitement and stimulation were succeeded by intervals of pallor and lethargy, and the circadian nature of these changes creates a further parallel between the vampire and the consumptive. Unique to this disease were the daily spikes in the patient's low-grade fever, which was usually near normal during the day but rose in the evening. This caused fluctuations in the consumptive's physical and mental state, for they came to life at night when the increase in temperature stimulated their mind and increased their energy: as Dr Edward Blackmore observed, 'the excitement of the fever is highly pleasurable to some patients and seems to be connected with the singular exhilaration of the spirits'.[61] When the fever went down again in the morning, however, they would be left weak, listless and literally drained by their night sweats. Hence many consumptives lived a kind of nocturnal existence evocative of that of the vampire, able to socialise or work during the evening but frequently exhausted and bed-ridden during the day.

Even those vampires who do not physically resemble the consumptive diathesis may display the disease's symptoms. One of the most well-known vampires in Victorian fiction, Le Fanu's Carmilla, 'has nothing in her appearance to indicate an invalid'[62] – though she is, of course, 'slender' (p. 34) – but her extraordinary physical weakness and constant fatigue baffle the novel's narrator, Laura, who befriends her. After 'a mere saunter' of a walk Carmilla becomes 'almost immediately exhausted' and has to rest (p. 37). Indeed her most defining features are her listlessness and 'languor' – a word used by Le Fanu to describe her nine times in twelve pages (pp. 34–45) – occasionally interposed with intervals of feverish passion:

Sometimes, after an hour of apathy, my strange and beautiful companion would take my hand, and hold it with a fond pressure, renewed again and again, blushing softly, gazing in my face with languid and burning eyes, and breathing so fast that her dress rose and fell with the tumultuous respiration ... her hot lips travelled along my cheek in kisses ... Then she has thrown herself back in her chair, with her small hands over her eyes ... (p. 36)

This passage demonstrates the essential duality and changeability of the vampire's behaviour, 'apathy' transforming suddenly into 'tumultuous' emotion and back again in a way evocative of the fluctuating state of the consumptive. It also, however indicates the transgressive sexuality which the novel associates with vampirism. There is an erotically charged romantic friendship between Carmilla and her victim, Laura, who feels a mixture of 'love growing into adoration' and 'abhorrence' for her mysterious houseguest. This mixture of fascination and disgust is reminiscent of Dracula's hold over Lucy Westenra – Le Fanu's story was of course a source for *Dracula*[63] – and both Lucy and Laura are at once virginal victims and deviant lovers willing to be seduced. Laura's reluctant but irresistible homosexual love for Carmilla is her equivalent of Lucy's polyandrous desires for the male heroes in *Dracula*. Also like Lucy, she is initially susceptible to the vampire because she has had a 'nervous' disposition since her childhood (p. 20). In both novels, then, the combination of mental delicacy and unnatural appetites seem to invite the vampire's embrace, just as in medical literature they were believed to invite consumption. Soon Laura, too, enters a decline, as Carmilla's vampiric signifiers, 'lassitude and melancholy', are transferred to her. The link between vampirism and disease is further explored by mention in the novel of the superstitions of the village people, who, in an interesting echo of Bell's research, believe that the unexplained deaths of a number of young girls are caused by a vampire. Laura's educated father brushes aside these beliefs in favour of his more practical explanation that there has been an outbreak of disease: 'All this ... is strictly referable to natural causes. These poor people infect one another with their superstitions, and so repeat in imagination the images of terror that have infested their neighbours' (p. 41). This speech reveals the way in which the vampire myths arise out of real-life pathological origins, but of course this little piece of folkloric history is subverted when the peasants' superstitions are proved correct, and it is revealed that it really is the vampire who is preying on the local people.

An examination of all these Victorian vampire stories confirms that there is a literary identification between the consumptive and the vampire as well as between the consumptive and the vampire's prey. Of course this can be considered the logical conclusion of this whole paradigm, for in the same way that the initially innocent, when themselves drained of blood, in their turn will drink the blood of another, the consumptive is also at once victim and predator, afflicted with the disease, and simultaneously passing it on to others. As Marie Mulvey-Roberts has observed, 'the literary vampire provides us with the most comprehensive symbol of disease',[64] but she might have specified that it is contagious disease in particular that vampirism is the perfect metaphor for, as the Undead infects his victims with vampirism as he feeds from them. This is, of course, a deliberate act, and this is the most sinister aspect of the vampiric metaphor in relation to consumption, for it contains the inherent implication that contagion is not a passive process beyond the patient's control, but rather that they are responsible for the transmission of their illness to others. As I have mentioned, several critics have suggested that vampirism in *Dracula* is meant to function as a symbol of syphilis, and this certainly was a disease in which the carrier was blamed and socially vilified. I suggest, however, that given the preoccupation with consumption displayed in the novel, the vampire plot therein was actually a response to the new social anxiety about consumption which consolidated in the 1890s. By this period Koch's announcement about the infectiousness of the disease, which had initially been disputed and resisted, had entered into public consciousness, and there was a new need to protect oneself again the contaminating consumptive, whom 'fellow men have learnt to look upon . . . as lepers, and fear any sort of association with'.[65] This is indicated by the heated debates throughout the 1890s over what state control could be exerted over consumptives and whether tuberculosis should have been included in, or should be added to, the Infectious Diseases Notification Act of 1889, which held that those infected with certain diseases must be reported to the government. Sir Arthur Ransome, Chief Physician to the Manchester Hospital for Consumption and Diseases of the Chest, was among those who believed that urban authorities should have the power to 'periodically cleanse and disinfect the rooms inhabited by phthisical persons, and to segregate them from other people'.[66] Even those physicians who, like Alfred Hillier, felt that notification was inappropriate for long-term chronic illnesses like phthisis, still believed in the need to control and isolate the consumptive in order to prevent him being a danger to others:

And when it is borne in mind that in the sputum of the consumptive the chief danger to the public health exists, it will be readily recognised how vitally important the conduct of the consumptive patient is. One of the first duties of a medical man dealing with a consumptive today is to see that the patient is properly instructed in the measures rendered necessary to his own and the public health, by his condition.

... it will be tolerably clear from what has already been written, that consumptives of both sexes and all classes should recognise that they are called upon to entirely adapt their lives, for the sake of themselves, their families, and their neighbours ....

We [should] encourage the voluntary isolation of all consumptives in suitable sanatoria ...[67]

Hillier's writing reveals that society believed consumptives had control over the spread of their disease, and that they were thought to have a moral obligation to protect others from it. Their lives must be 'entirely adapt[ed]' in order to protect 'the public health'. Implicit here is the suggestion that if consumptives fail to follow medical advice and persist in their usual lifestyle – which presumably many of them did – they will knowingly and maliciously infect others. Other physicians go into more detail about the dangerously contaminating behaviour of patients who seem to have no desire to protect the healthy from their illness. C. Braine-Hartnell condemns the behaviour of 'the vast majority' of consumptives who 'spit anywhere and everywhere', thus exposing others to the dangers of their germ-ridden sputum.[68] Similarly Dr Henry Bowditch criticises husbands who are 'so miserably exacting or thoughtless as to demand that [their wife] should sleep with them throughout their illness', as their selfishness means it is likely that she will become infected.[69] (In an interesting link with vampirism, it seems to be during the night and while asleep that people are believed to be most at risk from phthisis: inexplicably, many doctors advise against relatives sleeping in the same room as a consumptive patient, even though they may be spending just as much potentially infectious time together during the day.)[70] Even more revealing is Arthur Ransome's view of the wilful spread of the disease:

we might, I think, fairly hope that in a few years there would be a considerable reduction of the phthisis death rate; but ... there will probably still remain a large number of persons, actually suffering from the disease, who will escape from the net of precautions that we have endeavoured to cast around them, and in their heedlessness and contempt of danger to themselves and others, they will continue to spread the seeds of disease.[71]

When not confined and controlled by the medical 'net of precautions' – itself a suggestive image which constructs the phthisical patient as a dangerous beast or monster – consumptives are clearly believed to be a danger to themselves and others.

All this we can see manifested in the consumptive imagery used to portray vampires in Victorian novels. Vampires are feared and despised because they are bringers of illness and death, but, as Mina reminds the men in *Dracula*, should also be pitied, for they suffer too: 'That poor soul who has wrought all this misery is the saddest case of all . . . You must be pitiful to him too, though it may not hold your hand from his destruction' (p. 308). In similar fashion, the plight of consumptives demands sympathy – Ransome goes on to express and advocate compassion for those afflicted – but they are nonetheless viewed with suspicion and revulsion because of their capacity 'to spread the seeds of disease'. That the tubercular female vampires of fiction are restored to health and strength after preying on their victims implies, or perhaps constructs, an additional anxiety regarding the motives of the consumptive, for implicit in the vampiric metaphor is the possibility that patients might attempt to get rid of their affliction by passing it on to others. This is of course an idea without medical validation or justification – no disease can simply be purged from one body when it is passed into another – but it is one which has understandable resonance in a society only beginning to understand how germs worked. Transference to other animals was in fact a traditional means of ridding oneself of phthisis: J. D. Rolleston describes a folk cure in which 'the patient is made to sleep with a dog or cat because these animals are supposed to attract the disease to themselves'.[72] (It should be noted that here, once again, sleep is required for the infection to take place: consumption never seems to be transmitted during the waking hours.)

Late Victorian medical writings reveal the extent of the fear and paranoia which was directed towards consumptives in the 1890s. However, as I discussed in Chapter 1, this changing public attitude was symptomatic of a more general national anxiety about masculinity, the health of the nation – especially the upper classes, in the aftermath of the Oscar Wilde scandal – and the preservation of the empire, as the *fin de siècle* approached. All this is very pertinent to *Dracula*, a novel which, as Geoff Wall has observed, is 'a persistently anxious text', preoccupied with the threat posed to the British Empire by racial decay and the possibility of invasion.[73] Elaine Showalter identifies syphilis as the primary pathological force which undermined the strength and productivity of British men,[74] but of course consumption was an equally valid, if less shameful, threat to national efficiency, as I have shown elsewhere. It is useful to recall here a popular tract which I discussed in Chapter 1 and which was published the same year as *Dracula*, Josiah Oldfield's *Flesh Eating: A Cause of Consumption*, which makes apparent that the kind of imperialist fears Stoker articulates were actually part of social discourse about consumption in this decade. Oldfield warns that consumption 'was eating its way to the heart of the nation' and that if it were allowed to continue, 'modern, civilised races' would lose 'the power of progress and even of cohesion, and have been overwhelmed by other races, barbarous indeed, but not *effete*'.[75] Stoker too represents the struggle for survival of a 'modern and civilised' country, threatened by attempted colonisation by the primitive and 'barbarous' but more reproductively successful Count. His representation of vampirism is a warning about the potential consequences of consumption: just as there can be no human offspring in *Dracula* until all the vampires have been killed, Britain will become barren or 'effete' if certain diseases which undermine masculinity and contaminate the bloodline are not stamped out.

It is apparent that the parallel which both folklore and fiction create between vampirism and phthisis has disturbing implications for those who are afflicted with the latter. The comparison reinforces and articulates already existing social perceptions about consumptives, suggesting that they are predatory, dangerous and sexually deviant, that they invite their illness just as the vampire's victims subconsciously invite his embrace, and that they are responsible for the spread of their disease. It also suggests equally damaging new ideas which are implicit in such a metaphor, namely that the transmission to others is not through carelessness or selfishness – as the medical literature suggests – but rather through a deliberate, even evil desire to pass on the 'devil's taint', to consume others as they are themselves consumed, and to, perhaps, grow stronger and more powerful in the process. Of course this may not just function on a literal, physical level: the vampiric metaphor is particularly apt when applied to the psychological power consumptive invalids exert over their friends and family, an aspect of the disease I have discussed with regard to Mrs Ward's *Eleanor*. The consumptive can be considered vampiric on many levels, and Salli J. Kline has summarised the effects of this kind of vampiric symbolism in her book *The Degeneration of Women*:

> When a human being is metaphorically equated with a vampire the receiver of the symbol automatically actualises all the possible connotations, associates them with the person in question, and experiences a horrific loathing of that individual, as if he or she were an actual vampire ... the figurative vampire is a hyperbolic metaphor, and ... such metaphors clearly suggest a radical intolerant attitude on the part of those who employ them.[76]

Given the sinister possibilities attached to this literary identification between phthisis and vampirism, it is disturbing to consider that it is not only in Victorian novels that this symbolic 'vamping' of the consumptive occurs. The crossover between the fictional and the wider social view of the disease is so extensive that we can see the same images and comparisons in medical writing on phthisis as well. Indeed the idea of the consumptive as a vampiric figure may have been first represented by a physician, for one of the most famous early works on consumption, Thomas Beddoes's 1799 *Essay on the Causes, Early Signs of, and Prevention of Pulmonary Consumption*, pre-dates the conception of the Victorian literary vampire, and yet, as Michael Bell has also noted, contains a classic and often quoted characterisation of the consumptive which is strongly reminiscent of what would become the traditional portrait of the vampire:

The emaciated figure strikes one with terror; the forehead covered with drops of sweat; the cheeks painted with a livid crimson, the eyes sunk; the little fat that raised them in their orbits entirely wasted; the pulse quick and tremulous; the nails long, bending over the ends of the fingers . . . the breath offensive, quick and labourous . . .[77]

This may have been the image which gave birth to the phthisical vampire, and certainly the vampiric traits depicted here can be found in Victorian novels of the Undead. Indeed, interesting symptomatic similarities between the literary vampire and the consumptive can be found in a large number of medical texts throughout the century, and frequently can be considered the source for the phthisical nature of the Undead in fiction. For example, Dr R. J. Culverwell notes that oddly shaped hands and long curved fingernails are a typical accompaniment to this disease: 'A particular state of the nails has been described as appertaining to Phthisis Pulmonalis. The nails are curved, the extremity of the last phalanx appears swollen and the fingers become more or less deformed', he wrote in 1883.[78] Count Dracula, of course, possesses just such 'deformed' hands: his are noticeably unattractive, 'coarse and squat', with long pointed fingernails (p. 18). Similarly, Beddoes's mention of the 'offensive' breath of the consumptive is echoed by Dr James Weaver's observation in 1887 that 'there is always a particularly objectionable odour about such a patient',[79] and both invoke the unpleasant smell of the Undead, the 'bitter offensiveness' which Jonathan Harker notices in the breath of the female vampire (p. 38) and the 'deathly, sickly odour' he finds in Dracula's lair (p. 47). Both vampire and consumptive smell of, and are associated with, blood and death, the former because his very existence is a product of both, the latter because his lungs are decaying and rotting away inside him, and he is, in this sense, a living Undead.

Another symptomatic similarity revealed by Victorian medical literature is the pathological appetite displayed by both consumptives and vampires.

The 'total loss of appetite'[80] which most phthisical patients experienced was a troublesome aspect of the disease and one which was frequently a subject of medical discussion, but a number of Victorian physicians express their views on this matter in somewhat suggestive language. The consumptive's appetite is 'indifferent or unnatural', notes Dr Thomas Gurney;[81] Robert James Culverwell adds that while the 'appetite begins to fail and there is distaste for food', 'the thirst is almost always intense'.[82] 'Unnatural' appetites and 'intense thirst' are terms that have been used to describe the feeding behaviour of vampires, and so lend somewhat sinister overtones to these supposedly clinical descriptions of the consumptive.

If we can accept that Victorian medical literature seems to draw upon the features of vampirism in its construction of a portrait of consumption, it is perhaps not surprising that some physicians advocated a treatment for the disease which was not very far removed from that which restores the vampire to health and strength – a diet of fresh blood. *The Lancet* mentions in 1865 a 'French remedy', the results of which 'are stated to be marvellous', in which a Dr Montargis 'is accustomed to send his phthisical patients to the Parisian abattoirs to drink the fresh blood as it flows from the slaughtered cattle . . .'.[83] This is animal rather than human blood, admittedly, but is still drunk fresh from the vein. We can understand the appeal of blood in general as a cure for phthisis, given the anaemia which accompanied the disease, but it is more difficult to comprehend why it is recommended that blood should be drunk straight from the animal in such a vampiric fashion. Other physicians do not encourage their patients to go to quite such gruesome lengths to regain health, but still believe in the healing and restoring power of very fresh blood. For example, de Lacy Evans argues that 'many people have been greatly benefited by drinking the warm blood of animals', and stresses that 'the blood must be freshly drawn to be of any service'.[84] Raw meat, too, is useful, and again 'the flesh from newly-killed animals is the best'. This emphasis on the need for still living or at least still warm blood is a suggestive one, for physicians do not seem to offer a factual explanation why 'older' blood should be less beneficial. Indeed the treatment seems to really be about capturing and benefiting from the life force of the dying animal rather than having any more concrete haematic reason, as De Lacy's explanation indicates: 'There is no doubt that newly-drawn blood is invigorating, sometimes exciting, and that from it many people have experienced a great increase in power.'[85] Again there seems to be a hint of a vampiric subtext here, for 'exciting' implies an unusually strong enjoyment of, or response to, the consumption of blood. The use of the word 'power' instead of 'health' or 'strength' is also not something we would expect to see in this context, and it creates an association with the vampire who does indeed experience 'a great increase in power' by drinking from his prey. It is notable that there is is a shocking real-life case in which this blood cure turns a consumptive into an actual vampire: the famous 'Garder Crime', which took place in France at the turn of the century, involved a consumptive who stabbed an eight-year-old boy in the throat and drank his blood while he was dying, in the hope his young vitality might cure the disease.[86] In this instance the vampiric metaphor associated with consumption actually becomes reality, a process facilitated by the medical profession's construction of phthisis as a vampiric disease.

Medical literature seems to create a picture of a consumptive who in ways resembles a vampire; fictional writing portrays a vampire evocative of the consumptive. This seems to be a symbiotic process, for just as the fiction of the period was clearly influenced and informed by medical discourse, the writing of physicians was shaped by the consumptive myths and images portrayed in novels. Such an identification speaks volumes not only about society's perception of the consumptive, but also about the medical view of the disease itself. Through the use of the vampiric metaphor phthisis becomes more than just a disease: it is transformed into a monster preying on humanity. This is of course an especially poignant image for those physicians who were constantly battling with it for their patients' lives, as displayed by Dr S. Warren, who uses powerful vampiric imagery to describe the ravages of tuberculosis:

By what infernal subtlety hast thou contrived hither to baffle the profoundest skill of science, to frustrate utterly the uses of experience, and disclose thyself only when thou hast irretrievably secured thy victim and when thy fangs are crimsoned with its blood?[87]

The only weapons in the doctor's arsenal – 'science' and 'experience' – seem to be useless in the fight against consumption, which remains invisible until it has secured its victim. Warren's diction is significant: 'infernal subtlety' suggests something satanic, but also devious and hidden, and this neatly encapsulates one of the most important aspects of this disease. The silent, gradual and seemingly reason-less decline consumption induces is suggestive of the manifestations of a force which is unknown, secretive and evil – even occult – in nature. Whether in fact or fiction, or myth or medical writing, and even after its cause was identified by Koch, consumption always seems to have a strange, supernatural quality. This was a feature which endured throughout the nineteenth century and was noted not only by laymen but by more pragmatic men of science. Dale, for example, may or may not know of the folkloric belief that held that consumption was actually vampirism, but he certainly is aware that phthisis has a mysterious, even paranormal, quality, for in his analysis it becomes more demon than disease:

There is something unearthly or 'uncanny' about the struggle between soul and body, so gradual, quiet and solemn, that day by day and grain by grain the mortal part wastes and withers away, and standing by, you feel almost helpless in the presence of so insidious and so destructive a foe . . .

It has swept off whole families as if by a swift and pestilent plague, and youth and beauty and worth have passed away, as if touched by some sudden lethal witchcraft.[88]

Dale views phthisis as a 'struggle' between spirituality and physicality, or mind and body. This analysis suggests why in the vampiric paradigm the disease gains a moral dimension, and why its representation in fiction takes the form of a battle between good and evil. This is especially true because of the particular nature of phthisis, which may well appear to be evil in its destructive power: it seems most often to afflict 'youth and beauty', as though out of a vampiric desire to claim as its own the youngest and most desirable members of the population. It is because it resembles 'lethal witchcraft' in this way that tuberculosis forms an important and useful addition to novels of the uncanny, like *Trilby, Carmilla* and *Dracula*, which are concerned with bridging the gap between the world of pathological realism and the supernatural world of monsters and nightmares. Being half disease, half demon, consumption, it seems, has equal resonance in both.

CHAPTER 6

'A kind of intellectual advantage': consumption and masculine identity in Henry James's The Portrait of a Lady

I have previously argued that consumption was generally perceived to be a 'female disease' and that the consumptive in nineteenth-century literature and art was usually represented as a woman. As I indicated in Chapter 1, the disease afflicted men and women equally, but this statistical reality seemed to be discounted by the medical profession and popular culture alike. This had not been the case in previous eras, however: Lawlor has written about important male consumptives in eighteenth-century novels by Sterne, Smollett and Henry Mackenzie (though he also notes the inevitable emasculating effects of this illness in each case) and of physicians like Cheyne who do not gender the disease.[1] As a result of changing notions of masculinity and a movement away from heroes of sensibility, though, male fictional consumptives are by the Victorian period few and far between. Paul Dombey is not a man but a child, and an angelic and somewhat feminised one at that. Rather less angelic but notably effeminate and also a child, is Linton Heathcliff in *Wuthering Heights*. One of the few adult consumptives, the hero of Mary Ward's *Robert Elsmere*, only dies of the disease: he does not live with it for more than a few pages of this long novel, and Ward, in contrast to her purposes in *Eleanor*, is clearly not concerned with exploring his illness in much detail. In this novel consumption appears to function simply as a good death for a man who has been consumed by altruism and has spent his energy and health working and caring for others. We might note, however, that Elsmere describes himself as 'a man no longer' when he becomes ill.[2] This association between phthisis and compromised masculinity, and indeed between pthisis and self-sacrifice – itself a conventionally feminine attribute – link Ward's hero to the subject of this chapter, Ralph Touchett in Henry James's *The Portrait of a Lady*. Ralph is an important figure, as a rare literary example of the adult phthisical male whose decline is central to the narrative. As a novel by an American *Portrait* does differ from the other texts in this study, but seems to demand inclusion because it is not only set in England and Italy, but was written there also. By 1881 Britain had been James's home for more than six years and was to remain so until he died, having recently adopted British citizenship, in 1915.

At first glance James's treatment of the disease in *Portrait* seems to differ greatly from the representation of female consumptives in other novels. Unlike tubercular heroines such as Trilby or Eleanor, Ralph is not beautified, or glamorised by his disease, as his first appearance in the novel, walking in the grounds of Gardencourt, makes very clear. We are told that he looks 'ugly' and 'sickly', though also 'charming' – for the first chapter of *Portrait* he is in fact called 'the ugly young man' – and that he is 'loosely and feebly put together',[3] all in all forming a type of masculinity which is contrasted unfavourably with his friend, the handsome and apparently virile Lord Warburton. He would appear an unlikely fictional hero, but Ralph does, however, have the strong mind and pure spirit which are traditionally associated with, and are considered to be the compensation for, the feeble consumptive body. He is the most 'generous' and perceptive character in the novel, and possesses a 'wonder of wisdom' which makes him justifiably its most important male figure (p. 466).

I have identified that consumption in literature frequently functions as an expression of the pathological nature of Victorian society. In the Condition of England novel phthisis is used as a metaphor for industrial capitalism; in Du Maurier's *Trilby* it becomes a signifier of the destructive power of sexual desire. In *Portrait* this social element is continued, but James is not only concerned with the sickness of a community: it is, rather, the whole male gender which seems to be floundering in the world represented here. The novel represents modern masculinity as intrinsically weakened, feminised and diseased, and hence it is appropriate that its central male character is afflicted with consumption, generally perceived to be a female illness and one which undermines both the vitality and virility of its male sufferers. Ralph's physical illness therefore acts as a symbol of the emotional and spiritual sickness of the men around him.

That a kind of crisis of masculinity exists in the novel is made plain by its opening chapter which, before the portrait of Isabel unfolds, sets before the reader a portrait of three men. Two are invalids, and all three are having afternoon tea on the lawn, even though 'they are not of the sex which is supposed to furnish the regular votaries of the ceremony' (p. 19). Robert K. Martin has suggested that this opening scene is indicative of 'an unregulated, or deviant, system of gender relations'[4] and certainly it is an incongruous picture of masculinity indulging in a domestic, feminine ritual. Women are not merely absent from this picture, but have been replaced within it

and their traditional household roles have been transferred to men. Ralph
pours the tea, old Mr Touchett enjoys it, and all three engage in idle chat.
Conventional gender relations are further undermined by Ralph's adoption
of the role of 'sick-nurse' (p. 24), as he fusses over the comfort and wellbeing
of his elderly father. The cigarettes he and Lord Warburton smoke are the
only small assertion of masculinity in this scene. Given this setting, it
is unsurprising that the ensuing conversation establishes that there is a
fundamental problem with the affluent classes of Victorian manhood, a
problem voiced by old Mr Touchett:

> 'I'm never bored when I come here,' said Lord Warburton. 'One gets such
> uncommonly good talk.'
> 'Is that another sort of joke?' asked the old man. 'You've no excuse for being
> bored anywhere. When I was your age I had never heard of such a thing.'
> 'You must have developed very late.'
> 'No, I developed very quick; that was just the reason. When I was twenty
> years old I was very highly developed indeed. I was working tooth and nail.
> You wouldn't be bored if you had something to do, but you young men are
> too idle. You think too much of your pleasure. You're too fastidious, and too
> indolent, and too rich.' (p. 25)

This exchange indicates that wealth, self-indulgence and luxury (of which
the tea drinking may be a symbol, and see Chapter 2) are responsible for
the condition of the male characters in *Portrait*: their inherited riches do
away with the need for a work ethic, resulting in idleness, boredom and
even hedonism – 'You think too much of your pleasure . . .' – and finally
in effeminacy. In William Veeder's words, James's society 'equates business
with life, it is defining "presence" in a way appropriate to bourgeois patriarchy . . . a male who is not in business is feminine in gender because he
is signed by, is singled out for, nonexistence'.[5] Mr Touchett's above condemnation of modern masculinity is of course a representation of the late
Victorian anxiety about the damaging, feminising social effects of affluence and decadence – it could equally well describe a character from Oscar
Wilde – and it is this anxiety that James expresses through the pathologised
figure of Ralph.[6] As I have discussed, it is one of the many paradoxes around
consumption that luxury as well as deprivation was believed to be a cause of
the disease; that, as Burton-Fanning suggested, 'there are two kinds of consumption, that of the rich and that of the poor'.[7] Ralph's illness is clearly the
former, and in fact it is significant that he first becomes ill during the brief
period when he works at his father's bank, a point which both indicates his
fundamental unsuitability for the working world and reinforces the association that I have suggested existed between phthisis and capitalism. It is

notable, however, that Ralph's withdrawal from work is forced upon him by his disease, and so it is consumption which brings about his indolent lifestyle, and which simultaneously gives that life a sense of purpose, as Madame Merle points out in a very important and revealing passage:

Look at poor Ralph Touchett: what sort of a figure do you call that? Fortunately he has a consumption; I say fortunately, because it gives him something to do. His consumption's his *carrière*, it's a kind of position. You can say 'Oh, Mr Touchett, he takes care of his lungs, he knows a great deal about climates.' But without that who would he be, what would he represent? . . . 'He's very cultivated,' they say: 'he has a very pretty collection of old snuff-boxes.' The collection is all that's wanted to make it pitiful. I'm tired of the sound of the word; I think it's grotesque . . . . But I persist in thinking your cousin very lucky to have a chronic malady so long as he doesn't die of it. It's much better than the snuff boxes. If he weren't ill, you say, he'd do something? – he'd take his father's place in the house. My poor child, I doubt it; I don't think he's at all fond of the house. (p. 218)

This passage represents a reversal of the conventional way of thinking about phthisis as the force which consumes and destroys masculinity, activity and productiveness (although that representation is also at work within the text). Here, however, consumption is represented by Madame Merle as constructive rather than destructive, as a solution to the problems of modern masculinity. In this society idleness and displacement are so pathological in themselves that consumption is a kind of cure, and so Ralph is 'lucky to have a chronic malady' because it gives him an identity and a form of career. To be a man devoid of those things is, socially speaking, much worse than to be physically ill. Consumption is not only a '*carrière*', however; it is a refuge from responsibility – in Ralph's case it provides an escape from his unwanted place in his father's firm – and this is an important point which I will return to.

For the wealthy and indolent, the alternative to having a consumption, Madame Merle suggests, is having a collection. This is, however, a 'grotesque' hobby which is equated to phthisis in the above passage as it is throughout the novel. Gilbert Osmond and Ned Rosier are both symbolically linked with Ralph's disease, both being afflicted by a different kind of 'consumption': they are obsessed with the acquisition of possessions, and devote their lives to expanding and then displaying their collections of furniture, porcelain and art. This conspicuous consumption of 'treasure' is the defining feature of both men, for Rosier's bibelots are 'the best thing about him' (p. 562) and Osmond has 'nothing in the least solid to offer . . . but a dozen or two of early masters and a more or less pert little daughter' (p. 301). Just as Ralph's illness has become his vocation, in the absence of a 'real' profession collecting has become the sole occupation of Osmond and Rosier. This is, of course, as destructive to the outside world as consumption is to the internal body, and indeed, in Madame Merle's ironic terms, illness is actually a preferable lifestyle – 'it's much better than the snuff-boxes' (p. 218). That James considers this kind of consumerism just as damaging and pathological as Ralph's disease is indicated by the way it inevitably spreads to things other than inanimate objects. The novel reveals how, in this world of acquisitions, women are consumed just as art is: they are thought of only as prizes to be bargained for, acquired and displayed. Through this process of commodification, women even *become* art, and so heterosexual love itself is rendered emotionally sterile. Rosier is genuinely in love with Pansy, but his adoration is limited and flawed because it is clearly that of a collector for the ultimate ornament:

> He had made to a certain extent good use of his time; he had devoted it in vain to finding a flaw in Pansy Osmond's composition. She was admirably finished; she had had the last touch; she was really a consummate piece. He thought of her in amorous meditation a good deal as he might have thought of a Dresden shepherdess. Miss Osmond, indeed, in the bloom of her juvenility, had a hint of the rococo which Rosier, whose taste was predominately for that manner, could not fail to appreciate. (p. 386)

Pansy is of course 'a consummate piece' because Osmond has brought her up to be so. Like Rosier, Osmond treats his daughter as a valuable possession, on a par with his 'old masters', as Mrs Touchett's comment, quoted above, indicates, but one whom he is willing to part with for 'a high price'. This proprietorial attitude has eroded and replaced any healthy and loving father/daughter relationship, and so destroys Pansy's happiness when her wishes get in the way of another of Osmond's acquisitions – that of an aristocratic husband for her. The novel creates a sense of the damaging consequences of consumerism taken to extremes. This is also displayed by Osmond's treatment of Isabel, the 'young lady who had qualified herself to figure in his collection of choice objects'. His behaviour towards her is almost literally consumptive in a disturbing fashion:

> His egotism had never taken the crude form of desiring a dull wife; this lady's intelligence was to be a silver plate, not an earthen one – a plate that he might heap up with ripe fruits, to which it would give a decorative value, so that talk might become for him a sort of served dessert. (p. 378)

The metaphor here indicates that, to Osmond, Isabel's mind and personality are something to devour, even to ingest. He is thus the true 'consumptive' in the book and the most pathological of all *Portrait*'s men. Isabel herself comes finally to realise that he is 'malignant' (p. 456) and associates him with death: with an echo of vampirism, being married to him is described as 'being shut up with an odour of mould and decay' (p. 463). But then, as we shall see, all the men in the novel are associated with death in one way or another.

It is becoming apparent that there is no example of a healthy, active, successful male in *Portrait*, but the closest James seems to come to creating such a figure is Lord Warburton. William Veeder argues that it is the dislocation of the expatriate male community that James is concerned with exploring in this text,[8] and it is true that Madame Merle's analysis of the position of men, quoted above, refers to those Americans who don't 'live in their own land' and are 'trying to arrange themselves' in Europe (p. 217 and p. 218). However, the representation of Lord Warburton reveals that the crisis of masculinity in the novel is not restricted by nationality, for he is Englishness epitomised, and has a definite home and an important and defined identity as an English peer. He is also, of course, the physical opposite of the delicate and effeminate Americans in the text: 'remarkably well made', with a 'fortunate, brilliant, exceptional look' (pp. 21–2). His physical supremacy does not, however, preserve him from the same kind of emotional and social sickness which afflicts the other male characters, a point Veeder notes but does not elaborate on.[9] Indeed the text establishes a clear parallel between Warburton's spiritual condition and Ralph's physical one, suggesting that his boredom and dissatisfaction is like an illness – he is 'sick of life' – and one which is, like Ralph's, a disease of wealth. Again this is implicit right from the opening pages of the novel:

> 'He's a very good nurse – for a sick-nurse. I call him my sick nurse because he's sick himself.'
> 'Oh, come, daddy!' the ugly young man exclaimed . . .
> 'Were you ever sick, Lord Warburton?' his father asked.
> Lord Warburton considered a moment. 'Yes sir, once, in the Persian gulf.'
> 'He's making light of you, daddy,' said the other young man. 'That's a sort of joke.'
> 'Well there seem to be so many sorts now,' daddy replied, serenely. 'You don't look as if you had been sick, any way, Lord Warburton.'
> 'He's sick of life, he was just telling me so; going on fearfully about it,' said Lord Warburton's friend. (p. 24)

This is the first of many references and enquiries about Lord Warburton's health that occur in the text, references which are incongruous considering his clearly apparent vitality of body. For example, when speaking of Warburton to Isabel, Ralph describes his friend as being 'in a bad way', a comment which would be more appropriate to his own condition, and which prompts Isabel to enquire 'I suppose you don't mean in health?' (p. 89). Later in the novel Isabel's contemplation of his feelings for her significantly uses a metaphor of disease: 'It was the resignation of a healthy, manly nature, in which sentimental wounds could never fester. British politics had cured him; she had known they would' (p. 414). Moreover, Warburton undergoes a kind of symbolic death at the same time as Ralph undergoes a literal one, as indicated by Isabel's reaction to the news of his engagement when she returns home to Ralph's deathbed: 'Isabel felt as if she had heard of Lord Warburton's death. She had known him only as a suitor, and now that was all over. He was dead for poor Pansy; by Pansy he might have lived' (p. 608). Through his failure to win Pansy or Isabel Warburton is negated into unimportance, even nothingness, and in his final appearance in the novel, appropriately enough at Ralph's funeral, he has become a corpse-like non-entity who is 'strangely inexpressive' in appearance, and whom Isabel 'felt sorry for' (p. 621). Warburton is as lost and dislocated as any expatriate, but his displacement is caused not by geography but by the changing politics of the English class system: as a 'radical of the upper class' he does not know whether to 'abolish himself as a nuisance or maintain himself as an institution' (p. 90). The way in which this problematic and unstable position undermines his virility is displayed through his sexual failures. He is rejected and pitied first by Isabel, who thinks of him only as 'poor Lord Warburton', and then by Pansy Osmond, who is herself 'limited' yet still does not want him. Indeed his pursuit of the latter reveals that English politics have *not* 'cured him' after all, for his feelings for Pansy are a perverted and misplaced form of love: he wishes to marry her mainly to be close to Isabel, her stepmother. Hence he remains emotionally 'sick' to the end of the novel. His final engagement to 'Lady Flora, or Lady Felicity, or something of that sort' is not something we can consider likely to be a success, or even really believe in, as Isabel herself does not: ' "Are you very sure he is to be married?" Isabel asked . . .' (p. 621).

Sexual failure afflicts all the men in the novel. 'Little' Ned Rosier is not allowed to marry Pansy; Caspar Goodwood cannot win Isabel despite repeated attempts before and after her marriage. Gilbert Osmond does marry her but their relationship proves to be passionless, 'as dry as a burned-out fire' (p. 465). Furthermore, the only offspring of their union dies at a young age. That this was inevitable and that there will never be another child is implied by Ralph when he condemns Gilbert as a 'sterile dilettante' (p. 373), a term which encapsulates both his personality and his reproductive shortcomings. This sterility extends to the other male characters as well, however, for apart from Pansy, born many years before the novel opens, there are no children in the text, even though the Touchett and Warburton families seem to be in need of heirs. Such infecundity is of course inseparable from the economic unproductivity that I have suggested defines all *Portrait*'s men: because of indolence and luxury they become effeminate, and as effeminate beings they are barren. Through the figure of Ralph, however, James turns reproductive failure into eugenic discourse, for Ralph makes a conscious and altruistic choice not to have children because of his disease. And as that disease is symbolic of the failings of a whole society, a question is raised as to the advisability of that society perpetuating itself.

Ralph tells his father that one of his few, but 'strongly' held, 'convictions' is that 'people in an advanced stage of pulmonary disorder had better not marry' (p. 203). This is a view which clearly arises out of a belief in the hereditary nature of phthisis, and an anxiety about the passage of the disease to children from consumptive parents. Ralph's refusal to contemplate marriage is in fact a form of social Darwinism: a means of protecting society from the consequences of his consumption. That he is concerned with the breeding of healthy offspring is revealed by his other 'conviction', which is 'that people, on the whole, had better not marry their cousins' (p. 203). This is a statement which indicates an awareness of, and anxiety about, the potentially pathological consequences of inter-breeding. His father's response that there is nothing incestuous about 'a cousin that you had never seen for more than twenty years of her life' (p. 203) is clearly missing the biological point. Adherence to eugenic principles is one means of promoting the health of society and on this topic the novel reflects what Fred Kaplan identifies as an important preoccupation in the James family. Marriage without health was regarded by the Jameses as nothing less than a 'civic crime': Henry's brother William had urged their other brother Bob to abandon an engagement to a sick cousin because 'it is a true crime against humanity for anyone to run the probable risk of generating unhealthy offspring'.[10] A completely contrasting and more traditional cure for social ills is offered by old Mr Touchett, who suggests that marriage in general is the panacea both for Ralph's consumption and for the social sickness it represents. This is because he believes a healthy life for men is one that adheres to traditional, bourgeois principles, hence it must embrace the work ethic, heterosexual love and domesticity:

The best thing you can do, when I'm gone, will be to marry . . . You're a great deal better than you used to be. All you want is to lead a natural life. It is a great deal more natural to marry a pretty young lady that you're in love with than it is to remain single on false principles. (pp. 202–3)

This clearly suggests that as 'natural life' brings health, Ralph's pathological existence must be unnatural in some way. This may be a veiled comment about Ralph's possible homosexuality, for, as Robert K. Martin suggests, he was 'of the character and physical type that constituted the male homosexual as he was constructed in the years surrounding this novel'.[11] In fact it is possible to read much of the eroded masculinity in *Portrait* as a manifestation of, or consequence of, deviance from the heterosexual norm. It is at any rate significant that Mr Touchett's attitude towards Ralph's disease matches that held by the Victorian medical profession. As I have discussed in previous chapters, sexual misbehaviour was thought to be a possible cause of consumption, and certainly was damaging to the health of those already consumptive. Marriage was the best protection from sexual immorality of any kind, and hence Mr Touchett's conception of marriage as the most 'natural' cure for Ralph's consumption was an idea shared by contemporary physicians, even though the latter often disguise their more political agenda behind a litany of practical benefits for the patient. As Dr W. Roemisch indicates in *How to Guard Against a Return of Phthisis*, 'as a rule, marriage is favourable to the health of a husband previously consumptive. The domestic life, the better care, the avoidance of restaurants and clubs are great advantages, provided that the wife is sensible.'[12] Rohden echoed this view in 1875 with the observation that the consumptive's wife 'is his insurpassable nurse, imperceptibly infusing mental benefits with the loving offices of her hands' (p. 540). Rohden here suggests that even if marriage cannot cure the consumptive, the wife is the most proper and fitting person to nurse him, and that there are mental and presumably spiritual benefits to be gained from this relationship.

The Portrait of a Lady is deeply interested in these kinds of questions: the novel has a subplot devoted to debating Ralph's treatments, his best chance for recovery, and – inseparable from both – the question of who is responsible for his health. Regarding this James seems to reiterate the prevalent medical view by suggesting that Ralph's lonely and nomadic invalid existence would indeed benefit from domesticity and especially from some feminine care. At intervals during the novel it becomes apparent that he is unable or unwilling to look after himself properly. Isabel has to remind him to rest – 'You're very tired; you must go home and go to bed' (p. 172) – and, even more importantly for the consumptive patient, to eat – 'Shall you not come up for breakfast? . . . You ought to eat, you live on air' (p. 375). Of course being nursed by a woman has notable advantages for Ralph: as Miriam Bailin notes, for the Victorian male being 'under the care of a woman permits imaginative, if not actual, access to traits that were associated with femininity and allowed a retreat from those associated with manliness'.[13] Certainly much of Ralph's charm and moral worth stems from his deliberate embracing of 'feminine traits', as I will discuss. However all this reveals that Madame Merle is not actually correct when she identifies Ralph's consumption as a useful '*carrière*'. She says phthisis has shaped him into a man 'who takes care of his lungs and knows a great deal about climates' (p. 218), but in fact Ralph does not succeed even in the loose approximation of a career that is the life of a professional invalid. Indeed he fails to satisfy either of Madame Merle's definitions. He is careless enough about his lungs to prompt the concern of Isabel, Lord Warburton, and finally Henrietta Stackpole, who becomes his nurse on his last journey home. In addition, we are told that just before the novel opens his condition has been irrevocably worsened because of an error in his judgement 'about climates', as he had 'remained later than usual in England and had been overtaken by bad weather before reaching Algiers. He arrived more dead than alive . . .' (p. 57).

This all suggests that Ralph is not really any more successful at being an invalid than at being a banker. It is unsurprising, however, that he should be ambivalent about a life spent in the pursuit of health when this is the antithesis of the kind of productive masculine career his father has advocated. Ralph's awareness of the measures he must take to preserve his life seems to be undermined by the innate belief that care of one's health is a much more appropriate occupation for a woman than for a man. It is significant that the points in the novel at which he is entirely responsible for his own wellbeing, and cut off from the concern and care of Isabel and others, are those periods when his illness noticeably worsens. This is most apparent on his arrival back from a winter spent alone in Corfu, a place whose climate is intended to restore him, but from which he returns no longer merely ill but actually 'distressfully dying'.

This forms an interesting comment not only about Ralph's inability to care for himself, but also on the travelling-for-health lifestyle which was commonly adopted by well-to-do consumptives in the nineteenth century, and of which James was himself an observer when travelling in Europe. *Portrait* displays an interest in Ralph's pathological pilgrimages: his movements, destinations and even travel arrangements are frequently mentioned by the novel and discussed by the other characters. The novel interacts with the question of whether the search for health abroad is actually worthwhile: Ralph's situation seems to imply that it is not. This was a much-debated medical topic throughout the century, with some physicians advocating foreign travel as the best hope of a cure, and others more sceptical about whether there were actual physical benefits to be had from a warm climate, or even if there were, whether they were enough to outweigh the disadvantages – both physical and emotional – of being so cut off from the healing environment of the home. Dr John Parkin, for example, raised these questions in 1875, just five years before *Portrait* was written:

> Of what benefit, we may ask, can it be for a patient to leave his native shores, the comforts of home and the solace of friends, in the hope of avoiding those causes of disease that thus appear to be in operation everywhere?[14]

This is really another variation on the creed of 'domesticity as cure' advocated by Mr Touchett: the patient is better off amid 'the comforts of home' and with the 'solace of friends' – and presumably of his wife – than he would be as a nomadic traveller. It is interesting, however, that the Corfu episode can be read as a demonstration of the validity of this advice, for Ralph's rejection of the 'natural life' of marriage and home in favour of the pursuit of health in the warm counties of Europe has disastrous consequences for his health. Mr Touchett suggests that married life might save Ralph; it is at least true that the bachelor life destroys him.

Ralph's self-imposed exile from the 'comforts' and 'solace' of his friends is damaging not only to his health, however. It has far-reaching consequences within the novel because it is during his absence that Isabel decides to marry Gilbert Osmond. Ralph returns too late to prevent their engagement, and he is the only person who might have succeeded in reasoning with Isabel, as Mrs Touchett indicates (p. 362). This suggests that consumption is responsible for the central tragedy of the novel, for if it were not for Ralph's disease Isabel's fall could have been averted. Phthisis is after all also the reason Isabel obtains the fortune which attracts Osmond: Ralph gives half of his inheritance to her because his disease prevents him from enjoying it himself. He tells his father that 'it is impossible for a man in my state of health to spend much money, and enough is as good as a feast' (p. 201) and that he wishes Isabel to be able to meet 'the requirements of *my* imagination' (p. 207, italics mine). In other words, he is limited and confined by his invalidism and wishes to live out his hopes and ambitions through Isabel. That 'a young lady with sixty thousand pounds may fall a victim to the fortune hunters' is 'a risk [which] has entered into [his] calculations', but which he is nonetheless 'prepared to take' (p. 207). Of course it proves a bad gamble, and so Ralph, who will not consider marrying his cousin in case it puts her in danger from his consumption, is actually the reason she becomes consumed by marriage to the emotionally pathological Gilbert Osmond.

If Ralph's consumption is is partly to blame for Isabel's tragedy, it is also the means by which he makes amends. As Katherine V. Snyder has observed, his 'consumption contributes to his portrayal as a kind of martyr, an innocent whose death symbolically, though not unproblematically, enables others to live'.[15] This is most apparent when Ralph is on his deathbed, a moment in the text which proves a turning point for Isabel. His end not only brings about an escape – however temporary it may prove to be – from Osmond; it allows her to unburden her troubles to the dying man, and to finally acknowledge the truth about her marriage. In addition, Ralph's final prophecy – 'I don't believe that such a generous mistake as yours can hurt you for more than a little' (p. 613) – implies a renewal of hope for her. Most of all, his death itself has the effect of making Isabel, who until this point is 'almost as good as being dead' (p. 596) herself, feel alive and 'grow young again' (p. 613). As Ralph says, 'there's nothing makes us feel so much alive as to see others die. That's the sensation of life – the sense that we remain. I've had it, even I. But now I'm of no use except to give it to others' (p. 611). Synder offers an important reading of this deathbed scene:

Ralph represents himself as making the ultimate sacrifice, as giving his life so that Isabel may live vicariously through witnessing the spectacle. This donation of self is not only self-abnegating; it is also self-fulfilling in much the same way that we have come to understand a particular style of bourgeois Victorian femininity . . .[16]

Synder's analysis suggests that Ralph's always endangered masculinity is finally completely eroded, in that in dying he appropriates the sacrificial role traditionally occupied by the dying Victorian woman. But of course this is the cultural nature of consumption: it not only represents its victims as feminine; it also constructs them as spiritual, saintly, even Christ-like, elevated and even empowered by their willing self-sacrifice. (James's close friend Mrs Humphry Ward would use this very same representation of the dying several years later, in *Eleanor*.) Ralph's death is the last of several immolations he makes in the novel, beginning with the giving up of half his fortune to his poorer cousin, and compounded by his adoption of celibacy in order to protect others – whether potential wives or future offspring – from his illness. Given the book's advocation of marriage as a possible cure for consumption, this is really Ralph's ultimate sacrifice, for it is a relinquishing not only of his sexuality but also of his best chance for recovery.

This all seems to reinforce the classic cultural stereotype of the spiritual consumptive, but in fact all Ralph's sacrifices are 'self-fulfilling' or even self-serving, as well as noble, and this not only because they construct him as a superior soul. We have seen that his giving up his fortune was at least partially selfish, as it was done not only for the good of Isabel, but for his own amusement. More significantly, though, Ralph's illness-induced decision to become 'a man who is no longer a lover' (p. 199) is also not entirely altruistic, and this identifies one of the most important themes in the novel. James clearly appreciates the beneficial possibilities of such a position as Ralph's, and is aware of the unique power of illness to confer it. Consumption may limit, even destroy, Ralph's sexual prospects, but it also allows him to escape the bonds of matrimony which eventually enshroud almost all the other characters, and this is no inconsiderable asset within a novel which as Robert K. Martin describes is 'the most anti-marital of all marriage fictions'.[17] 'There are no happy marriages'[18] represented in *Portrait*, only the unhappy union of Mr and Mrs Touchett, who spend their time in different continents, the infidelity-filled travesty of marriage that exists between the Count and Countess Gemini, and the 'dark, narrow alley' of Isabel's relationship with Osmond. As we have seen, consumption, for the thoughtful and socially considerate patient, facilitates, even demands, bachelorism: the only alternative involves the unacceptable risk of passing the disease to one's children if the disease was indeed hereditary, or one's spouse if it proved to be infectious, as it did within a couple of years of *Portrait*'s publication. Hence phthisis is the best excuse that Ralph can give to a world which considers him obligated to take a wife. Henrietta indicates that 'it's everyone's duty to get married' (p. 110), and this concept of the 'duty marriage' is particularly relevant to Ralph, given the aforementioned wishes of his elderly and beloved father, and the fact that he is the last of the family and its name will die with him. Consumption allows him to defy such social and personal demands and expectations, justifying a certain amount of emotional detachment both to the people who believe he should marry, and to himself.

In particular Ralph's disease may be viewed as a convenient means of withdrawal from a potentially complex and painful emotional relationship with his cousin. He is 'more interested in . . . [Isabel] than in any one else on earth', but he is reluctant to become more than a 'brother' to her, telling his father that he is 'not in love with her but . . . should be if – if certain things were different' (p. 202). As 'certain things' means his state of health, Ralph is suggesting here that his disease intervenes between himself and his cousin, that it is the only thing which prevents him being in love with her. Yet this is an oversimplification of much more complicated emotions towards Isabel, as revealed by the passage in which she herself asks him what his intentions are towards her:

'Are you thinking of proposing to me?'
'By no means. From the point of view I speak of that would be fatal; I should kill the goose that supplies me with the material of my inimitable omelettes. I use that animal as the symbol of my insane illusions.' (p. 170)

The language used in this seemingly light-hearted exchange gives it the sense of being weighted with hidden meaning. On one level, the suggestion that a proposal would 'kill the goose that supplies me with the material' – Isabel – suggests a repetition of Ralph's fear that marriage may be dangerous to her because it could lead to infection by his disease. But, more significantly, proposing 'would be fatal' to Ralph's position as spectator, and by association to Ralph himself, whom we are told is kept alive solely by his observation of his cousin:

What kept Ralph alive was simply the fact that he had not yet seen enough of the person in the world in whom he was most interested: he was not yet satisfied. There was more to come; he couldn't make up his mind to lose that. He wanted to see what she would make of her husband, or what her husband would make of her. This was only the first act of the drama, and he was determined to sit out the performance. (p. 425)

Isabel is here once again suggested as a cure for Ralph's illness, but significantly is more acceptable to him, and hence more successful as a remedy, when she functions as a spectacle and source of entertainment rather than as possible wife and nurse. Consumption allows Ralph to remain an observer of his cousin's marriage rather than a participant in it. This is a state which is contrary to the demands and desires of conventional, healthy masculinity – as Mr Touchett says, 'when I cared for a girl – when I was young – I wanted to do more than look at her' (p. 205) – but is one which Ralph seems to find satisfactory. He declares his love to Isabel when she is on the point of marrying Osmond, but again uses his illness as a protective barrier, to qualify his emotions and eliminate any sense that he will act upon them. ' "I love you, but I love without hope," said Ralph quickly, forcing a smile and feeling that in that last declaration he had expressed more than he intended' (p. 373). It seems that it is never Ralph's 'intention' to risk the possibility of any kind of non-platonic relationship with Isabel, and so his only wholehearted expression of love comes when he is dying and about to be safely out of reach of sexual and emotional demands forever: 'if you've been hated you've also been loved. Ah, but, Isabel, *adored!*' (p. 614).

Ralph's choice of a life of invalidism and illness over one of matrimony suggests that, in the world of the novel, marriage may be more fatal that the disease which protects him from it. Indeed, his self-enforced removal from the marriage plot is symptomatic of the whole novel's anxiety about heterosexual relationships and the impact those relationships have upon the individual. This anxiety finds its most direct expression through the representation of Isabel, a heroine whose reactions and experiences are shaped by her fear of the all-consuming and uncontrollable nature of love and especially of sexual desire. She is reluctant to express any of the 'inspired and trustful passion' she feels, which is compared to a 'large sum stored in a bank which there was a terror in having to begin to spend. If she touched it, it would all come out' (p. 336). This 'terror' is illustrated further by Isabel's desire 'to see but not to feel': she wishes to see the world, but not 'as the young men want to see it . . . I don't wish to touch the cup of experience' (p. 171). She seeks to preserve the emotional detachment of the spectator, and of course sexuality is potentially threatening to this position, demanding involvement and necessitating the loss of perspective. Hence it compromises her spiritual freedom, even her sense of self. This is made plain in Isabel's final scene in the novel, which involves a famous confrontation with the phallically named Caspar Goodwood, and in which the full extent to which desire may function as a powerful, dangerous force is brought home to her:

She had never been loved before. She had believed it, but this was different; this was the hot wind of the desert, at the approach of which the others dropped dead . . . It wrapped her about; it lifted her off her feet, while the very taste of it as of something potent, acrid and strange, forced open her set teeth. (p. 625)

Isabel fears passion because it seems to take her over and imprison her: it is invasive, even to the point of being a form of rape – 'it . . . forced open her set teeth' – and overwhelming – 'it lifted her off her feet'. Isabel believes that to give in to it would be fatal – 'to let him take her in his arms would be the next best thing to her dying' – but is at the same time aware that in such submission there is a 'kind of rapture' (p. 627). So her final escape from Goodwood's attempted 'act of possession' seems to be represented as a personal triumph, over the power of both his desire and her own, a liberation of her soul from the demands of the body that almost succeed in claiming it. It is in this sense a choosing of life over moral and spiritual death. Her momentary temptation by passion is nearly her spiritual downfall, for she is 'wrecked and sinking' in the 'rushing torrent' of sexual possibilities and then blinded by the 'white lightning' of Caspar's embrace. However, 'when darkness returned she was free' (p. 627). The encounter with Caspar sends her fleeing away from passion and back onto the 'very straight path' of sexual purity and uncompromised spiritual independence. The loveless marriage she returns to at the end of the novel is both the high price she is willing to pay for this integrity and the best means of safeguarding it. Life with Osmond may be lonely and isolated, but it is morally and socially correct, and because it is 'dry' and 'sterile' Isabel is protected from the dangerous sexuality which demands the relinquishing and merging of the self with and to another person.

Isabel's need to liberate herself from the shackles of the corporeal and to rise above the temptations of sexual desire is clearly linked to Ralph's illness, for, as I have suggested elsewhere, consumption was traditionally believed to create this kind of asceticism in its sufferers by rendering the body weak, feeble and redundant, but the mind and spirit strong and pure. Even if Ralph's motives for celibacy are possibly self-serving, this state still seems to absolve him from the taint of deviant hyper-sexuality which usually mars the consumptive's purity. He is in this sense the personification of the spiritual consumptive, having been led by his disease to give up all bodily pleasures: his aforementioned refusal to eat can be viewed as an indication of the full extent of his rejection of physical appetites. His body becomes increasingly irrelevant, 'blighted and battered' (p. 364), as the novel progresses, so by its end his existence is almost purely intellectual: he had 'given up walking . . . he sat all day in a chair' yet 'his conversation had been better than ever' (p. 425). We can see how his disease has allowed him to leave behind the demands of the flesh and hence achieve the position of intelligent and perceptive but fundamentally detached observer which Isabel so wishes to emulate.[19] Given the novel's construction of sexuality as a dangerous and overwhelming force which compromises one's sense of self, we can not pity him his isolated, asexual position, nor can we be surprised that Isabel indicates some envy towards it:

He was so charming that her sense of his being ill had hitherto had a sort of comfort in it; the state of his health had seemed not a limitation, but a kind of intellectual advantage; it absolved him from all professional and official emotions and left him the luxury of being exclusively personal. The personality so resulting was delightful; he had remained proof against the staleness of disease . . . Such had been the girl's impression of her cousin, and when she had pitied him it was only on reflection. (p. 364)

This passage captures the advantages which consumption confers. Ralph's illness gives him an 'intellectual advantage', a clarity of mind and perception, because it frees him from the 'official emotions' – pride, jealousy, vanity and most of all desire – which burden the other, more earthly characters in the novel. Such mundane preoccupations cloud judgement and compromise purity of spirit, the former bringing about the downfall of

Isabel and the latter the moral sickness of Gilbert Osmond and Madame Merle. Ralph may have the sickliest body in *Portrait*, but he possesses the healthiest soul. He initially resents being forced to become a passive spectator of life rather than an active participant in it, likening his new invalid existence to 'reading a good book in a poor translation' (p. 57). In time, however, he comes to appreciate how illness increases the pleasures of observation and perception: 'With the prospect of losing them the simple use of his faculties became an exquisite pleasure; it seemed to him the joys of contemplation had never been sounded' (p. 57). 'Contemplation' is more than just a compensation for invalidism, however, for as we have seen, it renders Ralph the most superior character in the novel, with the special status of the outsider.

In this way Ralph can be considered an autobiographical figure, for his approach to illness is evocative of James's own. James viewed ill health as a useful tool for a writer, because of the outsider's perspective it granted, and in fact his conception of a successful artist was bound up with sickness. This is indicated by a review he wrote in *The Nation* in 1868, in which he described William Morris as 'a supremely healthy writer', a critical comment because James believed that 'to call a man healthy nowadays is almost an insult – invalids learn so many secrets'.[20] There were more prosaic advantages to the invalid state, however, because, like Ralph, James was allowed by his illness a withdrawal from familial and social duties, a means of escape from the more unattractive obligations and expectations of life. This view of illness as an escape route from banality and family responsibility was of course shared by James's sister Alice, who spent most of her life searching for a suitable affliction which would lend her glamour and enable her to travel, as Jean Strouse has documented.[21] Alice's early hypochondria and nervous illness were finally replaced by all-too-real breast cancer: Henry was, however, more fortunate. Throughout his youth he suffered from what Kaplan describes as a 'useful backache' which not only gave him a valid reason for not participating in the Civil War, but also 'allowed him to do what he most wanted to do – spend his time reading and writing'.[22] This was accompanied from 1867 onward by chronic constipation, as well as by frequent migraines and occasional urinary infections. This might not seem a serious litany of health problems, but it was enough to necessitate James's removal to Europe for therapeutic reasons, a trip financed by his parents because it was represented as a pilgrimage for health. Illness hence both facilitated foreign travel and allowed James to leave the confines of close-knit but demanding family behind him. We might recall Madame

Merle's pronouncement that Ralph was 'lucky to have a chronic malady so long as he doesn't die of it'.

It is consumption in particular rather than disease in general which offers the most direct parallel between *Portrait* and James's life, however, for phthisis functioned for James in the same way as it does for Ralph: as a means of protecting and removing oneself from the complexities of a problematic relationship with a female relation. Much has been written about the 'vivacious and intelligent' Minny Temple, Henry James's younger cousin, who died of phthisis in 1870, when she was only twenty-four.[23] James and Minny shared a close romantic friendship for ten years before her death, and James admired and loved her lively personality and 'wonderful, ethereal brightness of presence'.[24] Critics and biographers believe that Minny was the inspiration for the young, high-spirited American women of James's fiction,[25] particularly Milly Theale in *The Wings of the Dove*, whose name is so similar to Minny's, and Isabel Archer in *The Portrait of a Lady*. *Portrait* has been read as a kind of wistful rewriting of Minny's fate,[26] for by coming to Europe, seeing the world and marrying, Isabel experiences all the things Minny wishes to but cannot, owing to her ill health. Of course, as experience proves to be a 'poisoned drink' for Isabel, the novel gives a sense that Minny's illness and early death may have saved her from suffering as well as denied her a future. But even though Isabel is given all the opportunities that health endows, consumption is still present in the novel, only displaced onto Ralph. As Ernest Sandeen has observed, 'Ralph plays the role of scapegoat, of atoning redeemer' and 'his close relation to his author indicates that . . . James in the person of Ralph Touchett had entered his own story to take upon himself the disease which cut short his cousin's earthly career and so had made possible for her a new life in Isabel Archer'.[27] It is significant, however, that tuberculosis has the same effect in James's art as it did in his life: it intervenes between two cousins of the opposite sex and restricts, limits and finally terminates their loving relationship.

An examination of the author's letters reveals that his portrayal of Ralph's illness and the way it facilitates sexual or matrimonial detachment from Isabel has much in common with James's own feelings about Minny Temple. Fred Kaplan has suggested how Minny's death from consumption was an 'absolute remedy' to the difficulty she presented to her cousin: that of a young, single woman he was very close to, but did not wish to have a more than platonic relationship with, and had no desire to marry. His own mysterious ailments were for a long time his reason for not pursuing a more conventional relationship with her, as an extract of a letter to his brother William reveals:

> She never knew how sick and disordered a creature I was . . . I always looked forward with a certain eagerness to the day when I should have regained my natural lead, and friendship, on my part at least, might become more active and masculine.[28]

There is a clear parallel with Ralph and Isabel here, for James sets out to construct himself as, in Ernest Sandeen's words, 'not qualified as a suitor' for Minny because of his ill health.[29] This is a deceptive letter, however, for James's feelings toward her were ambivalent, and even when his health did improve there was no more 'active and masculine' romance between them. Indeed, there could not be, as he wrote to William that he was 'never' actually in love with her. Hence his reaction to the news of her death, as expressed in a letter to his mother, is suggestive:

> But who complains that she's gone or would have her back to die more painfully? She certainly never seemed to have come into the world for her own happiness – or that of others . . . to have known her is certainly an immense gain: but who would have wished her to live longer on such a footing – unless he had felt within him (what I felt little enough!) some irresistible mission to reconcile her to a world to which she was essentially hostile? . . . No-one who ever knew her can have failed to look at her future as a sadly insoluble problem – & we almost all had imagination enough to say, to ourselves at least that life – poor narrow life – contained no place for her.[30]

Fred Kaplan suggests that James represents Minny as 'essentially hostile' to the world because she possessed an unfeminine independence and restlessness of character. Given the sexual reluctance of the semi-autobiographical Ralph in *Portrait*, however, one wonders if it was in fact James's own life which 'contained no place for her'. Minny's frequently expressed desire to come to see James in Italy suggested the possibility of a threat to his bachelorhood, but her consumption intervened and she never made the trip.[31] This may be why his grief about her death seems in his letters to be tinged with relief that consumption has resolved the 'sadly insoluble problem' she presented: 'there is absolute balm in the thought of poor Minny and *rest* – rest and immortal absence . . . how profoundly inconsequential, in her history, continued life would have been!'.[32] For James, 'immortal absence' is a comforting 'balm' to his anxiety about the future of their relationship, for Minny has 'gone where there is no marriage', and marriage would have been disastrous not only to James's freedom but also to his struggling literary career. Consumption has other benefits as well, of course, for it was a 'remedy' for her feminine shortcomings. Her illness has transformed her in James's mind from someone socially subversive into the passive feminine ideal she had never been in life: 'I now become sensible how her image softened & sweetened by suffering & sitting patient and yet expectant.'[33] Consumption has fashioned her into a 'graceful invalid', and, as such, a suitable and enduring muse for the complex but always feminine women in James's fiction. In this way her death can be seen as a precursor of Ralph's, for both are constructed by James as willing sacrifices made to benefit those left behind. Just as Isabel experiences a renewal of life and vitality by witnessing the death of a loved cousin, James gains a more concrete gift: literary inspiration. He writes that the thought of Minny 'has operated in my mind as a gentle incentive to action & enterprise', and it seems that, as Kaplan suggests, Minny becomes 'a property of the literary imagination . . . having proved unsuitable for life, she had now been appropriated for art'.[34]

It is ironic that the portrayal of a male consumptive in *The Portrait of a Lady* emerges as a portrayal of a female consumptive after all. It seems that the disease can never be really disassociated from its identification with femininity. But in the gender paradox that surrounds this disease James finds the medium through which to articulate the crisis he perceives to be at the heart of modern masculinity. It is clearly apparent how the consumptive can function as a comprehensive metaphor for all the different forms of, and reasons for, masculine malaise in *Portrait*: his dispossession and restlessness are like those of the expatriate, his sense of social separatism recalls that of the bachelor and possible homosexual, and his enforced indolence evokes the wealth-imposed boredom of the upper classes. Ralph's disease is a product of these influences, a consequence of ignoring his father's prescription for the moral and physical health of men, namely hard work, responsibility and marriage. Of course not only do the other men in the novel also fail to adhere to this lifestyle, the author does too, and so Ralph can be read as an expression of James's anxieties about his own position of bachelor and author, anxieties linked to guilt and relief over the convenient death of Minny Temple and her subsequent 're-appropriation as art'. Ralph is also, however, a reflection of his creator's desires, because, through his illness he achieves the position James wants – that of the ideal artist. He is detached yet perceptive, sickly yet intelligent, isolated yet liberated and loved. Ralph represents the kind of consumptive fantasy which has become familiar throughout this book: he is a Christ-like figure whose 'blighted and battered' body is a physiological testament to the spiritual sickness around him, and who bears the physical manifestations of a society's suffering. This representation in *Portrait* is, however, inseparable from James's personal fantasy about the sacrificial potential of the consumptive, whose willing death brings about new life – or, in Minny's case, new life through art.

Conclusion

What emerges from a study of the literary representations of consumption is a sense of this disease as a hyperbolic metaphor: a signifier of gender and class issues, a female disease, and one which was associated with industrial capitalism in complex ways. There is clearly an evolution of these metaphors as the century progresses, as the romantic and mysterious disease became known to be bacterial and gradually became accepted as infectious. Texts in the early Victorian period seem to accept, and reinforce, the Romantic view of the consumptive as pure, saintly and 'too good to live', though this can be either a consequence of their disease or the quality that invites it in the first place. Hence it is the typical affliction of innocent, pious children, like Helen Burns in *Jane Eyre*, or Dickens's child heroes, from little Nell to little Dick to Paul Dombey. It is also often the means by which working-class adolescents are refined and transformed into admirable heroes who can be admired, pitied and identified with by the bourgeois readership, like Bessy in *North and South* and Smike in *Nicholas Nickleby*. In the mid-century *Bildungsroman*, in fact, the path towards adulthood of the hero or heroine is often parallelled by the path towards death of the consumptive friend. This doubling process has interesting effects on character construction, empathising the vitality and strength of the novel's protagonist – Jane Eyre is, for example, 'more tenacious of life' than Helen Burns – but also more wilful and flawed, and less spiritual. Hence Jane, Margaret Hale and the like sin and are in error and need to live and be tested, rather than simply be rescued from existence by a good death. This is still one of the functions of the disease in the 1880s, when Ralph's decline in *Portrait of a Lady* finally serves to make Isobel 'feel more alive', more immersed in life and in a society she has become distanced from. So, generally in these novels, the consumptive is the foil to and the better half of the the central character, and it is as if their disease teaches them precociously what their healthy double takes a lifetime – or at very least the whole of the novel – to learn.

I have suggested in this work that this construction of consumption as a spiritualising disease is echoed by the medical writing of the time, and that the descriptions of the typical consumptive in fiction seem to be reproduced and reinforced by doctors who turned to cultural beliefs because they were bereft of scientific knowledge about this illness. There are striking similarities, both theoretically and rhetorically, between the two genres, with many physicians using cultural and literary stereotypes as tools for diagnosis, for example. It could be observed, however, that the medical profession's belief that the behaviour and lifestyle of consumptives was usually pathological in one way or another – that they were, in fact, the instigators of their own illness – does not seem directly represented in the fiction of the early Victorian period. Novelists like Dickens continue to hold firmly to the idea that consumptives are spiritual angels. However, it is notable that in the novels I have examined here blame is still attached to this disease: if consumptives are not responsible for their own illness their society is. Paul Dombey may be himself an innocent but within the world of the novel his disease is the symbolic product of a corrupt, pathological way of life associated with the modern capitalism his father personifies. Bessy Higgins's illness is constructed by Gaskell as the result of deprivation brought about by her working conditions and the unhealthy, nutrient-poor and yet indulgently sugar-rich diet of the industrial working classes. Both are, then, victims of the capitalist's economic greed. Paul is simultaneously indulged and overworked, denied a healthy childhood by Mr Dombey's impatience to make him a servant of Mammon; Bessy is exploited by the factory system for which she is simply a diminutive, expendable cog in a huge machine. Both are 'weary' (Gaskell, p. 103; Dickens, p. 214) despite their youth, of the modern world and their very different, but equally regimented and soulless, roles within it. Both are liberated by their consumption, which disrupts and thwarts the usually inexorable process of the capitalist apparatus, and allows them both to finally escape it. And, in both cases, their death serves as a lesson and an example to those left behind. Mr Dombey and Mr Higgins are hard secular men who have immersed themselves without reservation in the working world, with damaging consequences for their humanity, but the death of their innocent offspring serves as a softening, educating experience for the latter, and a humbling punishment for the former. Those who contract the disease are not the only ones reformed and refined by its spiritualising presence, it seems.

Later in the century literary representations of the disease became more complex. In ways which reflected what had long been the medical opinion of phthisis, the late Victorian novelist began to problematise the saintly, 'too-good-to-live' image of the consumptive. It still, more than ever, retains its Romantic connotations as a glamorous, refined disease, associated with beauty and heightened sensibility, but, in novels such as Mary Ward's *Eleanor*, it is also symbolically associated with sexual desires and mental illness, as the logical conclusion of such sensibility. Ward is happy to draw upon some of the conventional cultural stereotypes in her portrayal of the charming, delicate and upper-class consumptive, but subverts and challenges others. As Eleanor is the heroine of Ward's novel, it represents a detailed study of her disease, rather than simply utilising the consumptive myth for secondary characters, as in the earlier texts I have examined. Ward appears intrigued by the psychological implications and contradictions implicit in an illness associated on the one hand with increased sensitivity and strong emotions and on the other with spirituality, purity and moral superiority. Her heroine is consumed by inappropriate desire as well as by disease, but society denies her a sexual identity for eugenic reasons, and expects her, as an invalid, to be passive, motherly and altruistic, though she is in reality increasingly vengeful, tyrannical and frustrated by her weakening body and the limitations of her life. Eleanor can in fact be considered to be struggling as much with the social and cultural expectations and myths which surround consumption as with the disease itself. Though she returns, when dying at the end of the novel, to the conventional self-sacrificing role society expects of her, this is undercut by the subversive tendencies she displays throughout. Possibly anorexic, certainly emotionally unstable, indulged by the fashionable life, drained by intellectual endeavour and deprived of the stabilising influence of family and home responsibilities, the nomadic Eleanor has exactly the kind of pathological lifestyle which physicians believed invited consumption. Her characterisation, then, utilises medical beliefs – in a phthisical diathesis and in personal responsibility for disease – and hence represents an evolution of the usual literary representation of the consumptive. Even her final guise, that of self-sacrificing, fasting saint, *seems* to perpetuate existing cultural myths about the spiritual superiority that accompanies the disease, but can actually be regarded as the final manifestation of the kind of wilful social rebelliousness which invited it in the first place.

George Du Maurier's *Trilby*, although also written in the 1890s, seems to rely more heavily on traditional consumptive stereotypes associated with the early Victorian period (perhaps engaging with cultural myth rather than medical fact because it is more Gothic fantasy than realist novel). As we have seen, the initially robust and sexual Trilby is purified and refined by the progression of her disease, which transforms her from vulgarly healthy grisette to the epitome of feminine grace and beauty. However, Du Maurier, like Ward, is primarily concerned with interrogating the cultural production of the disease. His novel may appear to reinforce the transforming power of the consumptive aesthetic, but – even while being clearly enthralled by the delicate loveliness of its heroine – it exposes how damaging fashionable frailty can be, and how pathological and predatory the male sexuality whose appetites it gratifies. It is this appetite which really consumes Trilby, and her illness can be laid at the door of the the bourgeois sensibility which rewards and fetishises delicacy and purity over mental and physical health and strength. In this way *Trilby* can be considered to be exposing the dangers of the cult of invalidism – while still seduced by the compelling appeal of the consumptive woman.

The position of the consumptive man, in contrast, is anything but appealing. Lawlor has written that, for the male Romantic poets afflicted with the disease, the 'consumptive metaphor was both enabling and disabling, a mark of distinction and a stigma, indicative both of the sensitivity and intensity of genius and yet the feminine weakness accompanying such a position'.[1] Lawlor is referring to Keats, but we can see these kinds of myths and ideas still at work much later in the century, in James's *The Portrait of a Lady*. Ralph Touchett is certainly 'feminised' by disease in this novel, and consequently is denied – or denies himself – all the acquisitions of masculine success: career, marriage, children, and even his inheritance. However, Ralph's perceptiveness, intelligence and altruism compensate for the material achievement and bodily strength he lacks: he may not be a Romantic poet, but he resembles one in many ways. By the standards of late Victorian masculinity, however, the unproductive, barren and dependent Ralph, like any male consumptive, is a failure, but James's novel reveals that he is not the only one. In fact Ralph is symbolic of a whole generation of idle, affluent men in the novel who contribute nothing to their society, and live vampirically, in one way or another, off the wealth acquired by others. Once again, consumption and capitalism seem bound up with one another in the Victorian novel.

An alternative version of the late-century literary consumptive combines the social anxieties which surrounded the male sufferer with the strange seductiveness associated with the female. The most sinister of all this disease's guises takes the form of a kind of monstrous hybrid of vampire and consumptive, in which the pallid and emaciated invalid becomes the predatory daemon. This inexplicable and stealthy disease had always seemed almost supernatural, to physicians and laymen alike, and hence for the Victorian novelist it provided an appropriate pathological paradigm through which to frame their representation of vampires. Of course such a representation must be a manifestation of the increasing awareness and acceptance, in the years following Koch, that tuberculosis was an infectious disease. Fundamental social anxieties around contagion are symbolised by the consumed body which becomes in turn a consumer of others. No longer just a victim to be pitied, the consumptive is a threat to the lives of those around them; their very continued existence necessitates the infection of those they meet. In this regard consumptives had much in common with the glamorous and compelling, yet sinister and terrifying, figure of the vampire, which captured the public imagination in the last years of the century. Furthermore, returning to an economic reading of this disease, consumptives can also be regarded as social vampires, given that their invalid lifestyle means they produce nothing, are usually unable to work, and hence live parasitically off a society which they contribute nothing to and which they, figuratively, drain dry. And once again, physicians used and perpetuated this construction of tuberculosis. Greater medical knowledge about the disease, rather than prompting a shift towards facts, logic and science, seemed to give rise to more anxiety and myth-making about an illness which was infectious yet mysteriously took years to gestate, and which it was impossible to quarantine against. Amid the eugenic fears which dominated the end of the century, tuberculosis was more socially terrifying than ever. In this representation, however, it was now lacking even the refined and benevolent spirituality and grace which had traditionally accompanied it. Hence the vampiric paradigm not only demonised consumptives, but deprived them of a fantasy which had long been their only compensation, as they suffered and died from a disease which was as monstrous as any vampire, but whose abilities to consume and destroy were all too real.

Epilogue 'A truly modern illness': into the twentieth century and beyond

By the end of the Victorian era, consumption's metaphors and associations had begun to change. The mysterious, ethereal wasting disease which had seemed to single out poets, children and beautiful women in the eighteenth and nineteenth centuries had become by the 1900s an identifiable bacterial infection, known to be transmissible and to be linked to low immunity, a rather more prosaic explanation than those which had previously been offered. Even the name changed after the turn of the century: in a reflection of the new advances in medical knowledge, consumption or phthisis, both slightly vague and generalising terms which meant 'wasting' and hence described one of the *symptoms* of the disease, gave way to tuberculosis or 'TB', which reflected its known *cause*, the *Mycobacterium tuberculosis*. Koch's identification of this bacterium in 1882 had, by the twentieth century, not only been accepted by an initially resistant medical profession, but had filtered through into public consciousness, and permanently altered the perception of the disease. Consumption's transformation into TB did not just occur on a symbolic level, however, but had very tangible consequences for patients, whose experience of the illness dramatically changed. A new body of tubercular literature reflected and shaped these changes, drawing on the nineteenth-century representations of consumption I have explored in this study, but ultimately constructing the disease in very different ways. There is much more work to be done on this modern consumptive genre, but such explorations lie outside the reach of this present work.[1] In this section, then, I will briefly interrogate these novels in order to reveal the ways in which they appropriated some of consumption's traditional metaphors and disregarded others, and how they reflected the process by which one of the world's oldest as well as most romantic and symbolic diseases became, as Katherine Ott puts it, 'a truly modern illness' which is still with us today.[2]

It was not only Koch's identification of the cause of tuberculosis which began the dissipation of the disease's traditionally inscrutable, even mystical quality after the turn of the century. 'With the use of technology to assess the patient's condition, the mystery of diagnosis was largely removed': many insights were offered by new treatments which penetrated and revealed the tubercular body, even though they could not yet cure it.[3] X-rays, which were discovered by Wilhelm Rontgen in 1895, began to be widely used for chest examinations in hospitals in Europe from 1901 onwards, though it was not until the 1920s that they were fully accepted in England as an important tool in the diagnosis of tuberculosis. By enabling the examination of the consumptive's internal organs, the X-ray rendered the disease visible and the extent of it ascertainable, literally casting light where previously there was only the darkness of diagnosis by percussion. The resulting pictures displayed the pathology of the disease to physicians and patients alike, and this transparency heralded a change in consumption's metaphorical power. The disease's mystery and romance was further eroded by the new interventionist approach to the treatment of consumptives which was ushered in in the twentieth century, with the advent of collapse therapy. This included the artificial pneumothorax, which involved puncturing the infected lung in order to induce collapse, and the surgical removal of some ribs or of the phrenic nerve (which controls the diaphragm) also in order to restrict the movement of the chest. Both procedures arose out of the belief that resting the lung allowed it time to heal, and enabled it to calcify and confine its diseased tissue. The success of such surgical practices was always very questionable – the risk of infection was high and there were no convincing statistics indicating long-term recovery in the majority of cases – but they remained popular with the medical profession until well after the arrival of streptomycin in the 1940s indicated that a real cure had been found.[4] The popularity of collapse therapy must be partly due to the way it facilitated the medical exploration of the consumptive's body: thoracoplasty in particular opened the whole chest up to the gaze of the physician. Tuberculosis was no longer visible only in autopsy, and it was now commonplace to 'see', intervene with and even excise the disease at any stage of its development. Of course, these invasive methods had repercussions for the associated images of the consumptive, for where previously it been an ethereal, aesthetic illness, it now became identified with brutal and physically deforming surgical treatment. The typical consumptive no longer possessed the kind of glamorously slender and delicate body which had served as the inspiration for art throughout the nineteenth century, but rather one mutilated and scarred by the operations they had undergone, which was exposed to the public by the new prevalence of medical photography.

This increased medical interventionism had further repercussions for the cultural perception of the disease, as the social and environmental spaces in which consumption was experienced and treated changed too. As we have seen, middle-class consumptives traditionally spent their days searching for health in the warm, balmy climates of Mediterranean countries, or, in the absence of the money and freedom this necessitated, in the domestic sanctuary – or possibly prison – that was the Victorian sickroom. In the new century, however, tuberculosis was relocated to the sanatorium, heralding a defining change in the management of the disease, and producing a whole new set of metaphors and associations. Institutionalisation signalled that tuberculosis was now regarded as a widespread social problem and that suffering from it had become a public experience shared with a whole array of doctors, nurses and other patients, whereas previously consumption had necessitated the private, personal suffering of the individual. The state-funded sanatoria which opened across Britain after 1900 represented a widespread governmental desire to wage war on tuberculosis, the first attempt to do so in the disease's long history.[5]

Sanatoria were, of course, a necessary consequence of invasive, long-term treatment, as collapse therapy required that the patient should remain under constant medical supervision for a protracted period of time. More sinisterly, however, they were a reflection of the state's new awareness of tuberculosis transmissibility and of the need to protect the health of the nation by keeping consumptives out of society. 'Sanatoriums ... met the basic psychological need of a community to isolate its sick and diseased.'[6] Hence the primary function of the sanatorium was to confine the dangerous consumptive until they were no longer infectious: curing their disease was desirable but always a secondary objective. This is indicated by the continuing prevalence of these institutions throughout Britain, and their continued funding by the government, even when statistics began to suggest that they were largely unsuccessful in their attempts to arrest the disease. F. B. Smith suggests that, given the limited impact of sanatoria on the problem, the money given to them could have been more efficiently spent 'on food and rent subsidies' for consumptives at home,[7] but this approach did not facilitate the primary aim of tuberculosis management: to reassure the public by removing and isolating the dangerously infectious members of the population. Hence a patient's release from the sanatorium was not based so much around their improved physical health, as on whether or not their sputum tested negative for infectious bacilli.

Sanatoria remain the defining image of twentieth-century consumption: as Smith indicates, they 'loomed large in the public perception of

tuberculosis care' more than they did as a solution to the actual problem of tuberculosis.[8] This 'perception' owes much to the new body of
tubercular literature which was set in and around them between 1893 and
1958. Thomas Mann's *The Magic Mountain*, a novel which 'has fixed the
association between tuberculosis and sanatoria in the minds of succeeding
generations',[9] is perhaps the most famous example of the sanatorium novel,
but this genre also includes Brian Bulman's *The House of Quiet People* and
A. E. Ellis's *The Rack*,[10] texts which seem to have been largely neglected
by contemporary criticism. Jeffrey Meyers's *Disease and the Novel*, which is
primarily concerned with the work of Thomas Mann, contains an important chapter on *The Rack*, but considers disease in Mann and Ellis as a
general pathological entity and does not examine the very specific choice of
consumption in both novels. Meyers does, however, touch upon consumption's enduring capacity to act as a social metaphor with his useful argument
that in these texts illness is 'both literal, and symbolic of the pathological
state of Europe' at this time.[11] In this era, then, tuberculosis is associated
with fascism and with the consuming destructiveness of modern warfare.
The Magic Mountain was published in the 1920s, but is set in 1914, and ends
with the outbreak of Wolrd War I (interestingly, and perhaps indicating the
extent of its perceived relevance to wartime, a second edition was issued
in Britain at the end of World War II). *The Rack* occupies a similar retro-
spective, contemplative position, being published in 1958 but set around
1946 and *The House of Quiet People* was published in 1939 and set several
years earlier. These novels represent the sanatorium as not merely a place of
treatment for those afflicted with tuberculosis, but for those whose bodies
and minds have been consumed by the ravages of war, and in this regard
it functions as a powerful metaphorical space, a microcosm of the modern
world.

In *The Rack*, Paul Davenport and his friends are all former soldiers and
most of them have contracted their disease during their time in the army;[12]
the same is true of Jopachim in *The Magic Mountain*, who looks 'as if [he]
had just come back from manoeuvres'.[13] Military metaphors abound in
both texts, and consumption and war are symbolically bound up with one
another. Paul's disgust at receiving unexpected treatment, for example, is
described as 'the moral indignation with which a civilian after the sound-
ing of the "All Clear," hears the sound of enemy engines' (p. 71). Hans
Castorp mistakes a man with tuberculosis in his knee for a war veteran,
implying that combat and phthisis are interchangeable, in that they both
have the same effect on the human body.[14] Even the restrictive, ordered
nature of the sanatorium is reminiscent of army life – 'it had about it the

precision of a military inspection' (p. 71) – and, as Meyers has observed, of
the fascist state: 'The barbaric doctors, who hate and oppress the patients,
are the dictators of the sanatorium ... '.[15] Indeed, the nightmare world
of the sanatorium, in which the Englishman is imprisoned, is evocative
of the kind of fascist society which would exist if the war had not been
won. This is reminiscent of another mid-century novel which makes an
association between tuberculosis and fascism, George Orwell's *Nineteen
Eighty-Four*, in which Winston Smith's consumptive frailty is a direct consequence of the mental and physical hardship inflicted upon him by Big
Brother.[16]

The most poignant and emotive use of the wartime comparison, however,
is the association between the sanatorium and another space in which
the socially undesirable could be isolated from the rest of society – the
concentration camp. Ellis makes the link explicit in *The Rack* by revealing
that a number of the residents at *Les Alpes* were survivors of the camps, and
that

> the conditions in which they lived had induced TB of the bone or lung, or some-
> times both. One form of imprisonment had been exchanged for another; where
> they had been confined to cells, they were now confined to beds, where they had
> lain in fetters, they now lay in plaster casts. They had previously existed in daily
> dread of summary death; it was now only the method, not the threat which had
> altered. (p. 102)

Tuberculosis here becomes not only a symbol of war, but a direct and
tangible consequence of it, a product of the deprivation which follows
in the wake of conflict in general and Nazism in particular. Even more
disturbingly, it functions as a means of continuing and perpetuating the
control and punishment of the bodies of the persecuted, long after peace
has been declared.

These novels suggest that not only are consumption's 'metaphors of illness' changing, but also the locus of the disease's symbolic importance is
shifting. The consumptive patient as individual is less central in these texts
than in Victorian fiction; instead the place in which consumption is housed
and treated has assumed a new importance. Yet it is notable that the sanatorium novel still has much in common with its predecessors and at times
draws heavily on earlier representations of illness. The most important link
between the 'old' consumptive text and the new is the way the sanatorium
is represented as a state of existence which is entirely self-contained, which
has its own rules, its own aims and objectives, its own triumphs and failures, all very different from those of healthy society. As William J. Heaney

recalls in his autobiographical text *House of Courage*, an account of the time he spent in the Dublin Sanatorium, it was

a world in itself: an inner world, if you will, where the bulk of one's personal, outer world problems had no place ...

I would try to shut out all thought of the outside world, in the interests of the now all important business, of getting my health back.[17]

This representation of illness in the sanatorium has much in common with Victorian narratives of consumptive invalidism, which also frequently represent the experience of sickness and suffering as a feverish existence divorced from reality and disassociated from the concerns of the 'outside world'. The dying Eleanor Burgoyne, for example, abandons civilisation and social convention to immerse herself in a moral 'wilderness', a fantasy of escape and revenge, in *Eleanor*. Lucy's quasi-consumptive illness in *Dracula* takes the form of a dark, supernatural nightmare in which the normal world is taken over by the presence of evil. And, of course, time itself ceases to have meaning in the blurred final days of Paul Dombey in *Dombey and Son*:

How many times the golden water danced upon the wall; how many nights the dark, dark river rolled toward the sea in spite of him; Paul never counted, never sought to know ... whether they were many days or few, appeared of little moment now, to the gentle boy. (p. 295)

Phthisis's capacity to consume temporality, which I discussed in more detail in chapter 2, still has resonance in the twentieth century as well. *The Magic Mountain*'s Jopachim, in response to Hans Castorp's observation that 'time must go fast, living up here', says it is 'Fast and slow, as you take it ... it doesn't go at all I can tell you. You can't call it time.'[18] This sense that the consumptive somehow experiences the passage of days and weeks differently is a useful vehicle for this novel's discourse about the philosophy of time, but is indicative of a much more general issue: the separation from the rest of the world which illness, and especially long-term illness like consumption, brings about. It seems that the literary invalid always inhabits their own, separate sphere, where reality is distorted by pain and fever and where other considerations are pushed aside by the need for self-preservation.[19] This is one of the reasons why invalids are frequently represented as ethereal and spiritual, as they are perceived to be detached from, and outside of, the everyday world and its mundane concerns. In this context the metaphorical value of the sanatorium in literature becomes apparent, for it gives tangible form to this separate sphere, summing up and defining the invalidism experience, encouraging and facilitating the patient's detachment from society, and legitimising the pursuit of health as the most important, indeed the only, goal in life.

The sanatorium also consolidates the connection between consumption and capitalism which I have suggested was a defining feature of the disease throughout the nineteenth century. As Katherine Ott has suggested, consumption had always been an important contributor to the 'invalid trade', demanding as it did the production of a wide variety of goods, from special mattresses for its well-to-do sufferers to quack remedies for its poorer ones.[20] The private sanatorium, however, bringing all these goods and services together and under one roof, became a large, wealthy and world-wide business which controlled and profited from every aspect of the consumptive's care. In this sense it can be regarded as the ultimate expression of the financial exploitation of this disease: consumption is by the twentieth century no longer just a means of encouraging patients to buy certain items, but has become an entire industry in itself. The importance of the financial aspect in the treatment of consumption is made apparent in *The Rack*, which reveals how money is essential even within a hospital which allows a funded scheme for poor patients. Although his stay is initially paid for by the International Students Organisation, Paul Davenport struggles with financial worries throughout his time at *Les Alpes*. These are temporarily alleviated by a small inheritance he receives while there, which enables him to better his previously inadequate living conditions: private patients do not have to undergo the privations that the non-paying ones do, especially in terms of diet, which plays an important part in recovery from TB. It is only this money that allows him to remain and continue his treatment after his fellow students have had to return home, whether or not they are cured, because their allocated time has expired. By the end of the novel he too is being encouraged to leave by the staff, not because he is better but because his money is running out. Even in the mid twentieth century, it seems, consumption is still 'two diseases – that of the rich and that of the poor'.[21]

It is apparent that the sanatorium novel, while it represents the changes made in the medical approach to the disease in the new century, still shares a number of thematic preoccupations with the consumptive literature I have examined in this work, and, indeed, develops these concerns further in interesting ways. These twentieth-century narratives do differ from their earlier counterparts in one very significant aspect, however, in that they give a rather altered view of the importance of the consumptive within their society. In the Victorian literary sickroom the invalid is a powerful figure, whose phthisis singles them out from, and frequently renders them superior to, the other, healthy characters. As a 'disease of individuals' it indicates that its sufferers are distinctive, even special, and that they have a significant function in the novel, frequently as an agent of moral good. The consumptives I have studied are feeble in body but strong in mind and personality, influencing and even controlling others by inspiring a mixture of guilt, admiration and awe. For example, the dying Trilby's 'grace, charm [and] magnetism' command the love and devotion of all those around her: 'And whatever might be her fate ... the care of her till she died or recovered should be the principal business of their lives' (p. 251). Less benignly, but even more powerfully, the heroine of *Eleanor* manipulates Lucy and Manisty by constructing them as responsible for her suffering: '[Lucy] felt herself a kind of murderer' (p. 268). Even when she allows this guilt to pass, they are still obligated to her for their happiness: 'every hour he realised more plainly with what completeness Eleanor held him in her hands' (p. 464).

In *The Rack* and other sanatorium novels, however, the consumptive hero is no longer special and set apart from others, for his illness is shared by almost all the characters in the book. Paul Davenport is only one of many almost indistinguishable phthisical patients resident in *Les Alpes*, and within this context tuberculosis appears to become like a disease of the masses. By the end of the novel the other residents are nameless and faceless, merely 'some fifty weary invalids' who are 'fed in great quantities' into the great 'digestive system' that is the sanatorium (pp. 308–9). As simply fodder to the sanatorium machine, they, unlike their predecessors in the Victorian novel, are no longer powerful or authoritative in any way. Instead of controlling others, they are themselves controlled, their personal freedom handed over to the doctors and nurses who manipulate their bodies and supervise every aspect of their daily lives. Paul is not consulted or informed about most of the invasive procedures carried out upon him, and it seems that many of them are performed not with real hope for success, but actually 'to satisfy [the] curiosity' of the doctors (p. 188). Hence Paul refuses treatment several times during the novel (p. 84, p. 131 and p. 183) but always has it forced upon him. At one point he is even anaesthetised by the physician in order to make him comply, in a scene which displays how medical autonomy does away with all resistance (p. 132). He appears to be powerless on a day-to-day level as well, as his demands for a vegetarian diet, for example, are not met by the hospital staff and by the end of the novel he has been forced to take up meat. Fellow patients are no more influenced by Paul than the physicians: two of his friends at the sanatorium bring about their own deaths at least partly because Paul lacks the spiritual or emotional reserves to help them. Similarly, the whole concept of the consumptive as a powerful figure is undermined by *The House of Quiet People*, in which the hero's fiancée is initially drawn to him through guilt, but eventually leaves him for his healthy rival, whose child she bears. Bulman here reveals that guilt and pity, which are such compelling forces in *Eleanor*, are poor substitutes for the advantages health brings. In fact in the modern novel the consumptive invalid, far from being a wielder of influence and an object of desire, is in fact rendered passive, impotent and finally redundant by his disease.

This represents a significant shift in the representation of the consumptive invalid in the space of only a couple of decades. So what brought about this change in the literary patient, from controlling to controlled, proactive to apathetic, singled out and individual to merely isolated? It is presumably linked to the eroding of the romance and glamour associated with the disease which I have suggested took place in the early twentieth century, but this cannot be the only reason for the transformation. Rather, it seems likely that this was in fact a consequence of a parallel change in the disease's gender associations. I have argued in previous chapters that phthisis was perceived in the nineteenth century to be a female disease and was hence represented as such in the literature of the time, but this undergoes a notable reversal after the turn of the century, when novels begin to represent their central consumptive characters as male. The sanatorium novels I have looked at above all represent male consumptives, and so too does Winifred Holtby's *The Land of Green Ginger*, published in 1928. The Victorian notion of the consumptive invalid as a powerful figure seems to be bound up with the identification of that invalid as female, for illness, while of course highly repressive on one level, could nonetheless operate as a means by which women could resist their traditionally enforced roles and subvert patriarchy while appearing the epitome of self-sacrificing femininity. It facilitated the legitimate avoidance of the demands of husband, children and household, as well as being a means of demonstrating the patient acceptance of suffering which commanded the attention and respect of those around her. In other words, it was one of few means of self-assertion available to the disenfranchised. The male experience of illness, in contrast, involved the relinquishing of the strength, authority and autonomy usually associated with the male sex. In *The Land of Green Ginger*, Teddy Leigh's vitality and virility are sapped away by his consumption, as he becomes physically frail, sexually unattractive and unable to support his family, either financially or otherwise. Hence his disillusioned wife cares for him as though he were one of their children, runs their farm and their house, and 'could have carried his wasted body', so much stronger is she.[22] Patriarchal power is almost completely eroded by disease in this novel and, as in *The House of Quiet People*, there is a further threat to the consumptive's sexuality in the form of a healthy – and therefore more suitable and desirable – rival for his wife's affections.

Other novels suggest that means and place of treatment played as big a part in tuberculosis's undermining of masculinity as the disease itself, however, and this seems to be a particularly twentieth-century phenomenon. It is not the prospect of dying but the consequences of invasive treatment and the fear of revealing that he is 'a moral coward' in the face of physical pain which terrifies Paul Davenport (p. 43). He feels inadequate because he cannot display 'manly' courage about the procedures he must endure – 'the very sight of a needle now emasculated him' (p. 85) – and because he thinks he lacks the 'stoicism of his fellow patients'. The sanatorium compromised male identity because it functioned as a hierarchal power system in which the patient, especially the non-paying patient, occupied the lowest and least influential position, irrespective of their gender. Their wants and needs, even their individuality, must be given up to allow the 'medical machine' (p. 70) that cares for them to function efficiently, for in this world obedience is more important than sense of self. Furthermore, while the top of the sanatorium hierarchy – the main authority figure in these novels – was usually a male physician, the day-to-day running of the hospital and supervision of the residents was carried out by female nurses. Hence the patient did not merely have to give up their autonomy but had to submit to female authority and control on a daily basis.

It is apparent, then, why experiences of consumption in the twentieth century were frequently expressed as narratives of frustration, both sexual and mental, and why the sanatorium became a site of male anxiety and a metaphor for all that was unappealing about the modernising world – including the changing position of women in that world. But why should literature suddenly begin to represent male consumptives in the first place, after representing tuberculosis as a female disease for so long? Why did this gender shift take place after the turn of the century? Was it simply a long-overdue acceptance of the fact that men did in fact suffer and die from consumption just as women did?

The gendering of tuberculosis remains one of the most elusive mysteries which surround this disease, but, given that there is clearly a link between the twentieth-century 'tubercular' novel and the two World Wars, it seems more than probable that war transformed the literary consumptive as it did the national male psyche in general. As Joanna Bourke has observed, the trauma, both physical and mental, of modern combat brought about a new sense of the male body as a fragile, damaged, pathological entity. 'The wartime aesthetics of the male body (and the disciplines applied to it by military and medical authorities) spread into civilian society after the war. The male body was no more than the sum of its various parts and the dismembered man became Everyman.'[23] Mass injury and the effects of shell-shock meant that the British male was no longer associated with health. Indeed, the healthy male body was one untouched by war, and hence had its masculinity compromised in other ways: 'it was the bodies of those who remained at home that symbolised all that was degenerate in the male physique'.[24] Of course war has a more direct, literal effect on the incidence of tuberculosis as well, as the close, cramped conditions of trenches, field hospitals and army bases all facilitated easy transmission of the disease. So too did the decrease in immunity brought about by stress and falling levels of nutrition which accompanied war, but these were factors which affected women at home too. However, an increase in the amount of exercise women took, falling birth rates, and the decline in the popularity of corsets went some way towards reversing the traditional construction of the bourgeois woman as 'an innate, natural invalid'. The male body to some degree replaced that of the female as an object of medical concern, but of course men were not constructed as natural invalids, but rather as those who bear the consequences of a pathological society. Hence in these twentieth-century tubercular texts, the time and means of contraction of the disease are always fully documented, as though to reassure compromised masculinity by reinforcing the idea of TB as a transmissible infection, not an intrinsic failing within the body. These writers seek to leave behind the nineteenth-century construction of the disease as something very personal and specific, a consequence of individual susceptibility through emotional disturbance, but their attempts to do so are frequently compromised by their continued reliance on the old myths of consumption as a disease of sensibility. Even as they portray the infectiousness of TB and clearly establish it as an illness associated with the physical deprivation of war, they also cannot disregard the idea that the disease is somehow bound up with one's mental state. For example, *The Rack* chronicles Paul's depression in the same detail as it does his deteriorating physical condition, and by doing so implies that there is a very real link between the two. As Jeffrey Weeks has observed, the novel 'describes tuberculosis as a horrible, physical reality, but Paul's despair and insight, reached through suffering and love, also reveal how the psychological state of the patient affects his receptivity to, or rejection of, the slow destruction of tissue'.[25] Paul is 'receptive' to the destructive power of tuberculosis in a way that his equally ill but more positive and hopeful lover, Michelle, is not. Hence she recovers against the odds, while he remains in the sanatorium to die – though, significantly, the novel leaves it unclear whether it will be TB or suicide which finally takes his life.

What has emerged out of this study is the existence of tuberculosis as a useful, powerful metaphor for the most all-consuming social and cultural anxieties of whatever society it manifests itself in. It has a long history of association with capitalism, and a complex identity as both a disease of luxury and consumerism and a consequence of the social deprivation that accompanies industrialisation. It can also function as a means of articulating concerns about gender and sexuality: the pathological threat posed by the desirable woman or the homosexual male in the nineteenth century, the post-war construction of masculine identity in the twentieth. Some of its metaphors change over decades; others remain constant. TB ceased to become a common subject for fiction after the advent of widespread use of streptomycin in the 1950s seemed to establish its demise. When a cure is found for a disease it loses much of its metaphorical power. Cancer today encapsulates many of the images, symbols and paradoxes which surrounded phthisis in the past: as Susan Sontag has pointed out, our society today creates fictions about the cancer sufferer, theorising over what lifestyle choices and personality traits bring about their disease, in ways similar to those which preoccupied the Victorians about consumption. Tuberculosis's usefulness to art and literature as an aesthetic illness has been mainly replaced by leukaemia, which frequently appears in modern novels and films when a disease of purity, pallidity and pathos is required. However, just as TB has not been eradicated, neither has its potential to function as a signifier for social anxiety: at the present time it is acting in the media as a symbol of the fear of the pathological potential inherent in the asylum seeker. It is no longer a gendered disease, it seems, but still a very politicised one. As its incidence in Britain seems likely to continue to increase, it will be interesting to see how it continues to be represented in the fiction of today and tomorrow. Certainly its appearance in one recent novel, and resulting Oscar-winning film, John Le Carré's *The Constant Gardener* (2001), is highly significant in the context of this study. Although Le Carré depicts tuberculosis in its modern guise, as one of the main threats to survival in the third world, the focus of his text is on the consequences of corporate greed and the corrupting nature of the pursuit of wealth. His exploration of the corruption in the pharmaceutical industry juxtaposes the responsibility to treat those afflicted with TB with the possibility it offers for huge financial gain. It seems that at least one of the 'metaphors of illness' I have discussed here continues unchanged: tuberculosis is still at the heart of a 'lucrative invalid trade', and functions as a metaphor for the destructive power of capitalism in the fiction of the twenty-first century, just as it did in the nineteenth.

Appendix A: Phthisis mortality

Period	All ages	< 5 years	5–10	10–15	15–20	20–25	25–35	35–45	45–55
1851–60	2,679	1,305	572	1,025	2,961	4,181	4,317	4,091	3,466
1861–70	2,475	968	454	825	2,651	3,928	4,243	4,026	3,340
1871–80	2,116	767	358	664	2,036	3,117	3,619	3,745	3,132
1881–85	1,830	569	312	560	1,695	2,535	3,154	3,312	2,849
1886–90	1,635	502	271	488	1,420	2,144	2,691	2,985	2,656
1891–95	1,463	444	228	410	1,253	1,875	2,342	2,771	2,440
Reduction % between 1851–60 and 1891–95	45.4	66.0	60.1	60.0	57.7	55.2	45.7	32.3	29.6

Table showing mortality (rate of death per million living) from pulmonary tuberculosis in England and Wales in the second half of the nineteenth century. Taken from Sir Richard Thorne, *The Administrative Control of Tuberculosis* (London: Baillière, Tindall and Cox, 1899), p. 6.

Appendix B: Medical publications on consumption

Year	Number of medical books/pamphlets published about consumption
1800–10	11
1811–20	18
1821–30	9
1831–40	16
1841–50	50
1851–60	59
1861–70	68
1871–80	52
1881–90	61
1891	55

Numbers of medical books about consumption published in each decade of the nineteenth century. This was compiled by me using total records of medical publications held in the British Library.

Appendix C: Gender distribution of phthisis

Year	Both sexes	Male	Female
1851	277	269	285
1861	258	261	257
1871	232	239	226
1881	189	199	180
1891	156	173	140
1901	128	150	106
1911	104	121	87
1921	89	101	78

Mean annual death rate for both sexes from respiratory tuberculosis in England and Wales, per 100,000 living. Taken from F. B. Smith, *The Retreat of Tuberculosis* (Beckenham: Croom Helm, 1988), p. 7.

Notes

INTRODUCTION

1 As there are a number of names for this illness it is important to establish the terms which I will use to describe it throughout this work. As I indicate in this first paragraph, phthisis (which is from the Greek for wasting) is perhaps the oldest name for tuberculosis, but was still used, though mainly in medical circles, until the late nineteenth century. Consumption was the most well-known denomination from the seventeenth century on: it was primarily a layman's term, but was also used by physicians. The medical profession began to use the modern name, tuberculosis, around the mid nineteenth century, though it seems to be only after the tubercle bacillus was identified in the 1880s that this more scientific term began to replace consumption in general use. As all three terms were valid in the nineteenth century I use them all throughout this book. The abbreviation which remains with us today, TB, is an entirely twentieth-century variation, however, and so in order to be chronologically accurate I do not use it when discussing the disease in the Victorian era, only in my introduction and conclusion regarding the 'modern' illness.

2 A. J. E. Cave, 'The evidence for the incidence of tuberculosis in ancient Egypt' *British Journal of Tuberculosis* 33 (1939), p. 142. A mummy of the high priest of Amon, dated around 3000 BC, still displays the trace of a thoracic lesion which would today be considered a classic indication of tuberculosis. This is not an isolated case – other prehistoric skeletons have been found which display similar features of the disease.

3 F. B. Smith, *The Retreat of Tuberculosis* (Beckenham: Croom Helm Ltd, 1988), pp. 1–20. Death rates from pulmonary tuberculosis, or consumption, began to slowly decline around 1850, though as late as 1947 phthisis could still be held accountable for half of all deaths from disease. Other forms of tuberculosis peaked in the 1860s and began to decline from 1870 on.

4 Susan Sontag, *Illness as Metaphor* (New York: Farrar, Straus & Giroux, 1977), p. 30.

5 Claude Quetel, *History of Syphilis*, trans. Judith Braddock and Brian Pike (London: Polity Press, 1990), p. 8. Quetel identifies the 'social' diseases as insanity, syphilis, tuberculosis and alcoholism, because, in his words, they have 'provoked and continue to provoke changes in society and cultural responses'.

It is important to note at this point that the social diseases are bound up with one another: throughout this study of tuberculosis, syphilis, mental illness and alcoholism crop up again and again.

6 Sontag, *Illness as Metaphor*, p. 28.
7 David S. Barnes, *The Making of a Social Disease: Tuberculosis in Nineteenth-Century France* (London: University of California Press, 1995), p. 4.
8 Consumption is central to the plot of both Alexandre Dumas's *La dame aux camélias* and the opera *La Traviata*, which was based upon it, and Mürger's *La vie de Bohème*, which was adapted for Puccini's *La Bohème*.
9 See Beth in *Little Women*, Ruby Gillis in *Anne of the Island* and Eva in *Uncle Tom's Cabin*. It is worth noting here that consumption seems to be portrayed as a female disease in American literature just as it is in British.
10 See for example Frank Mort, *Dangerous Sexualities*, 2nd edn (London: Routledge, 2000); Joan Lane, *A Social History of Medicine* (London: Routledge, 2001) and Robert Woods and John Woodward, eds., *Urban Disease and Mortality in Nineteenth-Century England* (London: Batsford Academic and Educational, 1984).
11 Those critical works which deal with the hysteric or anorexic woman are too numerous to list here, but see especially Elaine Showalter, *The Female Malady: Women, Madness and English Culture* (New York, Pantheon Books, 1985); Anna Krugovoy Silver, *Victorian Literature and the Anorexic Body* (Cambridge University Press, 2002) and Helen Small, *Love's Madness: Medicine, the Novel, and Female Insanity* (Oxford: Clarendon Press, 1996).
12 I am assuming to a certain degree here (and throughout) that in the Victorian era 'invalid' and 'consumptive' are synonymous with one another in literature. Of course phthisis was not the only malady which facilitated the existence of long-term patients, but as it was one of the most common, probably the most lingering, and certainly the most symbolic of wasting diseases, it is not surprising that the invalid in fiction is usually either known to be consumptive, or is suffering from an unnamed disease which has consumptive resonance.
13 Leigh Summers, *Bound to Please: A History of the Victorian Corset* (Oxford: Berg, 2001).
14 www.who.int/tb/en/
15 Thomas Dormandy, *The White Death* (London: The Hambledon Press, 1999), pp. 377–92.
16 Quetel, *History of Syphilis*, p. 8.

I NINETEENTH-CENTURY MEDICAL DISCOURSE ON TUBERCULOSIS

1 Definite statistics for tuberculosis deaths are hard to come by prior to 1850, as most records seem to date only from then, but 'George Gregory, physician to the London Small Pox Hospital, calculated in 1840 from Rickman's survey of the London bills of mortality from 1657 that about 20% of all deaths had been regularly ascribed to consumption. His estimates confirm those developed by

William Woolcombe in 1808', quoted from Smith, *Retreat of Tuberculosis*, p. 4:
Gregory had published his findings in *The Lancet*, 11 April 1840.

2 Gregory's sample suggests that around 1830 the proportion of phthisis deaths
   fell from 22 per cent to 16 per cent (*Lancet*, 11 April 1840, p. 88). William Farr's
   statistics agree that the turning point in the disease came between 1831 and 1835,
   when deaths from the disease fell for the first time in many decades (*Lancet*, 22
   January 1842). The death rate continued to fall steadily throughout the century
   (see Appendix A).

3 Horace Dobell, *On Loss of Weight, Blood-Spitting and Lung Disease* (London:
   J & A. Churchill, 1878), pp. 163–4.

4 *Lancet*, 18 November 1826, p. 211. Highly critical reviews of new books about
   consumption are much more common in this period than in later years. See
   also the reviews of books by Dr J. Jenkins and Dr Murray in *The Lancet*
   (1 May and 17 July, 1830, p. 180 and p. 611).

5 *Lancet*, 26 June 1841, p. 494.

6 *Lancet*, 8 June 1844, p. 341, italics mine.

7 Cholera had its initial outbreak in 1831–3, and returned in 1846–9. There were
   in addition major epidemics of typhus and typhoid between 1836 and 1842,
   and again in 1846–9. For more detail see Anthony S. Wohl, *Endangered Lives*
   (London: J. M. Dent & Sons, 1983).

8 See M. W. Flinn, introduction, *Chadwick's Report on the Sanitary Condition of
   the Labouring Population* by Edwin Chadwick (Edinburgh University Press,
   1965), p. 11. Flinn suggests that in fact tuberculosis 'scarcely stirred the imagination of any social group in this period. It was so much a part of life, so
   inevitable, so little understood, that it was accepted mutely' and not feared the
   way cholera and other virulent, epidemic diseases were.

9 An interesting example of this shunning of the disease can be found in the
   words of Dr Elliotson, who states that he and the staff of St Thomas's hospital,
   London, never 'admit such cases [of phthisis] if we can avoid it' because 'the
   hospital is instituted for the cure or alleviation of disease', and in consumption
   'we can do neither'. *Lancet*, 19 June 1830, p. 440.

10 *Lancet*, 26 June 1841, p. 494.

11 Richard D. Altick, *The English Common Reader* (University of Chicago Press,
   1957), p. 84.

12 *Ibid.*, p. 85. Altick points out that Evangelicalism made many forms of entertainment disreputable, and 'in so scrupulous an atmosphere, the reading habit
   flourished'.

13 Dr Norman Moore, *A Lecture on the History of Medicine as Illustrated in English
   Literature* (London: Adlard and Son, 1903), p. 23. See also Alfred Hillier's
   discussions of medicine and contemporary fiction in *Tuberculosis: Its Nature,
   Prevention and Treatment* (London: Cassell & Co, 1900) and *The Prevention
   of Consumption* (London: Longmans & Green, 1903) which will be discussed
   in more detail on the following pages.

14 Moore, *Lecture*, p. 23.

15 *Ibid.*, p. 7.

16 See for example Dr Thomas Bartlett, *Consumption, its Causes, Prevention and
   Cure* (London: Hippolyte Baillière, 1855), p. 2. Bartlett states that 'the mind of

the philosopher' as well as the 'practised judgement of the physician', 'can in no case be more usefully occupied than in alloying the sufferings occasioned by this disease'. Successful treatment for phthisis, he implies, requires much more than simply medical expertise.

17 Moore, *Lecture*, pp. 12–13.

18 *Ibid.*, p. 23.

19 Sir Humphry Rolleston, *Associations Between Literature and Medicine* (London: Harrison & Sons, 1933), p. 5. Rolleston practised medicine in England for some forty years, dating from 1893 onward.

20 *Ibid.*, p. 28. Rolleston points out a correlation between Dickens's descriptions of doctors and those published by physician Albert Smith, the brother of a close associate of Dickens (pp. 32–3).

21 Hillier, *Prevention*, p. 80.

22 *Ibid.*

23 Edwin Alabone, *The Cure of Consumption*, 6th edn (London: Kemp & Co., 1880), p. 34. Following references to this will be cited parenthetically in the text.

24 John Balbirne, *The Water Cure in Consumption and Scrofula*, 3rd edn (London: Longman & Co., 1856), p. 9.

25 T. R. Allinson, *Consumption: Its Causes, Symptoms, Treatment and Cure* (London: F. Pitman, 1854), p. 1.

26 Balbirne, *Water Cure*, p. 9.

27 Charles Dickens, *Dombey and Son* (London: Penguin Books, 1995), p. 87. All following references to this will be cited parenthetically in the text.

28 Dr Elliotson in *The Lancet*, 19 February 1830, p. 690.

29 Dr Henry Bowditch, *Is Consumption Ever Contagious?* (Boston: David Clapp, 1864), p. 4.

30 Dr C. Candler, *The Prevention of Consumption* (London: Kegan Paul Trench & Co., 1887) p. 4.

31 George Sand, Chopin's lover and companion in Majorca, demonised the island's treatment of him in the book she later wrote about their experiences, *Un hiver en Majorique*.

32 Sir Richard Thorne, *The Administrative Control of Tuberculosis* (London: Baillière, Tindall and Cox, 1899), p. 66.

33 Mrs Henry Wood, *East Lynne* (London: Macmillan, 1900), p. 467.

34 John Hughes Bennett, *The Pathology and Treatment of Pulmonary Consumption*, 2nd edn (Edinburgh: Adam and Charles Black, 1859), p. 64. All following references to this will be cited parenthetically in the text.

35 It is also worth noting at this point that medical discourse about anorexia evolved at around the same time as the resurgence of writing about consumption; French physicians Louis-Victor Marce and Pierre Briquet first published case studies of anorexic patients in 1860, and, more famously, Sir William Gull and Dr Ernest Lasegue began to bring the disease to popular attention in the 1870s. This similar time scale for medical attention is just one of many links between the two diseases, which will be examined in more detail in later chapters.

36 See for example Allinson, and Dr Ludwig Rohden, 'Balneotherapy and Climatotherapy of Chronic Pulmonary Consumption', in Julius Braun, *On the Curative Effects of Baths and Waters*, trans. F. E. Burnnett, ed. Hermann Weber (London: Smith, Elder & Co., 1875). All following references to Rohden will be cited parenthetically in the text.

37 Clark Lawlor, *Consumption and Literature* (London: Palgrave, 2006).

38 *Ibid.*, pp. 64–73.

39 See Peter Melville Logan, *Nerves and Narratives* (Berkeley: University of California Press, 1997).

40 Dr F. W. Burton-Fanning, *The Open-Air Treatment of Pulmonary Consumption* (London: Cassell & Co., 1905), p. 16.

41 *Ibid.*, p. 17.

42 Roy Porter, 'Consumption: disease of the consumer society?' in John Brewer and Roy Porter, eds., *Consumption and the World of Goods* (London: Routledge, 1993), pp. 66–7.

43 Dr W. Roemisch, *How to Guard Against a Return of Phthisis* (London: Adlard & Son, 1907), p. 57.

44 Burton-Fanning, *Open-Air Treatment*, p. 25, italics mine.

45 See for example Candler, Bowditch, and the views expressed in *The Lancet*, 8 June 1844, p. 341.

46 See Appendix C.

47 Lawlor, *Consumption and Literature*, p. 56.

48 Dobell, *Loss of Weight*, p. 68.

49 Sir Richard Thorne, *The Administrative Control of Tuberculosis* (London: Baillière, Tindall and Cox, 1899), p. 32.

50 Dr John Henry Bennet, 'On the Connection Between Phthisis and Uterine Disease', *Lancet*, 27 May 1865, p. 561.

51 Andrew Motion, *Keats* (London: Faber & Faber, 1997), p. 496.

52 Just for the sake of medical accuracy it is worth saying here that haemorrhage was not actually an early symptom of consumption: the disease had usually been present for some time before any bleeding began. However, as the earlier symptoms (lethargy, fever, loss of weight) were less concrete and could have a number of causes, the blood became the defining symbol. And its appearance *was* frequently a 'death warrant', for by the time the lungs were breaking down into blood the disease had usually reached such an advanced stage as to be almost always fatal.

53 Dr R. E. Thompson, *The Different Aspects of Family Phthisis* (London: Smith, Elder & Co., 1884), pp. 88–90.

54 Dr Francis Cook also associates women and pulmonary haemorrhage, stating that '. . . spitting of blood occurs . . . more frequently among females than males'. *A Practical Treatise on Pulmonary Consumption* (London: John Churchill, 1842), p. 26.

55 Thompson, *Different Aspects*, p. 90.

56 Bowditch, *Is Consumption Ever Contagious?*, p. 8.

57 Rohden, 'Balneotherapy', p. 506.

58 Literary examples of beautiful and desirable consumptive women include Dora in Dickens's *David Copperfield,* Tennyson's 'May Queen', and the subject of a later chapter, George Du Maurier's Trilby.

59 Dr Rowland East, *The Two Most Dangerous Diseases of England* (London: John Lee, 1842), p. 30.

60 *Ibid.*, p. 30.

61 Hillier, *Prevention*, p. 13.

62 Bram Dijkstra, *Idols of Perversity* (New York: Oxford University Press, 1986), pp. 25–63.

63 Sir Arthur Ransome, *The Causes and Prevention of Phthisis* (London: Smith, Elder and Co., 1890) and *Tuberculosis: Its Nature, Prevention and Treatment* by Dr Alfred Hillier are two of a number of late-century texts which treat phthisis as a disease which affects both sexes equally. For example, Hillier discusses 'consumptives of both sexes and all classes' (Hillier, p. 129).

64 Oldfield's career as published author begins in 1892 and continues until 1952, and includes texts like *The Evils of Butchery* (1895), *Fasting for Health and Life* (1924) and *Eat and Get Well* (1928), all concerned with the association between meat-eating and cruelty, luxury, and moral and physical illness.

65 Josiah Oldfield, *Flesh Eating: A Cause of Consumption* (London: The Vegetarian Society, 1897), p. 56, italics his.

66 G. R. Seale, *The Quest for National Efficiency* (Oxford: Blackwell, 1971), p. 9.

67 Dr J. Burney Yeo, *The Results of Recent Researches in the Treatment of Phthisis* (London: J. & A. Churchill, 1877), p. 7.

68 Oldfield, *Flesh Eating*, p. 3.

69 *Ibid.*, p. 19.

70 See Christopher Berry, *The Idea of Luxury* (Cambridge University Press, 1994), pp. 59–70.

71 J. Hungerford Sealy, *Medical Essays No 1: Phthisis Pulmonalis, its History and Varieties* (London: Sherwood, Gilbert & Piper, 1837), p. 8.

72 Oldfield, *Flesh Eating*, p. 56.

73 H. G. Wells, *The Time Machine* (London: Everyman, 1995), p. 20.

74 Maria H. Frawley, *Invalidism and Identity in Nineteenth-Century Britain* (London: University of Chicago Press, 2004), p. 126.

75 Dr John Parkin, *Climate and Phthisis* (London: Longmans, Green & Co., 1875), pp. 95–6.

76 Dr Thomas Burgess, *The Climate of Italy in Relation to Pulmonary Consumption* (London: Longman & Co., 1852), p. 104.

77 Parkin, *Climate and Psthisis*, p. 97.

78 Dr S. D. Bird, *Australasian Climates and their Influence on Pulmonary Consumption* (London: Longman, Green, Longman, Roberts & Green, 1863), p. 100.

79 *Ibid.*, p. 147.

80 Burgess, *Climate of Italy*, p. 102.

81 Frawley, *Invalidism and Identity*, p. 114.
82 Burgess, *Climate of Italy*, p. 117.
83 Rohden, 'Balneotherapy', p. 538.
84 Dr John Francis Churchill, *Letters to a Patient on Consumption and its Cure by the Hypophosphites* (London: David Stott, 1888), p. 3.
85 *Ibid.*, p. 2.
86 *Ibid.*
87 A. B. de Guerville, *The Crusade Against Phthisis* (London: Hugh Rees, 1904), pp. 28–30.
88 Book review in *The Lancet*, 8 December 1865, p. 649.
89 The British College of Health, *Vaccination as the Cause of Fever and Consumption* (London: British College of Health, 1868), p. 7.
90 *Lancet*, 8 June 1844, p. 340.

2 CONSUMING THE FAMILY ECONOMY: DISEASE AND
CAPITALISM IN CHARLES DICKENS'S *DOMBEY AND SON* AND
ELIZABETH GASKELL'S *NORTH AND SOUTH*

1 Thomas Malthus, *An Essay on the Principle of Population* (London: Penguin Books, 1970).
2 Dormandy, *White Death*, p. 22.
3 F. W. Burton-Fanning, *Consumption and Factory Life* (Norwich: Gibbs and Waller, 1911), p. 2.
4 F. B. Smith, *The Retreat of Tuberculosis 1850–1950* (Beckenham: Croom Helm, 1988), p. 1.
5 Neil McKendrick, John Brewer and J. H. Plumb, *The Birth of a Consumer Society* (London: Hutchinson & Co., 1983), p. 100.
6 Porter, 'Consumption', p. 59.
7 Berry, *Idea of Luxury*, p. 103.
8 George Cheyne, *The English Malady* (New York: Scholars' Facsimiles and Reprints, Inc., 1976), pp. 19–20.
9 Burton-Fanning, *Open-Air Treatment*, p. 16.
10 John Murray, *A Treatise on Pulmonary Consumption* (London: Whittaker, Treacher and Arnot, 1830), p. 37.
11 See for example the 'low' diet advocated by Murray, *ibid.*, and Dr Thomas Gurney, *Diet in Disease* (London: Henry Renshaw, 1886), p. 15.
12 Arthur Latham and Charles Garland, *The Conquest of Consumption: An Economic study* (London: T. Fisher, 1910), p. 2.
13 Australia, for example, was believed to be relatively free from consumption: see Bird, *Australasian Climates*.
14 Dr George Thomas Congreve, *On Consumption of the Lungs, OR Decline and its Successful Treatment* [sic] (London: Elliot Stock, 1881), p. 2.

15 F. S. Schwarzbach, *Dickens and the City* (London: The Athlone Press, 1979), p. 101.

16 For further discussion of how Dickens represents and uses disease in his fiction, see Miriam Bailin's *The Sickroom in Victorian Fiction* (Cambridge University Press, 1994), pp. 79–108. She does not discuss Paul Dombey, however.

17 Schwarzbach, *Dickens and the City*, p. 106.

18 *Ibid.*, p. 107.

19 Edgar Johnson, 'The World of Dombeyism' in Alan Shelston, ed., *Dombey and Son and Little Dorrit: A Casebook* (London: Macmillan Publishers Ltd, 1985), p. 69.

20 Margaret Wiley discusses the implications of wet-nursing in Dickens further in her short essay 'Mother's Milk and Dombey's Son' (*Dickens Quarterly*, December 1996, p. 19). In particular she raises the interesting questions around Dickens's guilt at his complicity in this debate through his employment of a wet nurse for his family, and how this might be manifested in his work.

21 Lynda Nead, *Myths of Sexuality* (Oxford: Basil Blackwell, 1988), p. 27.

22 Breast milk was in fact considered a possible cure for consumption in the Victorian era. See J. Edgar Foster, *The Natural Prevention and Cure of Colds, Sore Throats, Asthma, Bronchitis and CONSUMPTION,* 6th edn (Ipswich: Eastern Counties Gazette, 1887), p. 13: 'Some extraordinary cures in consumption have been performed by woman's milk . . .'

23 Robert Freedman, ed., *Marx on Economics* (Harmondsworth: Penguin Books Ltd, 1962), p. 46.

24 They are also perhaps symbols of urbanisation. Lorna Weatherill has identified that the incidence of household ownership of timepieces, in the eighteenth century at least, was higher in London than elsewhere in the UK: 'people in towns are usually thought of as being more conscious of clock time and more literate'. *Consumer Behaviour and Material Culture in Britain* (London: Routledge, 1988), p. 77.

25 Nina Auerbach, 'Dickens and Dombey: A Daughter After All' in Shelston, *Casebook*, p. 100.

26 *Ibid.*, p. 99.

27 Sontag, *Illness as Metaphor*, p. 17.

28 *Ibid.*, p. 30.

29 Peter Ackroyd, *Dickens* (London: Sinclair Stevenson, 1990), pp. 58–129.

30 See David Trotter, 'Circulation, Interchange, Stoppage: Dickens and Social Progress' in Robert Giddings, ed., *The Changing World of Charles Dickens* (London: Vision Press, 1983), pp. 163–79.

31 Michael Goldberg, *Carlyle and Dickens* (Athens: University of Georgia Press, 1972), p. 50.

32 Peter Melville Logan, *Nerves and Narratives* (London: University of California Press, 1997), p. 1.

33 Porter, 'Consumption', p. 66. As Beddoes's text is not available I have had to rely on Porter's quotes from it.

34 Logan, *Nerves and Narratives*, p. 18.

35 McKendrick *et al.*, *Consumer Society*, p. 286.
36 Porter, 'Consumption', p. 67.
37 Congreve, *Consumption of the Lungs*, p. 4.
38 Berry, *Idea of Luxury*, p. 58.
39 Nead, *Myths*, p. 99.
40 William Acton, *The Functions and Disorders of the Reproductive Organs* (London: Frank Cass and Company, 1972).
41 Ackroyd, *Dickens*, p. 528.
42 *Ibid.*, p. 186.
43 *Ibid.*, p. 529.
44 Edgar Wright quotes from Gaskell's letters in *Mrs Gaskell* (London: Oxford University Press, 1965), p. 131.
45 See for example Wright, and John Geoffrey Sharp, *Mrs Gaskell's Observation and Invention* (Sussex: Linden Press, 1970).
46 Coral Lansbury, *Elizabeth Gaskell: The Novel of Social Crisis* (London: ELEK, 1975), p. 119.
47 Elizabeth Gaskell, *North and South* (London: Penguin Books, 1994), pp. 118–19. All following references to this will be cited parenthetically in the text.
48 Anon., *The Use of Sugar: The Primary Cause of Pulmonary Consumption* (London: Simpkin, Marshall & Co., 1860), p. 8.
49 *Ibid.*, p. 9.
50 Charlotte Sussman, *Consuming Anxieties* (Stanford University Press, 2000), p. 30.
51 East, *Dangerous Diseases*, p. 52.
52 Victoria de Grazia, ed., *The Sex of Things* (Berkeley: University of California Press, 1996), p. 1.
53 Logan, *Nerves and Narratives*, pp. 1–7.
54 *Ibid.*, p. 6.

3 THE CONSUMPTIVE DIATHESIS AND THE VICTORIAN INVALID IN MRS HUMPHRY WARD'S *ELEANOR*

 1 Where to travel to was not so much a personal choice as a crucial science, investigated and discussed by the specialists of the day. The Victorian pamphlets and books which compare and contrast the benefits and disadvantages of different countries and their climates are numerous and clearly form another type of tubercular 'industry' by themselves. See for example Bird, *Australasian Climates*, and E. Bibby, *Invalids Abroad: Hints on Travelling, Nursing, and Cooking* (London: Hatchards, 1879).
 2 Henry James, *The Wings of the Dove* (New York: Norton & Co., 1978), p. 76.
 3 *Ibid.*, p. 76.
 4 Mrs Humphry Ward, *A Writer's Recollections* (London: W. Collins Sons & Co. 1918), p. 346.
 5 Lawlor, *Consumption and Literature*, p. 154.
 6 James, *Wings*, p. 357.

7 William S. Peterson, *Mrs Humphry Ward: Victorian Heretic* (Leicester University Press, 1976), p. 2.

8 *Ibid.*, p. 2.

9 John Sutherland, *Mrs Humphry Ward: Eminent Victorian, Pre-Eminent Edwardian* (Oxford University Press, 1990), p. 203.

10 Vineta Colby, *The Singular Anomaly*: *Woman Novelists of the Nineteenth Century* (New York University Press, 1970), p. 123.

11 Ward, *Recollections*, p. 311.

12 Janet Penrose Trevelyan, *The Life of Mrs Humphry Ward* (London: Constable & Co., 1923), p. 104 and p. 105.

13 See Ward, *Recollections*, p. 323.

14 See Lawlor's discussion of Gideon Harvey's 1666 treatise on consumption. Lawlor, *Consumption and Literature*, pp. 18–24.

15 Gurney, *Diet in Disease*, p. 8.

16 Mrs Humphry Ward, *Eleanor* (London: Smith, Elder & Co., 1911), p. 40. All following references to this novel will be cited parenthetically in the text.

17 James, *Wings*, p. 357.

18 Trevelyan, *Mrs Humphry Ward*, p. 190.

19 Sutherland, *Eminent Victorian*, p. 213.

20 Bird, *Australasian Climates*, p. 78.

21 *Ibid.*, pp. 78–9.

22 Karl Pearson, *Studies in National Deterioration II – Draper's Company Research Memoirs: A First Study of the Statistics of Tuberculosis* (London: Dulau & Co., 1907).

23 Burton-Fanning, *Open-Air Treatment*, p. 17.

24 Ransome, *Causes and Prevention,* p. v.

25 *Ibid.*, p. 106.

26 I would take issue with Susan Sontag's classic definition of tuberculosis as a 'disease of liquids, the body turning to phlegm and mucus and sputum and finally blood' (p. 14) as opposed to cancer which is 'the body tissues turning to something hard'. Phthisis in fact does both: tubercle deposits form cavities surrounded by rigid calcified matter. These may gradually take over more and more of the lungs, transforming the healthy fibrous tissue into something hard and stony, and then may or may not be later broken down into blood or mucus. See Willoughby Marshall Burslem, *On Consumption* (London: John Churchill, 1852), pp. 12–15.

27 It is interesting to note here, however, that in *Eleanor* passion in men is, in contrast, purifying and strengthening – 'supreme longing . . . seemed to have driven out of Manisty all the other elements in his character – those baser, vainer, weaker elements' (p. 512).

28 Dijkstra, *Idols*, pp. 18–21.

29 *Ibid.*, p. 50.

30 In this regard Ward's novel, like Du Maurier's, can be seen to challenge Clark Lawlor's belief that 'the praise of spiritualised women fading into God's glory

is rarely, if at all, to be found after the 1880s' (Lawlor, *Consumption and Literature*, p. 189). As this chapter and the following one show, this version of the consumptive myth does in fact endure into the twentieth century.

31 Plato, 'Phaedo', in *Five Dialogues*, ed. John M. Cooper, 2nd edn, trans. G. M. A. Grube (Indianapolis: Hackett, 2002), p. 103.
32 Silver, *Anorexic Body*, p. 9.
33 Joan Jacobs Brumberg, *Fasting Girls* (Cambridge, Mass: Harvard University Press, 1988), p. 182.
34 *Ibid.*, p. 182.
35 Colby, *Singular Anomaly*, p. 124.
36 Pat Jalland, *Death in the Victorian Family* (Oxford University Press, 1996), p. 39.
37 Rudolph Bell has identified 'holy anorexia' in his book of the same name (Chicago University Press, 1985). His study of the self-starvation of Italian holy women over the centuries uncovers the historical belief that purity, autonomy and religious devotion could be achieved by the self-denial and bodily punishment of anorexic behaviour.
38 Dobell, *Loss of Weight*, p. 165.
39 Bennett, *Pathology and Treatment*, p. 17.
40 Silver, *Anorexic Body*, p. 15.
41 *Ibid.*, pp. 13–14.
42 William S. Peterson, *Victorian Heretic* (Leicester University Press, 1976) p. 104.
43 Walter Vandereycken and Ron van Deth, *From Fasting Saints to Anorexic Girls* (London: The Athlone Press, 1994), p. 25.
44 *Ibid.*, p. 25.
45 Bell, *Holy Anorexia*, p. 20.
46 Trevelyan, *Mrs Humphry Ward*, pp. 152–3.
47 *Ibid.*, p. 146.

4 'THERE IS BEAUTY IN WOMAN'S DECAY': THE RISE OF THE TUBERCULAR AESTHETIC

1 Sealy, *Medical Essays*, p. 2.
2 Dr William Dale, *A Popular, Non-Technical, Treatise on Consumption* (Harrogate: R. Ackrill, 1884), p. 15.
3 *Ibid.*, p. 14.
4 *Consumption and Literature*, p. 46.
5 *Ibid.*, p. 140.
6 Mario Praz, *The Romantic Agony*, trans. Angus Davidson, 2nd edn (London: Oxford University Press, 1970), p. 27 and p. 31.
7 Thomas Moore, *Life and Journals of Lord Byron*, vol. 1 (Hamburg: Lebel, Trittel & Wrutz, 1830), p. 195.
8 Dijkstra, *Idols*, p. 25.
9 *Ibid.*, p. 8.
10 *Ibid.*, p. 25.

11 Jan Marsh, *Pre-Raphaelite Sisterhood* (London: Quartet Books, 1985), p. 26.
12 William Allingham, *A Diary*, ed. H. Allingham and D. Radford (London: Macmillan & Co., 1907), p. 144.
13 Curvature of the spine was diagnosed in 1854 by a Dr Garth Wilkinson, but in 1855 Dr Henry Ackland, Radcliffe Professor of Medicine, could find no organic disease: according to Rossetti, Ackland professed that 'her lungs, if at all affected, are only slightly so'. This comment implies that Ackland was concerned with refuting the common expectation, on which Lizzie was recommended to him by Ruskin, that she had consumption. Again, however, what is important is not so much that she did not have consumption as that she and her friends thought she did, despite any medical evidence of the illness.
14 Georgie Burne-Jones, *Memorials of Edward Burne-Jones,* vol. 1 (London: Humphries, 1993), p. 219.
15 Marsh, *Sisterhood*, p. 183.
16 Oswald Doughty and J. R. Wahl, eds., *Letters of Dante Gabriel Rossetti*, vol. 1 (Oxford: Clarendon Press, 1965). See especially letters number 175, 177, 202, 324 and 345.
17 William Rossetti, *Dante Gabriel Rossetti: His Family Letters,* vol. 1 (London: Ellis & Elvey, 1895), p. 221.
18 Violet Hunt, *The Wife of Rossetti* (New York: E. P. Dutton & Co., 1932), p. 32. See also Joseph Knight's account of her in *The Life of Dante Gabriel Rossetti* (London: Scott, 1887) and Evelyn Waugh's *Rossetti, His Life and Works,* 2nd edn (London: Duckworth, 1975).
19 E. T. Cooke and A. D. Wedderburn, eds., *The Works of John Ruskin*, vol. xxxvi (London: George Allen 1909), p. 203. For a discussion of this and other folk treatments for consumption, see J. D Rolleston, 'The Folklore of Pulmonary Tuberculosis', *Tubercle* 55 (1941).
20 East, *Dangerous Diseases*, p. 22 and p. 30.
21 Doughty and Wahl, *Letters*, p. 364.
22 See Georgie Burne-Jones's admiration of her style, *Memorials*, p. 207, and also Hunt, *The Wife of Rossetti*, p. 32.
23 Dante Gabriel Rossetti, *Ruskin: Rossetti: Preraphaelitism. Papers 1854 to 1862,* ed. William Michael Rossetti (London: George Allen, 1899) p. 75.
24 Georgie Burne-Jones described Siddal as 'excited and melancholy' (*Memorials*, p. 220) when separated even momentarily from her husband's calming influence, and recorded her instability and grief following the stillbirth of her child: '[she was] sitting in a low chair with the childless cradle on the floor beside her, and she cried with a kind of soft wildness as we came in "Hush, Ned, you'll waken it!"' (p. 222).
25 For a list and full discussion of the many twentieth-century books – both factual and fictional – films and plays which take Siddal as their subject see Jan Marsh, *The Legend of Elizabeth Siddal* (London: Quartet Books, 1989).

26 J. G. Millais, *The Life and Letters of Sir John Everett Millais*, vol. 1 (London: Methuen, 1899), p. 144.

27 Jan Marsh, *Pre-Raphaelite Women* (London: Weidenfeld & Nicolson, 1987), p. 142.

28 Jalland has explored how consumption, perhaps more than any other disease, facilitated the 'good death' in the Victorian era. Jalland, *Death in the Victorian Family*, pp. 39–58.

29 Marsh, *Sisterhood*, p. 216.

30 See Dormandy, *White Death*, pp. 48–9.

31 Jalland, *Death in the Victorian Family*, p. 69.

32 Burne-Jones, *Memorials*, p. 231.

33 David G. Riede, *Dante Gabriel Rossetti Revisited* (London: Twayne Publishers, 1992), p. 79.

34 Henry James, *Henry James: A Life In Letters,* ed. Philip Thorne (London: The Penguin Press, 1999), p. 216.

35 Leonee Ormond, *George Du Maurier* (London: Routledge & Kegan Paul, 1969), p. 173 and p. 495.

36 Elisabeth Bronfen, *Over Her Dead Body* (Manchester University Press, 1993), p. 174.

37 *Ibid.*, 174.

38 *Ibid.*, 176.

39 Jan Marsh, ed., *Christina Rossetti, Poems and Prose* (London: Everyman, 1994), p. 52.

40 See Dijkstra, *Idols*, pp. 34–6, and Silver, *Anorexic Body*, pp. 127–135.

41 George Du Maurier, *Trilby* (London: Osgood & McIllvane, 1895), p. 2. All following references to *Trilby* are cited parenthetically in the text.

42 Hillier, *Prevention*, p. 14.

43 Sarah Grand upholds the Venus as the epitome of female beauty in her 1886 novel *The Heavenly Twins*, and the 1871 pamphlet *Figure Training* even includes a picture of the Venus dressed in contemporary clothes, to display her inadequacies as a modern-day role-model for the fashionable woman.

44 David Kunzle, *Fashion and Fetishism* (Totowa: Rowman & Littlefield, 1982), p. 136.

45 Summers, *Bound to Please*, p. 84 and p. 19.

46 Kunzle, *Fashion and Fetishism*, p. 5.

47 See *The Lancet*, 10 January 1880.

48 Sarah Hale, *Manners; Or Happy Homes and Good Society All The Year Round* (Boston: 1868), p. 39.

49 Showalter, introduction, George Du Maurier, *Trilby*, (Oxford: Oxford University Press, 1998), p. xviii.

50 Silver, *Anorexic Body*, p. 132.

51 *Ibid.*, p. 134.

52 See Dr Peter Gowan, *Consumption* (London: J & A. Churchill, 1878), pp. 78–80.

53 Ormond, *George Du Maurier*, pp. 445–7.

54 Silver, *Anorexic Body*, p. 128.

55 Athena Vrettos, *Somatic Fictions* (Stanford University Press, 1995), p. 104.
56 Marsh, *Pre-Raphaelite Women*, p. 146.
57 Kunzle, *Fashion and Fetishism*, p. 21.
58 *Ibid.*, p. 23.
59 Madame de la Sante, *The Corset Defended* (London: T. E. Carter, 1865), pp. 11–12.
60 See Dr Anna M. Galbraith, *Hygiene and Physical Culture for Women* (London: B. F. Stevens, 1895), p. 224, and Foster, *Natural Prevention and Cure*, p. 17.
61 R. B. D. Wells, *Woman and Her Diseases* (London: J. Burns, 1880), p. 12.
62 Summers, *Bound to Please*, p. 140.
63 Bartlett, *Consumption*, p. 30 and p. 54.
64 Kunzle, *Fashion and Fetishism*, p. 185.
65 *Ibid.*, p. 44.
66 Charles Reade, preface, *A Simpleton: A Story of the Day* (London: Chatto & Windus, 1886), p. iv. All future references to this will be cited parenthetically in the text.

5 CONSUMPTION AND THE COUNT: THE
PATHOLOGICAL ORIGINS OF VAMPIRISM AND BRAM
STOKER'S *DRACULA*

1 See Clive Leatherdale, *Dracula, the Novel and the Legend* (Wellingborough: The Aquarian Press, 1985), pp. 15–23. Leatherdale suggests that while 'legends of the dead returning to drink human blood have been found in nearly every culture where records have survived', the image of what we think of as the vampire begins to crystallise in the Europe of the Middle Ages.
2 Edward Tylor, *Primitive Culture*, 3rd edn, vol. ii (London: John Murray, 1891), pp. 191–2.
3 Leatherdale, *Dracula*, p. 41.
4 *Ibid.*, p. 41.
5 Juan Gomez-Alonzo, *Neurology* 51 (1998).
6 Colin Kaplan, ed., *Rabies: The Facts* (Oxford University Press, 1977), p. 38.
7 Maud Ellman, introduction, *Dracula*, by Bram Stoker (Oxford University Press, 1996), p. 17. For more discussion of this point see Christopher Frayling, ed., *Vampyres* (London: Faber, 1991), p. 6.
8 *Dracula*, p. 42.
9 James Twichell, *The Living Dead* (Durham, NC: Duke University Press, 1981), pp. 38–65.
10 John Keats, *The Poems of John Keats*, ed. Jack Stillenger (London: Heinemann, 1978), p. 357.
11 Michael E. Bell, *Food for the Dead* (New York: Carroll & Graf Publishers, 2001), pp. 7–38.
12 *Providence Journal*, 21 March 1892, p. 8.

13 Bell, *Food for the Dead*, pp. 65–8 and p. 244.

14 Bram Stoker, *Dracula* (Oxford University Press, 1996), p. 297. All following references to this will be cited parenthetically in the text.

15 Gowan, *Consumption*, p. 88: 'The frequency with which the disease attacks one member of a family after another . . .'.

16 Bell, *Food for the Dead*, pp. 240–8.

17 C. A Fraser, 'Scottish Myths from Ontario', *Journal of American Folklore* 6 (1893), p. 196, quoted in Bell, *Food for the Dead*, p. 245.

18 Carl Both, *A New and Effective Method of Treating Consumption* (Boston: E. P. Dutton & Co., 1868), p. 26.

19 C. W. de Lacy Evans, *Consumption – A Re-Investigation of its Causes* (London: Baillière, Tindall & Cox, 1881), p. 10.

20 Gowan, *Consumption*, p. 49 and p. 66.

21 J. Gordon Melton, *The Vampire Book* (Detroit: Visible Ink Press, 1994), p. xxiii.

22 See for example the blood spots in James Rymer, *Varney the Vampyre* (London: E. Lloyd, 1853), p. 6.

23 Bell, *Food for the Dead*, p. 234.

24 Lawlor, *Consumption and Literature*, p. 188.

25 Daniel Farson, *The Man Who Wrote Dracula* (London: Michael Joseph, 1975), pp. 233–5.

26 Elaine Showalter, 'Syphilis, Sexuality and the Fiction of the *Fin de Siècle*' in Ruth Bernard Yeazell, ed., *Sex, Politics and Science in the Nineteenth Century* (Baltimore: Johns Hopkins University Press, 1986), p. 99. See also Jeffrey L. Spear, 'Gender and Sexual Dis-ease in *Dracula*' in Lloyd Davis, ed., *Virginal Sexuality and Textuality in Victorian Literature* (Albany: State University of New York Press, 1993) and Robert Tracy, 'Loving You All Ways' in Regina Barreca, ed., *Sex and Death in Victorian Literature* (Basingstoke: Macmillan Press, 1990), pp. 32–59.

27 Tracy, 'Loving You', p. 46.

28 Showalter, 'Syphilis', p. 99.

29 Tracy, 'Loving You', p. 45.

30 Barbara Belford, *Bram Stoker* (London: Weidenfeld & Nicolson, 1996), pp. 319–21.

31 Paul Murray, *From the Shadow of Dracula* (London: Jonathan Cape, 2004), p. 269.

32 *Ibid.*, pp. 267–8.

33 *Ibid.*, pp. 25–6.

34 Leatherdale, *Dracula*, p. 81.

35 Peter Haining, ed., *Shades of Dracula* (London: William Kimber, 1982), p. 102.

36 'Vampirism in New England', quoted in Haining, p. 107.

37 *Ibid.*, p. 103.

38 *Ibid.*, p. 104.

39 *Ibid.*, italics mine.

40 Bell, *Food for the Dead*, p. 225.

41 William Hughes, *Beyond Dracula* (Basingstoke: Palgrave, 2000), p. 142.

42 *Ibid.*, p. 143.

43 A. C. Dutt, *Health Notes for the Seaside, with Special Reference to Whitby and District* (Whitby: Horne & Son, 1895), p. 19.

44 Diane Mason, 'The Secret Vice: Masturbation in Victorian Fiction and Medical Culture', diss., University of the West of England, 2003, p. 88.

45 It is also possible that he passes over Mina because she is an industrious, bourgeois schoolteacher, whereas Lucy is a wealthy, idle and somewhat spoilt daughter of the gentry, for as I discussed in Chapter 2, it was believed that consumption could be caused by the idleness and over-indulgence in luxury that characterised the lifestyle of the upper classes.

46 Tracy, 'Loving You', p. 43.

47 See for example Carol A. Senf, ed., *The Critical Response to Bram Stoker* (London: Greenwood, 1993), p. 70, and Phyllis A. Roth, 'Suddenly Sexual Women in Bram Stoker's *Dracula*' in Margaret L. Carter ed., *Dracula: The Vampire and the Critics* (London: UMI Research Press, 1988).

48 See Robert J. Culverwell, *On Consumption, Coughs, Colds, Asthma and other Diseases of the Chest* (London: The Author, 1834), p. 33.

49 Dr Daniel Henry Cullimore, *Consumption as a Contagious Disease* (London: Tindall, Baillière & Cox, 1880), p. 58.

50 John and William Hunter, *To Be Or Not To Be: Happiness or Misery, an Essay on Nervous Disability* (London: The Authors, 1854), p. 49.

51 Anna Krugovoy Silver has suggested that the vampire's 'emaciation can be read as ... a sign of the monster's excessive and unfillable appetite ...' (Silver, *Anorexic Body*, p. 118).

52 Rymer, *Varney*, p. 8.

53 Leslie Shepard, ed., *The Dracula Book of Classic Vampire Stories* (London: Robert Hale, 1977), p. 119.

54 Richard Dalby, ed., *Dracula's Brood* (London: Crucible, 1987), p. 219 and p. 220.

55 *Ibid.*, p. 224.

56 Dr Richard Sandon Gutteridge, *Consumption and its Cure* (London: T. J. Hutchins, 1892), p. 21.

57 Dalby, *Dracula's Brood*, p. 220.

58 *Ibid.*, p. 225, italics mine.

59 Elizabeth Gaskell describes the 'bright, feverish, glittering eyes' of the consumptive Esther in *Mary Barton* (London: Penguin Books, 1996), p. 391.

60 H. G. Wells mentions the 'the hectic beauty' of the consumptive in *The Time Machine* (p. 20) and Burgess is one of many physicians who describe phthisis sufferers as 'hectic patients' (*Climate of Italy*, p. 102).

61 Dr Edward Blackmore, *A Practical Treatise on the Forms, Sanability and Treatment of Pulmonary Consumption* (London: Longman, Rees & Co., 1832), p. 202.

62 Sheridan Le Fanu, *Carmilla* (London: Pilot Press, 1985), p. 34. All following references to this will be cited parenthetically in the text.

63 See Alan Johnson, 'Bent and Broken Necks: Signs of Design in Stoker's *Dracula*' in Carter, *Dracula*, p. 236, and Frayling, *Vampyres*, p. 304.

64 Marie Mulvey-Roberts, 'Dracula and the Doctors: Bad Blood, Menstrual Taboos and the New Woman' in William Hughes and Andrew Smith, eds., *Bram Stoker* (Basingstoke: Macmillan, 1998), p. 78.

65 Burton-Fanning, *Open-Air Treatment*, pp. 20–1.

66 Sir Arthur Ransome, *A Campaign Against Phthisis* (Manchester: John Heywood, 1892), p. 2.

67 Hillier, *Tuberculosis*, p. 127, p. 128 and p. 49.

68 C. Braine-Hartnell, *The Prevention and Cure of Tuberculosis* (Cheltenham: Norman, Sawyer & Co., 1900), p. 8.

69 Bowditch, *Is Consumption Ever Contagious?*, p. 14.

70 Other physicians who advise against sharing a bed with a consumptive include James Weaver, who says there is 'great danger to anyone who does so'. *A Practical Treatise on the Cure of Pulmonary Consumption* (London: J. & A . Churchill, 1887), p. 26.

71 Ransome, *Causes and Prevention*, p. 128.

72 J. D. Rolleston, 'The Folklore of Pulmonary Tuberculosis', *Tubercle* 22 (1964).

73 G. F. C. Wall, 'Different from Writing': *Dracula* in 1897', *Literature and History* 10 (1984), p. 15.

74 'Syphilis Sexuality', pp. 90–100.

75 Oldfield, *Flesh Eating*, p. 56, italics his.

76 Salli J. Kline, *The Degeneration of Women* (Rheinbach: CMZ-Verlag, 1992), pp. 21–2.

77 Dr Thomas Beddoes, *Essay on the Causes, Early Signs of, and Prevention of Pulmonary Consumption* (Bristol: Biggs and Cottle, 1799), p. 8, quoted in Bell, *Food for the Dead*, p. 236.

78 Culverwell, *On Consumption*, p. 33.

79 Weaver, *A Practical Treatise*, pp. 28–9.

80 Dale, *Treatise*, p. 32.

81 Gurney, *Diet in Disease*, p. 8.

82 Culverwell, *On Consumption*, p. 46.

83 *Lancet,* 10 July 1865, p. 496.

84 De Lacy Evans, *Consumption*, pp. 50–1.

85 *Ibid.*, p. 51.

86 Rolleston, 'Folklore', p. 58.

87 S. Warren, 'Passages from the Diary of a Late Physician', quoted in Hunter, *Happiness or Misery*, p. 448.

88 Dale, *Treatise*, pp. 6–7.

6 'A KIND OF INTELLECTUAL ADVANTAGE': CONSUMPTION AND MASCULINE IDENTITY IN HENRY JAMES'S *THE PORTRAIT OF A LADY*

1 Lawlor, *Consumption and Literature*, pp. 91–107, and p. 55.
2 Mary Ward, *Robert Elsmere* (London: Nelson's Books, 1888), p. 567.
3 Henry James, *The Portrait of a Lady* (Oxford University Press, 1995), p. 22. All other references to this will be cited parenthetically in the text.
4 Robert K. Martin, 'Failed Heterosexuality in *The Portrait of a Lady*' in John R. Bradley, ed., *Henry James and Homo-Erotic Desire* (London: Macmillan Press, 1999), p. 87.
5 William Veeder, 'The Portrait of a Lack' in Joel Porte, ed., *New Essays on The Portrait of a Lady* (Cambridge University Press, 1990), p. 99.
6 For an examination of decadence and disease in literature, see Barbara Spackman, *Decadent Genealogies* (Ithaca, N.Y.: Cornell University Press, 1989).
7 Burton-Fanning, *Open-Air Treatment*, p. 16.
8 Veeder, 'Portrait of a Lack', pp. 98–108.
9 *Ibid.*, p. 106.
10 Kaplan, *Henry James: The Imagination of Genius* (London: Hodder and Stoughton, 1992) p. 116.
11 Martin, 'Failed Heterosexuality', p. 88.
12 Dr W. Roemisch, *How to Guard Against a Return of Phthisis* (London: Adlard & Son, 1907), p. 57.
13 Bailin, *The Sickroom in Victorian Fiction* (Cambridge University Press, 1994) p. 40.
14 Parkin, *Climate and Phthisis*, p. 8.
15 Katherine V. Snyder, *Bachelors, Manhood and the Novel* (Cambridge University Press, 1999), p. 95.
16 *Ibid.*, p. 98.
17 Martin, 'Failed Heterosexuality', p. 87.
18 *Ibid.*
19 For further discussion of the watchful, all-seeing 'invalid looker-on', see Frawley, *Invalidism and Identity*, pp. 200–44.
20 Kaplan, *Henry James*, p. 97.
21 Jean Strouse, *Alice James: A Biography* (Cambridge, Mass.: Harvard University Press, 1999).
22 Kaplan, *Henry James*, pp. 55–6.
23 See Ernest Sandeen, '*The Wings of the Dove* and *The Portrait of a Lady*: A Study of Henry James's Later Phase' in William T. Stafford, ed., *Perspectives on James's The Portrait of a Lady* (New York University Press, 1967), pp. 187–205.
24 Henry James, *Henry James Letters*, vol. 1, ed. Leon Edel (London: Macmillan, 1974), p. 218.
25 See Nicola Bradbury, introduction, *The Portrait of a Lady*.
26 See Alfred Habegger, 'The Fatherless Heroine and the Filial Son', in Porte, *New Essays*.

27 Sandeen, 'Henry James's Later Phase', p. 190.
28 F. O. Matthiessen, *The James Family* (New York: Alfred A. Knopf, 1947), p. 260.
29 Sandeen, 'Henry James's Later Phase', p. 190.
30 Edel, *Henry James Letters*, p. 219 and p. 222.
31 Kaplan, *Henry James*, pp. 92–117.
32 Edel, *Henry James, Letters*, p. 219 and p. 222.
33 *Ibid.*, p. 221.
34 Kaplan, *Henry James*, p. 119.

CONCLUSION

1 Lawlor, *Consumption and Literature*, p. 138.

EPILOGUE 'A TRULY MODERN ILLNESS':
INTO THE TWENTIETH CENTURY AND BEYOND

1 The writings of Katherine Mansfield and D. H. Lawrence can also be considered a form of tubercular literature, for as long-term consumptives their work has distinctly pathological influences. However, as this study is confined to direct textual representations of consumption I have not discussed their novels here. For further discussion of this see Mary Burgan, *Illness, Gender and Writing: The Case of Katherine Mansfield* (Baltimore: Johns Hopkins University Press, 1994) and David Ellis, *D. H. Lawrence: Dying Game, 1922–1930* (Cambridge University Press, 1998).
2 Katherine Ott, *Fevered Lives* (Cambridge, Mass.: Harvard University Press, 1996), p. 2.
3 Lawlor, *Consumption and Literature*, p. 189.
4 For a detailed discussion of the success rate of collapse therapy and its longevity as a popular treatment, see Smith, *Retreat of Tuberculosis*, pp. 139–47.
5 H. Timbrell Bulstrode, *Report on Sanatoria for Consumption* (London: 1908).
6 Ott, *Fevered lives*, p. 150.
7 Smith, *Retreat of Tuberculosis*, p. 130.
8 *Ibid.*
9 *Ibid.*
10 See also Betty MacDonald, *The Plague and I* (London: Hammond, Hammond and Co., 1948), the autobiographical *House of Courage,* by William Heaney, and, for an earlier (1893) perspective on sanatoria, Beatrice Harraden, *Ships that Pass in the Night* (London: Lawrence and Bullen, 1893).
11 Jeffrey Meyers, *Disease and the Novel 1880–1960* (London: Macmillan Press, 1984), p. 105.
12 A. E. Ellis, *The Rack* (Harmondsworth: Penguin, 1961), p. 26. All further references to this will be cited parenthetically in the text.
13 Thomas Mann, *The Magic Mountain,* trans. H. T. Lowe-Porter (London: Secker, 1928), p. 6.
14 *Ibid.*

15 Meyers, *Disease and the Novel*, p. 105.

16 George Orwell, *Nineteen Eighty-Four* (London: Penguin Books, 2003), pp. 36–7. We are not directly told that Winston Smith is a consumptive, but he fits the conventional picture of the disease exactly, given that he is emaciated, frail and 'doubled up by . . . violent coughing' in the mornings. Of course, George Orwell himself had tuberculosis, and due to his inability to tolerate the newly available streptomycin, died of the disease in 1948, ten years after diagnosis. *Nineteen Eighty-Four* can hence be read as a tubercular narrative, and even, given its preoccupation with constant surveillance and enclosure, and the time its author spent in such institutions, as a version of the sanatorium novel.

17 William J. Heaney, *House of Courage* (Dublin: Clonmore & Reynolds, 1952), p. 21 and p. 39.

18 Mann, *Magic Mountain*, p. 14.

19 A good illustration of the emotional and social detachment of the invalid can be found in *Dracula*, when Dr Seward notes the instinct for self-preservation apparent in Lucy's mother. Mrs Westenra is dying of heart disease, and as a result seems not to want to realise the full horror of her daughter's condition: 'She was alarmed, but not nearly so much as I expected . . . Here, in a case where any shock may prove fatal, matters are so ordered that, from one cause or other, the things not personal – even the terrible change in her daughter, to whom she is so attached – do not seem to reach her . . . I saw again the hand of Nature fighting for life' (pp. 119–20).

20 Ott, *Fevered Lives*, pp. 87–99.

21 Burton-Fanning, *Open-Air Treatment*, p. 5.

22 Winifred Holtby, *The Land of Green Ginger* (Chicago: Cassandra Editions, 1978), p. 239.

23 Joanna Bourke, *Dismembering the Male* (London: Reaktion Books, 1996), p. 16.

24 *Ibid.*, p. 175.

25 Meyers, *Disease and the Novel*, p. 104.

Bibliography

PRIMARY TEXTS

Acton, William. *Prostitution*. 2nd edn. London: Frank Cass and Company Ltd, 1870.

Alabone, Edwin. *The Cure of Consumption*. 6th edn. London: Kemp and Co., 1880.

Alexander, John. *The Collapse Therapy of Pulmonary Tuberculosis*. Springfield, Ill.: Charles C. Thomas, 1937.

Allingham, William. *A Diary*. Ed. H. Allingham and D. Radford. London: Macmillan, 1907.

Allinson, T. R. *Consumption: Its Causes, Symptoms, Treatment and Cure*. London: F. Pitman, 1853.

Balbirnie, John. *Consumption, the Modern Youth Consumer: Its Nature, Causes, Prevention and Cure*. London: Darton and Co., 1856.

    The Water Cure in Consumption and Scrofula. 3rd edn. London: Longmans and Co., 1856.

Bartlett, Thomas. *Consumption, its Causes, Prevention and Cure*. London: Hippolyte Baillière, 1855.

Beddoes, Thomas. *Essay on the Causes, Early Signs and Prevention of Pulmonary Consumption*. Bristol: Biggs and Cottle, 1799.

Bennet, J. Henry. *Winter in the South of Europe*. 3rd edn. London: J. Churchill and Sons, 1865

    'On the Connection Between Phthisis and Uterine Disease'. *Lancet*, 27 May 1865.

Bennett, John Hughes. *The Pathology and Treatment of Pulmonary Consumption*. 2nd edn. Edinburgh: Adam and Charles Black, 1859.

Bibby, E. *Invalids Abroad: Hints on Travelling, Nursing and Cooking*. London: Hatchards, 1879.

Bird, Samuel Dougan. *On Australasian Climates and their Influence in the Prevention and Arrest of Pulmonary Consumption*. London: Longman and Co., 1863.

Blackmore, Edward. *A Practical Treatise on the Forms, Sanability and Treatment of Pulmonary Consumption*. London: Longman, Rees and Co., 1832.

Bodington, George. *An Essay on the Treatment and Cure of Pulmonary Consumption*. London: Orme, Brown, Green and Longmans, 1840.

Both, Carl. *A New and Effective Method of Treating Consumption.* Boston: E. P. Dutton and Co., 1868.

Bowditch, Henry. *Is Consumption Ever Contagious?* Boston: David Clapp, 1864.

Braine-Hartnell, C. *The Prevention and Cure of Tuberculosis.* Cheltenham: Norman, Sawyer and Co., 1900.

Braun, Julius. *On the Curative Effects of Baths and Waters.* Trans. F. E. Burnnett. Ed. Hermann Weber. London: Smith, Elder and Co., 1875.

Brontë, Charlotte. *Jane Eyre.* [1847]. Oxford University Press, 1975.

Brontë, Emily. *Wuthering Heights.* [1847]. London: Penguin Books, 1996.

Broughton, Rhoda. *Not Wisely But Too Well.* [1867]. London: Cassell and Company, 1967.

Bulman, Brian. *The House of Quiet People.* London: Macmillan Press, 1937.

Burgess, Thomas. *The Climate of Italy in Relation to Pulmonary Consumption.* London: Longman and Co., 1852.

Burne-Jones, Georgie. *Memorials of Edward Burne-Jones.* [1904]. London: Humphries, 1993.

Burslem, W. M. *On Consumption.* London: John Churchill, 1852.

Burton-Fanning, F. W. *The Open-Air Treatment of Pulmonary Consumption.* London: Cassell and Co., 1905.

Consumption and Factory Life (Norwich: Gibbs and Waller, 1911).

Candler, C. *The Prevention of Consumption.* London: Kegan Paul and Co., 1887.

Cave, A. J. E. 'The evidence for the incidence of tuberculosis in ancient Egypt' *British Journal of Tuberculosis* 33 (1939).

Chadwick, Edwin. *Chadwick's Report on the Sanitary Condition of the Labouring Population.* Ed. M. W. Flinn. Edinburgh University Press, 1965.

Cheyne, George. *The English Malady.* 1733. New York: Scholars' Facsimiles and Reprints, Inc., 1976.

Churchill, John F. *Letters to a Patient on Consumption and its Cure by the Hypophosphites.* London: David Sott, 1888.

Congreve, George T. *On Consumption of the Lungs, OR Decline and its Successful Treatment.* London: Elliot Stock, 1881.

Cook, Francis. *A Practical Treatise on Pulmonary Consumption.* London: John Churchill, 1842.

Cooke, E. T. and Wedderburn, A. D., eds. *The Works of John Ruskin.* London: George Allen, 1909.

Cullimore, Daniel Henry. *Consumption as a Contagious Disease.* London: Tindall, Baillière and Cox, 1880.

Culverwell, Robert J. *On Consumption, Coughs, Colds, Asthma and Other Diseases of the Chest.* London: The Author, 1834.

Dale, William. *A Popular, Non-Technical, Treatise on Consumption.* Harrogate: R. Ackrill, 1884.

De Guerville, A. B. *The Crusade Against Phthisis.* London: Hugh Rees, 1904.

De La Sante, Madame. *The Corset Defended.* London: T. E. Carter, 1865.

De Lacy Evans, C. W. *Consumption – A Re-Investigation of its Causes.* London: Baillière, Tindall and Cox, 1881.

Dickens, Charles. *Dombey and Son.* [1848]. London: Wordsworth Editions Ltd, 1995.

  David Copperfield. [1849]. London: Penguin Books, 1994.

  Hard Times. [1854]. London: Penguin Books, 1995.

Disraeli, Benjamin. *Sybil.* [1845]. Harmondsworth: Penguin Books, 1980.

Dobell, Horace. *On Loss of Weight, Blood Spitting and Lung Disease.* London: J. and A. Churchill, 1878.

Doughty, O. and Wahl J. M., eds. *Letters of Dante Gabriel Rossetti.* Oxford: The Clarendon Press, 1965.

Du Maurier, George. *Trilby.* [1894]. London: Osgood and McIllvane, 1895.

Dutt, A. C. *Health Notes for the Seaside, with special Reference to Whitby and District.* Whitby: Horne and Son, 1895.

East, Rowland. *The Two Most Dangerous Diseases of England.* London: John Lee, 1842.

Ellis, A. E. *The Rack.* [1958]. Harmondsworth: Penguin Books, 1961.

Foster, Edgar J. *The Natural Prevention and Cure of Colds, Sore Throats, Asthma, Bronchitis and CONSUMPTION.* Ipswich: Eastern Counties Gazette, 1887.

Garland, Charles H. and Latham, Arthur. *The Conquest of Consumption: An Economic study.* London: T. Fisher, 1910.

Gaskell, Elizabeth. *Mary Barton.* [1848]. London: Penguin Books, 1996.

  North and South. [1854]. Oxford University Press, 1998.

Gissing, George. *Workers in the Dawn.* [1879]. Sussex: The Harvester Press, 1976.

  The Nether World. [1889]. London: Eveleigh, Nash and Grayson, 1928.

Gowan, Peter. *Consumption.* London: J. and A. Churchill, 1878.

Gurney, Thomas. *Diet in Disease.* London: Henry Renshaw, 1886.

Gutteridge, Richard Sandon. *Consumption and Its Cure.* London: T. J. Hutchin, 1892.

Hale, Sarah. *Manners; Or, Happy Homes and Good Society All the Year Round.* Boston: 1868.

Harraden, Beatrice. *Ships that Pass in the Night.* London: Lawrence and Bullen, 1839.

Heaney, William J. *House of Courage.* Dublin: Clonmore and Reynolds, 1952.

Hillier, Alfred. *Tuberculosis: Its Nature, Prevention and Treatment.* London: Cassell and Co., 1900.

  The Prevention of Consumption. London: Longmans and Green, 1903.

Holtby, Winifred. *The Land of Green Ginger.* [1928]. London: Cassandra Editions, 1978.

Hunter, John and Hunter, William. *To Be or Not To Be: Happiness or Misery, an Essay on Nervous Disability.* London: The Authors, 1854.

James, Henry. *The Portrait of a Lady.* [1881]. Oxford University Press, 1995.

  The Wings of the Dove. [1902]. New York: Norton and Co., 1978.

  A Life in Letters. Ed. Philp Thorne. London: Penguin Press, 1999.

  Henry James Letters. Ed. Leon Edel. London: Macmillan, 1974.

Keats, John. *The Poems of John Keats.* Ed. Jack Stillender. London: Heinemann, 1978.

Le Fanu, Sheridan. *Carmilla*. [1872]. London: Pilot Press, 1985.

MacDonald, Betty. *The Plague and I*. London: Hammond and Co., 1948.

Malthus, Thomas. *An Essay on the Principle of Population*. [1798]. London: Penguin Books, 1970.

Mann, Thomas. *The Magic Mountain*. Trans. H. T. Lowe-Porter. London: Secker and Warburg, 1946.

Meredith, George. [1896]. *The Ordeal of Richard Feverel*. London: Archibald Constable and Co., 1909.

Millais, J. G., ed. *Life and Letters of Sir John Everett Millais*. London: Methuen, 1899.

Moore, Norman. *A Lecture on the History of Medicine as Illustrated in English Literature*. London: Adlard and Son, 1903.

Moore, Thomas. *Life and Journals of Lord Byron*. Hamberg: Lebel, Trittel and Wrutz, 1830.

Newsholme, Sir Arthur. *Fifty Years in Public Health*. London: George Allen and Unwin Ltd., 1935.

Oldfield, Josiah. *Flesh Eating: A Cause of Consumption*. London: The Vegetarian Society, 1897.

Orwell, George. *Nineteen Eighty-Four*. [1949]. London: Penguin Books, 2003.

Parkin, John. *Climate and Phthisis*. London: Longmans, Green and Co., 1875.

Ransome, Arthur. *The Causes and Prevention of Phthisis*. London: Smith, Elder and Co., 1890.

A Campaign Against Phthisis. Manchester: John Heywood, 1892.

Reade, Charles. *A Simpleton: A Story of the Day*. London: Chatto and Windus, 1886.

Roemisch, W. *How to Guard Against a Return of Phthisis*. London: Adlard and Son, 1907.

Rolleston, Humphry. *Associations Between Literature and Medicine*. London: Harrison and Sons, 1933.

Rossetti, William, ed. *Dante Gabriel Rossetti: His Family Letters*. London: Ellis and Elvey, 1895.

Ruskin: Rossetti: Preraphaelitism. Papers 1854 to 1862. London: Allen, 1899.

Rymer, James. *Varney the Vampyre*. London: E. Lloyd, 1853.

Sealy, J. Hungerford. *Medical Essays No. 1: Phthisis Pulmonalis, its History and Varieties*. London: Sherwood, Gilbert and Piper, 1837.

Smith, Fred. *Keep Your Mouth Shut: A Treatise on Breathing*. London: Baillière and Co., 1892.

Stoker, Bram. *Dracula*. [1897]. Oxford University Press, 1996.

Thompson, R. E. *The Different Aspects of Family Phthisis*. London: Smith, Elder and Co., 1884.

Thorne, Richard. *The Administrative Control of Tuberculosis*. London: Baillière, Tindall and Cox, 1899.

Trollope, Anthony. *Marion Fay*. [1882]. London: The Trollope Society, 1997.

Use of Sugar, the Primary Cause of Pulmonary Consumption. London: Simpkin, Marshall and Co., 1860.

Vaccination as the Cause of Fever and Consumption. London: British College of Health, 1868.

Ward, Mrs Humphry. *Robert Elsmere*. London: Nelson Books, 1888.

    Eleanor. London: Smith, Elder and Co, 1900.

    A Writer's Recollections. London: W. Collins, Sons and Co., 1918.

Weaver, James. *A Practical Treatise on the Cure of Pulmonary Consumption*. London: J. and A. Churchill, 1887.

Wells, H. G. *Tono-Bungay*. London: Waterlow and Sons Ltd, 1909.

Wells, R. B. D. *Woman and Her Diseases*. London: J. Burns, 1880.

Wood, Mrs Henry. *East Lynne*. [1861]. London: Macmillan, 1900.

Yeo, J. Burney. *The Results of Recent Researches in the Treatment of Phthisis*. London: J. and A. Churchill, 1877.

SECONDARY TEXTS

Ackroyd, Peter. *Dickens*. London: Sinclair-Stevenson Ltd, 1990.

Allett, John. 'Tono-Bungay: The Metaphor of Disease in H. G. Wells's Novel.' *Queens Quarterly* 93 (1986 Summer): pp. 365–74.

Altick, Richard D. *The English Common Reader*. Chicago: University of Chicago Press, 1957.

Andrews, Malcolm. *Dickens on England and the English*. Sussex: The Harvester Press, 1979.

Bailin, Miriam. *The Sickroom in Victorian Fiction*. Cambridge University Press, 1994.

Barnes, David. *The Making of a Social Disease: Tuberculosis in Nineteenth-Century France*. London: University of California Press, 1995.

Barreca, Regina, ed. *Sex and Death in Victorian Literature*. Basingstoke: Macmillan Press, 1990.

Belford, Barbara. *Bram Stoker*. London: Weidenfeld and Nicolson, 1996.

Bell, Michael E. *Food for the Dead*. New York: Carroll and Graf Publishers, 2001.

Bell, Rudolph. *Holy Anorexia*. Chicago University Press, 1985.

Bergonzi, Bernard. *H. G. Wells: A Collection of Critical Essays*. New Jersey: Prentice Hall Inc., 1976.

Borrello, Alfred. *H. G. Wells: Author in Agony*. Springfield, Ill.: Southern Illinois University Press, 1972.

Berry, Christopher J. *The Idea of Luxury: A Conceptual and Historical Investigation*. Cambridge University Press, 1994.

Bourke, Joanna. *Dismembering the Male*. London: Reaktion Books Ltd, 1996.

Bradley, John R., ed. *Henry James and Homo-Erotic Desire*. London: Macmillan Press, 1999.

Breward, Christopher. *The Hidden Consumer*. Manchester University Press, 1999.

Brewer J. and Porter, R., eds. *Consumption and the World of Goods*. London: Routledge, 1993.

Bristow, Joseph. *Sexuality*. London: Routledge, 1997.

Brewer, J., McKendrick, N. and Plumb, J. H., eds. *The Birth of a Consumer Society*. London: Hutchinson and Co., 1983.

Bronfen, Elizabeth. *Over Her Dead Body*. Manchester University Press, 1992.

Brumberg, Joan Jacobs. *Fasting Girls*. Cambridge, Mass.: Harvard University Press, 1988.

Burgan, Mary. *Illness, Gender, Writing: The Case of Katharine Mansfield*. Baltimore: The Johns Hopkins University Press, 1994.

Carter, Margaret L., ed. *Dracula: The Vampire and The Critics*. London: U.M.I. Research Press, 1988.

Colby, Vineta. *The Singular Anomaly: Women Novelists of the Nineteenth Century*. New York University Press, 1970.

Dalby, Richard, ed. *Dracula's Brood*. London: Crucible, 1987.

Davis, Lloyd, ed. *Virginal Sexuality and Textuality in Victorian Literature*. Albany: State University of New York Press, 1993.

De Grazia, Victoria, ed. *The Sex of Things: Gender and Consumption in Historical Perspective*. London: University of California Press, 1996.

Dijkstra, Bram. *Idols of Perversity*. New York: Oxford University Press, 1986.

Dormandy, Thomas. *The White Death*. London: The Hambledon Press, 1999.

Douglas, Mary. *Purity and Danger*. London: Routledge and Kegan Paul, 1966.
  Natural Symbols. London: The Gresset Press, 1970.

Dubos, Rene and Dubos, Jean. *The White Plague*. London: Victor Gollancz Ltd, 1953.

Ellis, David. *D. H. Lawrence: Dying Game, 1922–1930*. Cambridge University Press, 1998.

Farson, Daniel. *The Man Who Wrote Dracula*. London: M. Joseph, 1975.

Fraser, C. A. 'Scottish Myths from Ontario'. *Journal of American Folklore* 6 (1893).'

Frawley, Maria H. *Invalidism and Identity in Nineteenth-Century Britain*. London: University of Chicago Press, 2004.

Flint, Kate, ed. *The Victorian Novelist; Social Problems and Social Change*. Beckenham: Croom Helm Ltd, 1987.

Freedman, Robert. *Marx on Economics*. Middlesex: Penguin Books Ltd, 1962.

French, Roger, ed. *Medicine from the Black Death to the French Disease*. Aldershot: Ashgate, 1998.

Gallagher, Catherine. *The Industrial Reformation of English Fiction: Social Discourse and Narrative Form*. London: University of Chicago Press, 1985.

Gallagher, Catherine, and Laqueur, Thomas, eds. *The Making of the Modern Body*. London: University of California Press, 1987.

Giddings, Robert, ed. *The Changing World of Charles Dickens*. London: Vision Press, 1983.

Gilbert, Pamela K. *Disease, Desire and the Body in Victorian Women's Popular Novels*. Cambridge University Press, 1997.

Gilman, Sander L. *Making the Body Beautiful: A Cultural History of Aesthetic Surgery*. Princeton University Press, 1999.
  Death and Representations: Images of Illness from Madness to AIDS. London: Cornell University Press, 1988.
  Health and Illness: Images of Difference. London: Reaktion, 1995.

Goldberg, Michael. *Carlyle and Dickens*. Athens: University of Georgia Press, 1972.

Gould, Warwick and Staley, Thomas, eds. *Writing the Lives of Writers*. London: Macmillan Press, 1998.

Greer, Germaine. *The Politics of Human Fertility*. London: Martin Secker and Warburg Ltd, 1984.

Guy, Josephine M. *The Victorian Social Problem Novel*. London: Macmillan Press, 1996.

Haining, Peter, ed. *Shades of Dracula: Bram Stoker's Uncollected Stories*. London: William Kimber and Co., 1982.

Helman, Cecil. *Body Myths*. London: Chatto and Windus, 1991.

Hughes, William. *Beyond Dracula*. Basingstoke: Palgrave, 2000.

Hughes, W. and Smith, A., eds. *Bram Stoker*. Basingstoke: Macmillan, 1998.

Hunt, Violet. *The Wife of Rossetti*. New York: E. P. Dutton and Co., 1932.

Jalland, Pat. *Death in the Victorian Family*. Oxford University Press, 1996.

Judd, Catherine. *Bedside Seductions: Nursing and the Victorian Imagination 1830–80*. Basingstoke: Macmillan, 1998.

Kaplan, Colin, ed. *Rabies: The Facts*. Oxford University Press, 1977.

Kaplan, Fred. *Henry James: The Imagination of Genius*. London: Hodder and Stoughton, 1992.

Karlen, Arno. *Plague's Progress*. London: Victor Gollanez, 1996.

Kline, Salli J. *The Degeneration of Women*. Rheinbach: CMZ-Verlag, 1992.

Kunzle, David. *Fashion and Fetishism*. Totowa: Rowman and Littlefield, 1982.

Lane, Joan. *A Social History of Medicine*. London: Routledge, 2001.

Latimer, Dan. 'Erotic Susceptibility and Tuberculosis: Literary Images of a Pathology.' *MLN* 105, no. 5 (1990).

Lawlor, Clark. *Consumption and Literature: The Making of the Romantic Disease*. Basingstoke: Palgrave, 2006.

Leatherdale, Clive. *Dracula: The Novel and the Legend*. Wellingborough: The Aquarian Press, 1985.

Logan, Melville. *Nerves and Narratives*. London: University of California Press, 1997.

Lovel, Terry. *Consuming Fictions*. London: Verso, 1987.

Marsh, Jan. *Pre-Raphaelite Sisterhood*. London: Quartet Books Ltd, 1985.
  Pre-Raphaelite Women. London: Weidenfeld and Nicolson, 1987.
  The Legend of Elizabeth Siddal. London: Quartet Books Ltd, 1989.
  ed. *Christina Rossetti, Poems and Prose*. London: Everyman, 1994.

Mason, Diane. 'The Secret Vice: Masturbation in Victorian Fiction and Medical Culture'. Diss. University of the West of England, 2003.

Matthiesson, F. O. *The James Family*. New York: Alfred A. Knopf, 1947.

Melton, J. George. *The Vampire Book*. Detroit: Visible Ink Press, 1994.

Meyers, Jeffrey. *Disease and the Novel, 1880–1960*. London: Macmillan, 1985.

Micale, Mark S. *Approaching Hysteria*. Princeton University Press, 1995.

Moorman, J. *Tuberculosis and Genius*. London: University of Chicago Press, 1940.

Mort, Frank. *Dangerous Sexualities*. London: Routledge, 2000.

Motion, Andrew. *Keats*. London: Faber and Faber, 1997.

Murray, Paul. *From the Shadow of Dracula: A Life of Bram Stoker*. London: Jonathan Cape, 2004.

Nead, Lynda. *Myths of Sexuality*. Oxford: Basil Blackwell, 1988.

Nicol, D. M. *The End of the Byzantine Empire*. London: Edward Arnold Ltd, 1979.

Ormond, Leonee. *George Du Maurier*. London: Routledge and Kegan Paul, 1969.

Ott, Katherine. *Fevered Lives*. Cambridge, Mass: Harvard University Press, 1996.

Perrot, Philippe. *Fashioning the Bourgeoisie*. Trans. Richard Bienvenu. West Sussex: Princeton University Press, 1994.

Peterson, William S. *Mrs Humphry Ward: Victorian Heretic*. Leicester University Press, 1976.

Plato. 'Phaedo', *Five Dialogues*. Ed. John M. Cooper. 2nd edn. Trans. G. M. A. Grube. Indiapolis: Hackett, 2002.

Porte, Joel. *New Essays on The Portrait of a Lady*. Cambridge University Press, 1990.

Porter, Roy. 'Consumption: Disease of the Consumer Society', in John Brewer and Roy Porter eds. *Consumption and the World of Goods*. London: Routledge, 1993.

Bodies Politic: Disease, Death and Doctors in Britain 1650–1900. London: Reaktion, 2001.

Porter, Roy and Mulvey-Roberts, Marie, eds. *Literature and Medicine During the Eighteenth Century*. London: Routledge, 1993.

Praz, Mario. *The Romantic Agony*. 2nd edn. Trans. Angus Davidson. London: Oxford University Press, 1970.

Pykett, Lyn, ed. *Reading Fin de Siècle Fictions*. London: Longman, 1996.

Quetel, Claude. *A History of Syphilis*. Trans. Judith Braddock and Brian Pike. London: Polity Press, 1990.

Rolleston, J. D. 'The Folklore of Pulmonary Tuberculosis'. *Tubercle* 22 (1964).

Rotberg, Robert I., ed. *Health and Disease in Human History, A Journal of Interdisciplinary History: Reader*. London: MIT Press, 2000.

Roth, Phyllis A. *Bram Stoker*. Boston: G. K. Hall and Company, 1982.

Ryan, Frank. *Tuberculosis: The Greatest Story Never Told*. Bromsgrove: Swift Publishers, 1992.

Sales, Robert. *Jane Austen and Representations of Regency England*. London: Routledge, 1996.

Schwarzbach, F. S. *Dickens and the City*. London: The Athlone Press, 1979.

Searle, G. R. *The Quest for National Efficiency*. London: The Ashfield Press, 1971.

Senf, Carol A., ed. *The Critical Response to Bram Stoker*. Westport, Conn.: Greenwood Press, 1993.

Sharp, William. *Dante Gabriel Rossetti: A Record and a Study*. London: Macmillan, 1882.

Sharrock, Cath. 'Pathologising Sexual Bodies' in A. Medhurst and S. Munt, eds. *Lesbian and Gay Studies*. London: Cassell, 1997.

Shelston, Alan, ed. *'Dombey and Son' and 'Little Dorrit': A Casebook*. London: Macmillan Press, 1985.

Shepard, Leslie, ed. *The Dracula Book of Classic Vampire Stories.* London: Robert
    Hale, 1977.
Showalter, Elaine. *Sexual Anarchy.* London: Virago Press, 1992.
Shuttleworth, Sally. *Charlotte Brontë and Victorian Psychology.* Cambridge Univer-
    sity Press, 1996.
Silver, Anna Krugovoy. *Victorian Literature and the Anorexic Body.* Cambridge
    University Press, 2002.
Small, Helen. *Love's Madness: Medicine, the Novel, and Female Insanity.* Oxford:
    Clarendon Press, 1996.
Smith, F. B. *The Retreat of Tuberculosis.* Beckenham: Croom Helm Ltd, 1988.
Smith, Sheila M. *The Other Nation.* New York: Oxford University Press, 1980.
Snyder, Katherine V. *Bachelors, Manhood and the Novel.* Cambridge University
    Press, 1999.
Sontag, Susan. *Illness as Metaphor.* New York: Farrar, Straus and Giroux, 1977.
    AIDS and its Metaphors. Harmondsworth: Penguin Books, 1990.
Spackman, Barbara. *Decadent Genealogies.* Ithaca, N.Y.: Cornell University Press,
    1989.
Spongberg, Mary. *Feminising Venereal Disease.* London: Macmillan Press, 1997.
Stafford, William T., ed. *Perspectives on James's 'The Portrait of a Lady'.* New York
    University Press, 1967.
Stott, Rebecca. *The Fabrication of the Late Victorian Femme Fatale.* London:
    Macmillan Press, 1992.
Summers, Leigh. *Bound to Please: A History of the Victorian Corset.* Oxford: Berg,
    2001.
Surtees, Virginia, ed. *The Diaries of George Price Boyce.* Norwich: Real World, 1980.
    Rossetti's Portraits of Elizabeth Siddal. Oxford: Scholar Press, 1991.
Sussman, Charlotte. *Consuming Anxieties.* Stanford University Press, 2000.
Sutherland, John. *Eminent Victorian Pre-Eminent Edwardian.* Oxford University
    Press, 1990.
Tillotson, Kathleen. *Novels of the 1840s.* Oxford: Clarendon Press, 1954.
Trevelyan, Janet Penrose. *The Life of Mrs Humphry Ward.* London: Constable and
    Co., 1923.
Turner, Brian S. *The Body and Society.* Oxford: Basil Blackwell, 1984.
Twichell, James. *The Living Dead.* Durham, N.C.: Duke University Press, 1981.
Uglow, Jenny. *Elizabeth Gaskell: A Habit of Stories.* London: Faber and Faber, 1993.
Tylor, Edward. *Primitive Culture.* 3rd edn. London: John Murray, 1891.
Vandereycken, Walter, and van Deth, Ron. *From Fasting Saints to Anorexic Girls.*
    London: The Athlone Press, 1994.
Vrettos, Athena. *Somatic Fictions.* Stanford University Press, 1995.
Walkowitz, Judith R. *Prostitution and Victorian Society.* Cambridge University
    Press, 1980.
Wall, G. F. C. 'Different from Writing: *Dracula* in 1897'. *Literature and History* 10
    (1984).
Wear, Andrew, ed. *Medicine in Society: Historical Essays.* Cambridge University
    Press, 1992.

Weatherhill, Lorna. *Consumer Behaviour and Material Culture in Britain,* 1660–1780. London: Routledge, 1988.

Williams, A. Susan. *The Rich Man and the Diseased Poor in Early Victorian Literature.* London: Macmillan Press, 1987.

Winnifrith, Tom. *Fallen Women in the Nineteenth-Century Novel.* London: Macmillan Press, 1994.

Wohl, Anthony. *Endangered Lives.* London: J. M. Dent and Sons Ltd, 1983.

Woods, Robert and Woodward, John, eds. *Urban Disease and Mortality in Nineteenth Century England.* London: Batsford Academic and Educational, 1984.

Wright, Edgar. *Mrs Gaskell.* London: Oxford University Press, 1965.

Yeazell, Ruth, ed. *Sex, Politics and Science in the Nineteenth-Century Novel.* Baltimore: Johns Hopkins University Press, 1986.

Index

CAMBRIDGE STUDIES IN NINETEENTH-CENTURY
LITERATURE AND CULTURE

General editor
Gillian Beer, *University of Cambridge*

Titles published

For EU product safety concerns, contact us at Calle de José Abascal, 56–1°,
28003 Madrid, Spain or eugpsr@cambridge.org.